Story Crafting

LITERACY: MADE FOR ALL SERIES

Series Author: Arlene F. Marks

Literacy: Made for All is a classroom-ready, teacher-friendly resource for English and Writing teachers of Grades 9 through 12. Organized buffet style, it is designed to complement an existing English curriculum by providing a tested repertoire of strategies for teaching both writing skills and literary analysis techniques.

Benefits and Features:

- tested and proven effective at all learning levels, from Remedial to Pre-AP
- provides complete lesson plans including reproducible materials
- can be implemented as is or modified to suit individual teaching styles and/or students' needs
- each skill, assignment, or project begins by "teaching the teacher," giving an inexperienced teacher the knowledge to provide effective instruction first time out and the confidence to modify and experiment thereafter
- comprised of reading, writing, literary criticism, and language-study components
- moves students from writing effectively to reading analytically (approaching text from the authoring point of view), a proven, highly successful methodology
- can turn any English course into a Literacy course
- extremely versatile and cost-effective
- can deepen an existing English course or complete the framework for a new one

Titles in the Series:
Story Crafting: Classroom-Ready Materials for Teaching Fiction Writing Skills in the High School Grades (2014)
Enjoying Literature: Classroom-Ready Materials for Teaching Fiction and Poetry Analysis Skills in the High School Grades (2014)
Wordsmithing: Classroom-Ready Materials for Teaching Nonfiction Writing and Analysis Skills in the High School Grades (2014)

Story Crafting

Classroom-Ready Materials for Teaching Fiction Writing Skills in the High School Grades

Arlene F. Marks

ROWMAN & LITTLEFIELD
Lanham • Boulder • New York • Toronto • Plymouth, UK

Published by Rowman & Littlefield
4501 Forbes Boulevard, Suite 200, Lanham, Maryland 20706
www.rowman.com

10 Thornbury Road, Plymouth PL6 7PP, United Kingdom

British Library Cataloguing in Publication Information Available

Library of Congress Cataloging-in-Publication Data

Marks, Arlene F., 1947–
  Story crafting : classroom-ready materials for teaching fiction writing skills in the high school grades / Arlene F. Marks.
    pages cm. — (Literacy: made to order series)
  Includes bibliographical references.
  ISBN 978-1-4758-0733-2 (pbk. : alk. paper)—ISBN 978-1-4758-0734-9 (electronic)
  1. Language arts (Secondary)—United States—Activity programs. 2. Composition (Language arts) I. Title.
  LB1631.M3857 2014
  428.0071'2—dc23   2013044406

♾™ The paper used in this publication meets the minimum requirements of American National Standard for Information Sciences—Permanence of Paper for Printed Library Materials, ANSI/NISO Z39.48-1992.

Printed in the United States of America

Contents

PART IV: THE WRITING PROCESS:

Introduction

Welcome to *Literacy: Made for All*, a buffet-style reading and writing program for the high school grades.

This student-centered approach to the study of literature, language, and writing is based on certain classroom-tested precepts:

1. **That reading and writing are equally essential to the development of a student's understanding of and appreciation for literature.**
   Students who practice using a variety of rhetorical and literary techniques in their own work not only become much better equipped to identify examples of a particular writing strategy, they are also able to discuss more knowledgeably how and how well the strategy has been used.

2. **That literate readers are critical readers.**
   Because literate people understand and appreciate what words can do, they are not easily confused or manipulated by words. To be considered literate, therefore, students need to be able to assess the quality, the effect, and—most important—the *intent* of the language that is used to address them.

3. **That literature being studied must be read with purpose.**
   When we read strictly for entertainment, certain parts of the brain "gear down," sidelining the learning process. Students of literature, however, need to *think* about what they are reading. To ensure that this happens, they must read "with pen in hand," making notes or recording specific information as they go along.

4. **That discovery and learning come about when students feel confident enough to take risks and try new experiences.**
   Investigating something new always brings with it the risk of making mistakes. Children are taught from an early age to avoid mistakes if possible. However, students need to understand that while remaining in one's comfort zone may guarantee success, it also prevents growth, and while success may bring praise and make us feel good about ourselves, mistakes are how we learn.

At the same time, I have developed this program keeping in mind certain other rules of thumb, learned the hard way over years of teaching experience:

1. **Always begin with review.**
   No matter how basic the skill or how many grades ago the material should have been learned, there are bound to be students in your class who have never heard of it. That is why I've made laying the foundation a routine first step in each segment of *Literacy: Made for All*.

2. **The one who is doing the work is the one who is learning.**
   Since you already have the credit in the course you're teaching, this means the students should be the ones practicing the skills, doing the investigating, bouncing ideas off one another, and drawing the conclusions. *Literacy: Made for All* gives students plenty of opportunity to do all of these.

3. **Repetition works.**
   By this, I don't mean rote learning, but rather going back over already-charted territory. This kind of repetition hones skills and deepens understanding. It creates a level of comfort and encourages experimentation. And as long as you're

asking students to repeat something they've enjoyed or found interesting in the past, they'll cheerfully revisit favorite lessons, activities, and assignments, over and over. In fact, I've had students *request* them.

4. **Practice may not make perfect, but it does make permanent.**
   Like a tattoo on the skin, something learned is very difficult to erase from the mind. That is why students need to learn things correctly the first time. And that is why modeling and guided practice are essential preliminary steps in each segment of *Literacy: Made for All.*

IMPLEMENTING *LITERACY: MADE FOR ALL*

Literacy: Made for All is organized into units called **modules**, each focusing on a particular kind of writing or a particular type of reading material. Each module is divided into a menu of teachable segments, called **skills**, **projects**, or **assignments**, which provide the teacher with complete, classroom-ready lesson plans focusing on particular aspects of the material being read or written, as well as master copies of any student handouts included in the lessons. Extensions have also been added to deepen or differentiate the material for senior-level or enriched classes.

Literacy: Made for All is not a complete English course. It is designed to complement an English curriculum by providing a repertoire of strategies for teaching writing skills and literary analysis techniques suitable for the study of any type of text. The teacher can then select the most effective and appropriate segment(s) to introduce, reinforce, or illuminate classroom discussions of literary works.

There is no prescribed order or number of segments within a module. The teacher may select one or all of them, depending on the expectations to be fulfilled, the skill and interest levels of the students, the time allotted to the unit, and the instructional strategies preferred by the teacher.

When planning the English course at any high school grade level, the teacher may begin with any segment within the applicable module. However, for a final-year class destined for college or university, I highly recommend beginning with the ten-day segment from *ENJOYING LITERATURE* entitled "Literary Criticism 101," as critical thinking skills are essential to the understanding of literary and media works both within and outside of the classroom.

Each reading or writing segment consists of four phases:

Introduction

- The literary/media element or writing skill under study is introduced and explained.
- In the process, students are introduced to the appropriate literary terminology.

Modeling/Guided Practice

- The learning strategy is modeled by the teacher.
- Students practice with partners or in groups, with teacher guidance.

Practice

- Students attempt the modeled skill individually.

Product

- Students form groups for the purpose of sharing and discussing the results of their practice.
- If completing a reading assignment, each student then creates a tangible expression of her/his understanding, sharing it with the discussion group if time permits.

Student products may be written, visual, or auditory. At the teacher's discretion, the finished product of any segment may be collected for formative assessment or may serve as the summative evaluation for the unit, provided it is complete and in final-draft form.

There is no prescribed duration for a segment. Segments can be compressed or extended to occupy whatever length of time the students require or the reading material demands. I have found it most effective in my own classes to teach a writing skill and let students practice it in their own writing before asking them to find and analyze examples of the skill in a text under study. However, it is not necessary for a writing segment to be fully completed prior to commencing the study of a literary text—teachers can select segments from the relevant modules that allow writing and text analysis to be practiced simultaneously.

Each segment is a basic framework—a recipe, if you like, tested and proven successful in my classroom. If you're having an off day or not feeling especially creative—and we all have times like that—you can follow the recipe as is and be assured of a positive result. As with any recipe, however, you may wish to adapt the ingredients or the process to suit individual tastes or needs. Please feel free to modify, combine, or embellish these activities as much as you like in order to tailor them to your own classes. Above all, have fun with your students as they enjoy honing their literacy skills using *Literacy: Made for All*.

AIMS AND OBJECTIVES OF THE PROGRAM

Aims:

Students shall have opportunities to:

1. become aware of themselves as authors and come to realize the worth and uniqueness of their writing;
2. become proficient in the mechanics of written language and in the effective use of spoken and written language to think, learn, and communicate;
3. understand the role that language, literature, and the media play in the exploration of intellectual issues and in the establishment of personal and societal values;
4. develop critical skills and use them to respond to ideas communicated through the various media; and
5. prepare for productive community membership by taking personal responsibility for their progress toward self-directed learning.

Objectives:

Through this program, students will be encouraged to:

1. become better communicators of their own opinions and observations;
2. develop a greater understanding and acceptance of other points of view through discussions and shared writing assignments;
3. develop a better understanding of themselves;
4. hone and channel their creative abilities by practicing the creative process;
5. establish a personal writing style;
6. become effective editors of their own writing and that of others; and
7. plan writing projects by determining the purpose and format and then organizing their time to allow for effective editing techniques.

HOW TO IMPLEMENT *STORY CRAFTING*

STORY CRAFTING focuses on the creation, editing, polishing, and sharing of short stories and longer prose fiction. The first module, Getting Started, is a review of basic prose fiction writing skills. The second module, Writing Short Stories, may be used alone or treated as a continuation of the first module. The third module, Writing Longer Fiction, supplies additional necessary material for students who will be attempting longer and more complicated stories. This last series of skills is designed to supplement a Writer's Craft course but may be treated as an extension of the second module. Completing *STORY CRAFTING* is The Writing Process, a supplementary library of reproducible materials designed to help guide your students through the revising, editing, and polishing phases of producing a final draft work of fiction.

Each segment in a module is a Skill Set, containing up to several skill activities, arranged to be progressively more challenging and sophisticated. How deeply students delve into any of the Skill Sets will depend primarily upon their own interest and ability levels. Teachers may decide to do only the first activity of each Skill Set initially and then revisit selected segments later in the course to provide students with necessary reinforcement or "refreshers."

Here are some further recommendations to help ensure that both you and your students derive the greatest possible benefit from *STORY CRAFTING*:

1. Give students every opportunity to practice peer- and self-evaluation of their writing. Let them pair up or form groups to edit or critique one another's work. It may be beneficial as well to teach a preliminary lesson on ways to deliver constructive criticism.

    I have three effective rules for the English classroom, which you may find useful in yours:
    a. *Every person in this class is entitled to form her/his own opinions, and every expressed opinion has value. (But in order to earn marks, an opinion must be convincingly supported by examples or quotations.)*
    b. *Every expressed criticism of another student's work must be constructive. (A chart may be posted on the wall to suggest constructive openings for critical comments and to serve as a reminder that the purpose of criticism is to help the other author to improve.)*
    c. *Always try your best. (Areas where a student author needs to improve will thus be easier to identify. Also, trying one's best to be constructive at all times will speed everyone's progress toward fluent, effective, and (if desired) publishable writing.)*

2. Do not hesitate to repeat any of the activities in this program if, in your opinion, the students need more practice. Because the practical portion of each writing lesson depends almost entirely on the students' input, it will be different and interesting for them each time. Rather than feeling bored because of lesson repetition, students will become more familiar with the structure of the activity and therefore more confident about undertaking it. Increased confidence makes students more willing to take risks by experimenting with different styles and techniques in their writing. *This is what you want them to do—this is how they become more proficient communicators.* So, don't worry about repeating the segments in consecutive grades or even about repeating a particular activity in two or more consecutive English periods. As your students "get into" *STORY CRAFTING*, you may even find them asking to repeat an activity that they have particularly enjoyed.

ENJOYING LITERATURE and *STORY CRAFTING*, like your students' right and left legs, are designed to work together to move them along as naturally and efficiently as possible (in this case, toward literacy). *Literacy: Made for All* is non-prescriptive and non-grade-specific. It presents a methodology that can be used for the critical study of virtually any kind of literature and that will help your students to develop their expressive faculties as they become confident, discriminating, and *literate* readers, writers, and viewers.

Part I

GETTING STARTED

GRADE 9 (14 YEARS) AND UP

All story writing begins with ideas. Ideas are everywhere, but people often need to be taught how to recognize and capture them. By asking their imaginations the right questions and listening carefully for the answers, authors are able to make ideas grow into interesting situations and make situations grow into scenarios. Using language as a tool, an author can then mold a scenario into a story that will grip the reader, engage her/his emotions, and not let go until the problem is resolved, the villain/ess is vanquished, and all's right with the hero/ine's world once more.

This fiction-writing module is about getting and growing ideas. Here, your young authors will learn how to mine sources for interesting notions, how to develop notions into complete story outlines, and how to turn a first draft into a perfect final draft. In the process, they will also review the importance of theme, conflict, and story structure and will revisit and practice some descriptive writing techniques.

AIMS AND OBJECTIVES

Aims:

In this unit, students will have the opportunity to:

1. engage in interactive learning;
2. develop an understanding of both the creative process and the writing process;
3. understand the importance of each stage in the writing process;
4. appreciate the importance of pre-planning;
5. explore and appreciate the nature of reality;
6. enhance their decision-making and problem-solving skills; and
7. develop confidence in their own opinions and writing.

Objectives:

Students will be encouraged to:

1. engage in imaginative and original thinking;
2. take risks;
3. further develop their group learning skills;
4. practice analyzing causes and predicting outcomes of events both real and imagined;
5. understand the benefits and learn the strategies of organizing and outlining stories before writing;
6. feel comfortable with the revising, editing, and polishing process;
7. develop their critical editing skills;
8. evaluate the quality of their own writing; and
9. discuss life's problems and their solutions with their peers.

	SKILL SET	DESCRIPTION	NCCS ANCHORS ADDRESSED
1	Establishing an ideas file	Students learn how to develop and use an Ideas File as a source of writing inspiration.	W.4, W.5, W.10
2	What happened before and what happens next	Students explore the causes and effects of a variety of story-triggering incidents or situations and practice turning them into story ideas.	W.4, W.5, W.10
3	Developing the theme of a story	Students practice growing underlying themes that can help their fictional tales deliver important and powerful messages to readers.	R.2, W.3, W.4, W.5, W.10, L.6
4	Creating the illusion of reality	Students learn how to make characters, settings and plot events behave or transpire in realistic ways.	R.1, R.3, W.3, W.4, W.5, W.10
5	Dramatic Conflict: Creating story texture with multiple antagonists	Student authors practice putting multiple conflicts into a story to make it interesting and exciting for the reader.	W.3, W.4, W.5, W.10, L.6
6	Building scenes and using them to structure a story	Young authors will learn how to construct a fictional scene and will practice putting scenes in the best order to create an interesting story.	R.5, W.3, W.4, W.5, W.10, L.6
7	Writing Descriptively: Wake up your senses	Young authors reawaken their senses and establish a vocabulary of sensory words and phrases to enhance their descriptive writing.	W.4, W.10, L.3, L.5
8	Writing Descriptively: Use Figurative language	Student authors practice using similes and metaphors to make their descriptive writing more evocative.	W.4, W.5, W.10, L.3, L.5
9	Writing Descriptively: Use Descriptive language	Students learn to recognize and use words with specific connotations in order to make their writing more effective.	W.4, W.5, W.10, L.3, L.4
10	Putting Everything Together	Students take a story through the entire process from outlining to Final Draft.	W.3, W.4, W.5, W.10, L.1, L.2, L.3, L.5

Getting Started: Skill Set 1
Establishing an Ideas File

✍️ **YOU WILL NEED:**

- Large manila envelopes—1 per student (Skill 1)
- A container per class to hold the envelopes upright
- GSR 1—WHO, WHY, WHERE, HOW? CHART—1 per student (Skill 1)
- A selection of old magazines (Skill 2)
- Newspapers—a section per student (Skill 3)
- GSR 2—CLUSTERING AROUND QUOTATIONS WORKSHEET—1 per student (Skill 3)
- CLUSTERING AROUND QUOTATIONS on overhead transparency (Skill 3)
- An overhead projector (Skill 3)
- A newspaper article of the teacher's choice (Skill 3)
- GSR 3—"WHAT-IF" WORKSHEET—1 per student (Skill 4)
- "WHAT-IF" WORKSHEET drawn on the board (Skill 4)
- GSR 4—"WHAT-IF" SCENARIOS—1 copy, cut into strips (Skill 4)

PURPOSE

Authors find it handy to have an Ideas File they can skim through from time to time for inspiration. These ideas can help with story plotting, setting, character development, and vocabulary. Since the students will be writing longer stories than in previous years, it will be advantageous for them to learn how to develop, maintain, and use an Ideas File.

SKILL 1: WHO, WHY, WHERE, HOW?

Introduction

1. The teacher hands out one manila envelope to each student. The student then prints her/his name in bold letters on the top right-hand corner of the envelope.

    Senior students can be given several envelopes each, and categories can be printed on them, such as: Interesting Settings, Gadgets and Gimmicks, and Character Sketches; or, if students prefer, they can use genre classifications like Science Fiction, Crime and Mystery, Romance, and so on.

    The teacher explains that each student's envelope(s) will be her/his Ideas File for the year and that the envelopes belonging to each class will be stored upright in alphabetical order in that class's container. The teacher and class briefly discuss the purpose of these Ideas File envelopes, as outlined above.

It should be stressed that each student's Ideas File, like her/his first-draft notebook, is private and that neither the teacher nor any other students will be allowed to sift through it.

2. The teacher and class next discuss the nature of story ideas. Students should realize that ideas come from the imagination and that their imaginations can be triggered by virtually anything that the students see, hear, feel, or experience. Therefore, the best way for a writer to get story ideas is to ask her/himself questions about what s/he perceives and let her/his imagination make up answers to the questions.

Modeling/Guided Practice

1. To provide an example of this process, the teacher reads the following passage aloud to the class:

    You are on the bus, en route to a mid-morning appointment. The bus stops, and a passenger boards. This woman is in her sixties, at least, quite well dressed and impeccably groomed. She has a pleasant, smiling expression on her face . . . she looks as though she ought to be in a kitchen somewhere, baking cookies for a tribe of adoring grandchildren. Then you notice the large tattoo of a coiled snake on her right forearm.

2. The teacher elicits a list of questions that would run through the students' minds at the sight of this woman and writes them on the board, organizing them under the headings Who, Why, Where, and How. The students then brainstorm, letting their imaginations answer these questions until four or five distinct story ideas have emerged.

    FOR EXAMPLE: The woman might be on her way to a meeting with a government official who has been ignoring and patronizing her. Won't this tattoo make him see her in a different light! Or she might be a former biker's moll or war veteran, en route to a reunion. Or, *she* might be a *he* in disguise (great comedy potential here).

    For senior or enriched students, a different exercise may be used. The teacher can select two characters from totally disparate stories (such as James Bond and Snow White). Students can compile a list of questions that would run through their minds at the thought of this character combination, all beginning with Who, Why, Where, and How: Who brought them together and why? Where did they meet? How did they feel when they first saw each other? And so on. Students can then develop the answers to these questions to create a comedy, a romance, an adventure, or a fantasy story.

Practice and Product

1. Each student selects one of the story ideas and summarizes in a paragraph the story of the grandmotherly character with the tattoo (or synopsizes the story of the two disparate characters who have been brought together).

    These paragraphs can be collected by the teacher for diagnostic evaluation.

2. Each student is given a copy of the WHO, WHY, WHERE, HOW Chart and is encouraged to recall a person, thing, or event that stands out in her/his mind from the past few days (*may be something dramatic or just unusual, but it tweaked the student's curiosity at the time*). Each student records a summary of this information at the top of the chart, then proceeds to formulate questions and answers to complete the chart. The student can place this completed sheet in her/his Ideas File.

SKILL 2: QUESTIONS AND ANSWERS

Introduction and Modeling

1. The teacher hands out back issues of magazines to the students and explains that these can be excellent sources of story material.

    Students may need to be reminded that a story idea is just the author's imagination asking and answering questions about something that has caught the author's interest. Therefore, anything that makes them stop and wonder could be the beginning of a story.

2. The teacher demonstrates by finding an advertisement and wondering out loud about the people shown in the ad. *For example: What is she looking at (off the page)? What is he really thinking right now? How did they meet? And so on.* These questions can be written on the board, along with a couple of possible answers for each. The teacher then selects a couple of interesting answers and briefly summarizes the story they suggest.

Guided Practice

1. The students are instructed to leaf through the magazines until each person has found a picture, phrase, or piece of text that sparks her/his interest.

    Each student then takes a piece of lined paper and summarizes at the top of the page, in two or three sentences, what is in the selected advertisement or story/article.

2. Each student draws a line down the middle of the page, dividing it into 2 wide columns, and prints a large "Q" (for Questions) at the top of the left-hand column and a large "A" (for Answers) at the top of the right-hand column.

3. Students pair up with working partners to brainstorm and write in the "Q" column of Student A's chart all the questions that Student A's article/advertisement brings to mind. In the "A" column, they record all the possible answers that their imaginations provide to these questions. *(Hint: The more questions that are raised, the better the story will be.)*

4. Step 3 is repeated for Student B's article/advertisement, and the questions and answers are recorded on Student B's chart.

Practice and Product

1. Working independently, each student now writes a paragraph describing or summarizing the story suggested by the questions and answers on her/his chart.

2. Each working pair can get back together, and Students A and B can read their completed paragraphs aloud to each other.

3. Each student's "Q and A" sheet (with first-draft paragraph attached) is to be placed in her/his Ideas File.

SKILL 3: CLUSTERING AROUND QUOTATIONS

Introduction and Modeling

1. The teacher shows the class a newspaper article or advertisement that has caught her/his interest. Several suggestive phrases have been highlighted, and these are read to the class.

2. Using an overhead projector and a copy of the CLUSTERING AROUND QUOTATIONS Worksheet on a transparency, the teacher models how the worksheet is to be completed: A highlighted phrase selected by the class is copied into the first box. Then the students brainstorm ideas that are brought to mind by association with the phrase, and these are recorded on the transparency immediately below the first quote box. This process is repeated twice more, for two additional phrases selected by the class.

Practice

1. The teacher hands out sections of newspapers to the students, who are to skim through the pages until each person has found at least one picture (with caption), advertisement, or article that fires her/his interest.

2. Each student then highlights any words or phrases that could spark ideas (i.e., that raise questions for the student's imagination to answer). Students should be encouraged to find at least three quotes each.

3. The teacher hands out a CLUSTERING AROUND QUOTATIONS Worksheet to each student, who records her/his selected quotes in the boxes on the sheet. Each student then pairs up with a different working partner from the previous skill activity and brainstorms with the partner to complete both their worksheets.

Product

1. Working independently, each student now selects the most intriguing idea on her/his worksheet and summarizes in a paragraph or two the story it suggests.

    As an additional challenge, students can try to include the original quote.

2. When finished, each brainstorming pair can get back together, and students can read their paragraphs aloud to each other.

3. Each student's completed worksheet and first draft are attached together and inserted in her/his Ideas File.

SKILL 4: WHAT-IFFING

Introduction and Modeling

1. The teacher explains that today the class is going to do some "what-iffing" and that this kind of structured speculation is another good way for an author to develop story ideas. For example, suppose the students had just finished watching a video about the last ice age. Several "what-ifs" could run through their heads, such as (teacher writes the "what-if" on the board):

    What if another ice age began now?

    The teacher points out that this is a rather vague and generalized thought that will need to be elaborated to make it more immediate and concrete. *(For example, how would you know that an ice age was beginning?)* Teacher and students together can come up with a second version, which is then written on the board below the first one:

    What if it started snowing one winter and the snow just never went away?

2. The teacher sketches the WHAT-IF Chart on the board. The students then discuss who might be affected by this situation, such as: me, my family, the community, my country, the world. Each of these is written under the "Who" column heading on the chart on the board.

Guided Practice

1. The class is organized into as many groups as there are "Who" selections on the chart. Each group of students takes one of the line headings, and for two minutes they brainstorm questions to add to that line of the chart. When time is up, each group selects three or four questions from its list, and these are written in the appropriate box on the board.

2. Each group of students is then assigned the job of imagining answers to one of the sets of questions on the chart (not the line they worked on before) and writing these answers in the appropriate box of the chart when ready. When the chart is completed, the teacher and students can briefly discuss the kinds of stories that might be developed from its various lines.

    It should be pointed out to the students that not every aspect of a "what-if" will necessarily develop into a story or even be of interest to an author or a reader.

Practice

1. The students remain in their groups. Each student receives a copy of the WHAT-IF Worksheet, and each group selects or is given one of the WHAT-IF Scenarios.

2. The members of each group work together to complete their worksheet.
   Each member should ensure that s/he has a personal copy of the group's chart.

Product

1. Working independently, each student now selects from the group worksheet a story idea that has become important to her/him and writes the story in first draft. Once finished, these stories can be read aloud by their authors to the other members of their respective brainstorming groups.

2. Each student places her/his completed WHAT-IF Worksheet and first-draft story into her/his Ideas File.

EXTENSIONS

This Skill Set should be repeated periodically to keep students' "plotting muscles" strong and limber for story writing. "What-ifs" are everywhere. Students can jot down and develop thoughts that occur to them in other classes (*What if I had gills?*), or they can plot prequels, sequels, or spinoffs from other stories, or from favorite TV shows or movies. *(In a spinoff, a minor character from one story becomes the main character in another.)*

WHO, WHY, WHERE, HOW?

WHAT: _____

_____

WHO?	WHY?
WHERE?	**HOW?**

CLUSTERING AROUND QUOTATIONS

Quotation:

Quotation:

Quotation:

'WHAT-IF' WORKSHEET

First Idea: What if _____

More Specific: What if _____

WHO IS AFFECTED?	QUESTIONS	ANSWERS
1.		
2.		
3.		
4.		
5.		

"WHAT-IF" SCENARIOS

1. What if the world suddenly ran out of fossil fuel?

2. What if you won $17 million in the lottery?

3. What if you found out you had tested positive for HIV?

4. What if your parents announced that they were getting a divorce?

5. What if you didn't have to go to school to be educated, but were expected to learn a certain amount each day on a home computer?

6. What if, on your way to visit relatives in some distant city, you had an accident and hit your head and completely lost your memory?

7. What if there were no such thing as money and people just traded favors?

8. What if a space traveler crash-landed in your back yard?

9. What if you walked into a corner store to buy a pack of gum and were suddenly 'discovered' by a Hollywood talent agent?

10. What if you learned that dolphins and whales are really the most intelligent animals on the planet and they are getting fed up with humans?

Getting Started: Skill Set 2

What Happened Before and What Happens Next

✍️ **YOU WILL NEED:**

- A variety of newspapers (Skills 1 and 3)
- GSR 5—SAMPLE NEWSPAPER FILLER—1 per student (Skill 1)
- GSR 6—Q & A WORKSHEET—1 class set per skill
- Pictures of people in interesting situations—1 per group of 3 or 4 students (Skill 2)

PURPOSE

Authors know that in order to develop a story, they must build a chain of cause and effect. Each plot incident must be the logical result of a previous incident or circumstance and must also lead inevitably to the next incident. Among the questions that an author must ask her/his imagination in order to help a story grow are these two important ones: What caused this to happen? and What will happen next?

As they explore the causes and effects of a variety of story-triggering incidents or situations, students will begin to understand how the events in their own lives have been shaped by the past and how their actions in the present will have an effect on the future.

SKILL 1: USING THE NEWSPAPER

Introduction

1. The teacher hands out the SAMPLE NEWSPAPER FILLER and reads it aloud to the class:

   The unidentified body of a man was discovered this morning in a boxcar at the rail yards on Sullivan Avenue. Two teenagers taking a shortcut through the rail yard on their way to school found the body and immediately notified the yard foreman, who called police. The deceased was wearing a money belt containing a quantity of cut diamonds and other gems. Police have classified this as a suspicious death and are investigating the possibility of foul play.

2. There are two mysteries in this little article—the man and the diamonds—and both suggest story ideas. The teacher explains that if the story is going to be about the man, then the discovery of his body must be at the end. The author must put her/his imagination to work to figure out *what happened before*. Brainstorming a series of questions about what led up to the man's death would enable an author to investigate a great many story possibilities.

   If, on the other hand, the story is going to be about the diamonds in the money belt, the scene in the rail yard is just the beginning. The author must determine who really owns the diamonds and *what happens next*.

Guided (Group) Practice

1. Each student receives a copy of the Q & A WORKSHEET, and the class is organized, first in two equal sections (A and B) and then in groups of three or four within each section.

2. The groups in Section A will brainstorm questions and answers and fill in their charts for a story about the man—*what happened before*. The groups in Section B will do the same thing for a story about the diamonds and gems—*what happens next*.

    Each group member should make sure s/he has a personal copy of the group's completed worksheet.

Practice and Product

1. Working independently, each student then selects from her/his group's chart a story possibility that has become important to her/him and writes or summarizes that story.

2. Each student from Section A pairs up with a student from Section B. The partnered students then read their completed stories aloud to each other.

3. Each student places her/his completed Q & A WORKSHEET and first-draft story into her/his Ideas File. Students can spend what is left of the period looking through newspapers for fillers and articles that contain "little mysteries." These should be cut out and added to the students' Ideas Files as well.

SKILL 2: USING PICTURES

Introduction and Modeling

1. The teacher shows the class a picture of people in an interesting situation. This picture is attached to the board, leaving space on both sides. To the left of the picture, the teacher writes the heading BEFORE; to the right, s/he writes the heading AFTER.

    HINT: Pictures for this activity can be clipped out of newspapers or magazines or may be downloaded from public domain Web sites and printed out. If the picture chosen to model Skill 2 is too small to be seen easily from the back of the room, the picture can be copied or printed out onto an overhead transparency and the headings written on the blackboard to the right and left of the overhead screen.

2. The class then brainstorms a series of questions that are suggested by the picture about *what happened before* the depicted scene. These questions and the possible answers to them are listed on the board to the left of the picture, under the heading BEFORE.

3. The same procedure is repeated as the students brainstorm possibilities for *what happens next*, and their ideas are recorded on the board to the right of the picture, under AFTER.

Guided Practice

1. Students form groups of three or four. Each group receives a different picture, and group members discuss what is happening in the picture.

    If this skill activity is being done immediately following Using the Newspaper, then students should get back into the same groups.

2. Each student is given a copy of the Q & A WORKSHEET, and each group is assigned to work on either *what happened before* the picture was taken or *what happens next*. Student groups are to brainstorm questions and discuss possible answers, as modeled by the teacher. As they work, each student should ensure that s/he fills in a personal copy of the worksheet.

If this skill activity is being done immediately following Skill 1, then the groups that worked on what happened before *in the previous activity should switch to the* what happens next *scenario today, and vice versa.*

Practice and Product

1. Each group then selects the story idea that members feel is the most intriguing and develops it for dramatization. These will be improvised presentations, requiring a minimum amount of scripting and rehearsal.

    For a class inexperienced with (or nervous about) drama, the teacher may wish to write the following guidelines on the board:
    *   *This is a short sketch, so get into the action immediately.*
    *   *Each actor must know what happens, in what order, who does it, and how her/his character feels about it. Speech will then flow naturally.*
    *   *An actor can play more than one role but must be different somehow for each part (change voice, add a mannerism, alter clothing, etc.).*

2. Each group presents its dramatization for the rest of the class. The groups doing *what happened before* should present first. Each cast should freeze for three seconds, in the positions of the people in the picture, at the end of its presentation. Each cast doing *what happens next* should begin its presentation with a freeze.

3. Working independently, each student then writes a story suggested by one of the improvisations s/he has watched. *(This can be done in class, if there is time, or as homework.)*

4. Each student places her/his completed Q & A WORKSHEET and first-draft story in her/his Ideas File.

EXTENSIONS

The exercises in the first two Skill Sets can be used to pull stories out of just about anything. James Michener used to base entire novels on this technique, writing *what happened before* chapters to explain the presence in his stories of such things as a fossilized dinosaur bone, a volcano, an underground oil deposit, and so on. Science fiction writers routinely speculate about *what happens next* for such things as television, drugs, and computers.

Try challenging your students to write *what happened before* or *what happens next* stories about one of the people or any inanimate object involved in:

a sporting event	a fashion show
a court trial	a natural disaster
a television game show	an election
a parade or demonstration	a battle
an expedition	a circus or fair
a scientific discovery	a space voyage
a crime or criminal investigation	a final exam

SAMPLE NEWSPAPER FILLER

The unidentified body of a man was discovered this morning in a boxcar at the rail yards on Sullivan Avenue. Two teenagers taking a short-cut through the rail yard on their way to school found the body and immediately notified the yard foreman, who called police.

The deceased was wearing a money belt containing a quantity of cut diamonds and other gems. Police have classified this as a suspicious death and are investigating the possibility of foul play.

Q AND A WORKSHEET

Situation: _____

WHAT HAPPENED BEFORE?

QUESTIONS	ANSWERS

WHAT HAPPENS NEXT?

QUESTIONS	ANSWERS

Getting Started: Skill Set 3
Establishing the Theme of Your Story

✍ YOU WILL NEED:

- Superficial themes written on slips of paper—1 per group (Skill 1) (see **Practice** below)

PURPOSE

Young authors need to understand the importance of having a central idea and purpose for a story before beginning to write it. Theme provides direction, and a story that knows where it is going has a much better chance of taking the reader along with it. As students practice developing story themes, they will also come to realize that fictional tales can deliver important and powerful messages.

SKILL 1: THE UNDERLYING THEME

Introduction and Modeling

1. The teacher explains that there are two different kinds of themes in a story and discusses with the class the definition of each one:

   The *superficial* theme is simply a statement describing what the story is about. (e.g., *This is a story about a first meeting between a human and an alien on the alien's home world.*)

   The *underlying* theme answers the question, "What message do you want the reader to get from this story?" (e.g., *This is a story about the importance of not judging people by their appearance.*)

   It should be stressed to the students that in order to have an effect on the reader, a story must have both a superficial and an underlying theme.

2. The teacher illustrates the process by which an author develops the necessary themes for her/his story by first writing this very superficial theme on the board under the heading *Superficial Theme*:

   This is a story about a haunted house.

   Before an underlying theme can be determined, the students will have to develop a more specific idea of what the story will be about. To be useful, a superficial theme should summarize the WHO, WHAT, and WHERE of the story. For example:

   This is a story about some youngsters who spend the night in a haunted house.

   This second theme statement is written on the board below the first one.

19

3. The teacher then leads the class in a discussion of possible messages that could be conveyed in this story and the details or circumstances that would need to be included in each case. For example:

The message in this story could be that true character is revealed in a crisis. There would have to be a timid child in the group who shows that s/he is capable of great courage when circumstances require it and also a child who acts very brave but who is revealed to be fearful and afraid.

Several possibilities are written on the board under the heading *Underlying Themes*.

Practice

1. The class is then organized into groups of four or five students. Each group selects or is given one of the following superficial themes to develop:

This is a story about a summer camp.
This is a story about moving to a different city.
This is a story about falling in love.
This is a story about a part-time job.
This is a story about qualifying for a driver's license.
This is a story about a talent show.
This is a story about football (or some other sport).

2. Each group begins by expanding its theme statement with WHO, WHAT, WHERE details and recording this more specific statement on a sheet of paper. Group members then brainstorm several possible underlying themes for their story, and these are recorded on the paper as well.

3. Each group's work is shared with the rest of the class.
    Depending on the class, this may be done orally by a group spokesperson, by having groups pass their work around to other groups, or by posting work on the wall and letting classmates view it gallery style.

Product

1. Working independently, each student selects the superficial and underlying theme pair that interests her/him the most, develops it into a story, and writes the first draft.
    At the teacher's discretion, students may select theme pairs from the work of brainstorming groups other than their own.

2. Brainstorming groups can reassemble for the sharing of members' stories with group mates.

3. Each student should place her/his completed first-draft story in her/his Ideas File.

SKILL 2: FROM SYNOPSIS TO STORY

Introduction

1. The teacher points out to the class that superficial and underlying themes together provide the synopses that are found in TV guides and in film or book catalogues.

2. The teacher reads the following synopses aloud and asks the students to name the book or film being described in each case:
    a. This is the story of a beautiful Southern belle, who discovers after the Civil War that her emotional attachment to her family's plantation is even stronger than her love for her husband.
    b. This is the story of a man who is shipwrecked on an island, and who learns to survive with the help of an outcast native he calls Friday.

c. This is the story of the doomed love between two teenagers, whose deaths finally bring their feuding families together.

d. This is the story of a young man caught up in an interstellar war, who learns that his sworn enemy is really his long-lost father.

It should be noted that in each case, the first part of the synopsis is the superficial theme, and the second part brings in elements of the underlying theme. The dividing line tends to be a comma and/or the relative pronoun.

If the above examples would be too unfamiliar to students, the teacher should find or compose a list of synopses that they would recognize more easily.

Guided Practice

1. The teacher organizes the class into groups of three. Each group creates and records three theme statement synopses—one for a book, one for a movie, and one for an episode of a television show. Each must synopsize a known story, and each must be written on a separate piece of paper.

2. The headings BOOK, MOVIE, and TV are written across the top of the board, and the synopses are read aloud one by one to the class. This can be done by each group in turn or by a single designated reader pulling slips of paper out of a container in which all the synopses have been collected. As the students guess the title of each work being described, the title is written on the board in the appropriate column.

Practice and Product

1. Each student selects one story or story idea from her/his Ideas File and writes a theme statement synopsis describing both the superficial and underlying themes.
   Students should be encouraged to make their themes strong and include plenty of detail in the synopsis.

2. The class is now organized into groups of four or five. Each group member writes out her/his synopsis on a piece of paper and passes it to the student on her/his right.

3. The receiving student author then develops the synopsis into a one-page story that illustrates and embodies the underlying theme.

4. Within each group, each student author reads aloud her/his completed story and then the synopsis on which it is based. The group members discuss and compare each story and synopsis, noting the various ways in which the synopses have been "fleshed out" with details.

EXTENSIONS

Many of our old proverbs or sayings make good underlying themes for stories. In fact, most have already been translated into a variety of different tales and will continue to be used over and over again. How many different story ideas can your students think of to convey each of the following messages to a reader?

Don't judge a book by its cover.
All that glitters is not gold.
Money isn't everything.
Don't change horses in mid-stream.
Love conquers all.
Heroes are made, not born.

Two wrongs don't make a right.
It isn't whether you win or lose, but how you play the game.
If at first you don't succeed, try, try again.
The grass is always greener on the other side of the fence.
Never underestimate an opponent.

Getting Started: Skill Set 4

Creating the Illusion of Reality

✍ **YOU WILL NEED:**

- GSR 7—REALITY IN THE NEWS CHART—class set (Skill 1)
- REALITY IN THE NEWS CHART—on an overhead transparency (Skill 1)
- An overhead projector (Skill 1)
- Newspaper articles about an event—1 for the teacher (Skill 1), 1 brought by each student as homework from a previous class
- GSR 8—THE ILLUSION OF REALITY CHART—class set (Skill 2)
- Reality diagram drawn on the board (Skill 1, Introduction)

PURPOSE

Authors understand the importance of creating the Illusion of Reality for their readers with characters, settings, and plot events that behave or transpire in completely realistic ways. As they explore the nature of reality, student authors will learn how not only character, setting, and plot but also people, places/times, and real-life events depend on and influence one another.

SKILL 1: UNDERSTANDING REALITY

Introduction

1. The teacher indicates a diagram on the board, consisting of three overlapping circles with a shaded triangular area in the center, and titles it REALITY. Using Socratic questioning, the teacher then gets the students to identify the three circles as PEOPLE, PLACES/TIMES, and EVENTS. These labels are printed on the diagram.

2. The teacher points out that the circles overlap to show that each of these elements has an influence on the other two. For example, in the temperate zone, we don't try to grow crops outdoors during the winter—because PLACE/TIME influences EVENTS—and when we decorate our homes to suit our own tastes, we are PEOPLE influencing PLACES.
   The teacher asks the students to supply other examples of one element influencing another and lists them on the board.
   It should be stressed to the students that this network of influences is a basic principle of what we know as reality.

3. The teacher now points to the shaded area in the middle of the diagram and explains that this area of focus represents an individual's awareness of her/his world. For each person, this area could be labeled "you are here."

In the real world, there are billions of people that you do not know, many places you have not visited or heard about, and many events of which you are unaware. But in your area of focus, where the three circles overlap, these are the people you do know or know about; the places you have visited or read about; and the events that you have participated in, witnessed, or learned about. Here they all come together to form *your personal reality*. This is where each of us actually lives. The rest of the diagram is still present, but until something enters the area of focus and begins to affect us directly, we aren't really aware of it.

Modeling

1. The teacher reads a newspaper article aloud to the class.

2. With reference to the article just read and using the example REALITY IN THE NEWS CHART on the overhead transparency, the teacher and class discuss and record the information necessary to complete each section of the chart.
   By the time this step is done, students should have begun to realize how each element of the news story has had an influence on the other two.

Guided Practice

The students now refer to the newspaper articles that they were asked to bring. Each student receives a copy of the REALITY IN THE NEWS CHART and proceeds to read her/his article and fill in the chart. The teacher circulates, providing assistance if required.

If any element was not reported in the article, the student should be encouraged to complete the chart by imagining what it might have been and how it might have exerted an influence.

Practice

Each student now switches to a different color pen, selects one element from her/his chart, and changes it. On a separate sheet of paper, the student records how the influence of the new person, setting, or event would be demonstrated by the other elements of the story.

Product

Each student first-drafts the modified story as it would appear in tomorrow's newspaper. If there is time, students can pair up and share their stories with their partners.

SKILL 2: CREATING THE ILLUSION OF REALITY

Introduction

1. The teacher refers to the diagram of reality still on the board and asks the class, "What if I decided to write a book about my life? Where on the diagram would that book be located?"
   Answer: In the area of focus, because the author would be writing about her/his personal reality.
   But what if the teacher decided to write a novel? This is a fictional book. Where on the diagram would its people and places and events be located?
   Answer: Still in the area of focus. They couldn't exist anywhere else, but coming from the author's imagination they would be part of her/his personal reality.

2. The teacher repeats that these fictional people, places, and events cannot exist outside the author's area of focus . . . but the reader would really like to believe that they could. People read fiction because they want to "suspend their dis-belief"; that is, they want to believe, for as long as it takes them to finish the story, that what is described in the book could actually take place in the future or could have taken place in the past or could be taking place in the present. The author's job is to convince the reader to "suspend disbelief" by making the story feel like reality—by creating the Illusion of Reality *(teacher should write this phrase on the board)*—making sure that the world of the story contains

people, places/times, and events and that each of them influences the other two, just as they do in real life. In a work of fiction, they aren't called PEOPLE, PLACES, and EVENTS, but rather CHARACTERS, SETTING, and PLOT.

3. The teacher adds these labels to the diagram.

Modeling

1. The teacher explains that the students will be learning and practicing various techniques for creating the Illusion of Reality in their own stories. The teacher then writes the following on the board:

$$CHARACTER + SETTING = (RE)ACTION$$

2. The teacher points out that any time an author puts a character into a setting, the character is going to be affected somehow. How s/he reacts and what action s/he decides to take will depend on what sort of character s/he is. For example, if a character is leaving her/his favorite store through a security archway and suddenly the alarm goes off, what will the character do?

3. The teacher and class brainstorm at least eight different types of characters who might be shopping at that store (e.g., an uptight bank executive, a frazzled single mom with a cranky toddler, and so on). These are listed on the board. The teacher then leads a full-class discussion of all the different ways in which these characters might be affected and what action they might take in this particular setting. Together, teacher and students select their favorite possibility and record its particulars under the three elements of the equation in Step 1.

Guided Practice

Each student receives a copy of the ILLUSION OF REALITY CHART. The teacher and class together complete the first two lines of the chart, following the same process as was modeled above but for two new settings (e.g., a campground during a thunderstorm, a traffic accident at a busy intersection). The students then work in groups of three or four to discuss and complete the rest of the chart.

Practice and Product

1. Working independently, each student selects her/his favorite line of the chart and develops it into a short, action-packed scene that describes realistically both the setting and the character's reaction to it.

2. Students can reassemble in their groups to read their completed scenes aloud and constructively criticize one another's work (i.e., offer suggestions for improvement). Students should save their ILLUSION OF REALITY CHARTS in their Ideas Files.

SKILL 3: PUTTING PRE-WRITING SKILLS TOGETHER

Practice and Product

1. Each student retrieves her/his completed ILLUSION OF REALITY CHART from her/his Ideas File and selects one character and one setting from two different lines of the chart.

2. The student then jots down in point form a description of the character and a description of the setting and decides how the character would react to the setting and what action s/he might decide to take.

3. Each student then writes a paragraph based on the information above and develops it into a story outline by using the question-and-answer brainstorming technique from Skill Set 2 to imagine either *what happened before* or *what happens next*.

4. After completing the story outline, the student should be able to formulate both a superficial theme and an underlying theme for the story. These are written at the bottom of the story outline.

5. Each student should staple her/his ILLUSION OF REALITY CHART to her/his completed story outline and place these in her/his Ideas File.

EXTENSIONS

The surest way to get a reaction out of a character is to put her/him in a place where s/he doesn't belong. Ask your students to write paragraphs about ordinary people who unexpectedly find themselves:

in the middle of the jungle   at a diplomatic function
playing for a major league sports team   headlining a rock concert
in a hospital bed awaiting surgery   on a reality show
working for a mobster   arrested for a crime
caught in an extreme climate event   elected to office

REALITY IN THE NEWS

What is the headline of your newspaper article?

_____

_____

IDENTIFY

THE PEOPLE: _____

_____

THE PLACE/TIME: _____

_____

THE EVENT: _____

_____

NOW FILL IN THE CHART:

	PEOPLE	PLACE/TIME	EVENT
How do PEOPLE influence:			
How do PLACE/TIME influence:			
How does THE EVENT influence:			

THE ILLUSION OF REALITY

	CHARACTER (Name, Type, Short Desc)	SETTING (Where and When)	PROBABLE EMOTION	PROBABLE REACTION TO SETTING
1				
2				
3				
4				
5				
6				
7				
8				
9				
10				

Getting Started: Skill Set 5
Understanding Dramatic Conflict

✎ **YOU WILL NEED:**

- GSR 9—THREE TYPES OF CONFLICT WORKSHEET—class set
- Chart on the board:

Protagonist	Goal	Motivation	Antagonists
			1)
			2)
			3)

PURPOSE

Authors understand that a strong dramatic conflict is essential to effective storytelling. People enjoy reading about other people overcoming obstacles in order to achieve their goals. The more obstacles there are, the more satisfaction the reader derives from the character's final achievement. Student authors must therefore become aware that there are three kinds of conflict and that when all three are present in a story, the texture they create makes the story interesting and exciting for the reader.

INTRODUCTION AND MODELING

1. The teacher reviews with the class the four elements of a dramatic conflict: Protagonist (*the hero/ine*), Goal (*what the hero/ine wants to achieve in the story*), Motivation (*why the hero/ine wants or needs to achieve this goal*), and Antagonist (*an obstacle to be overcome*).

2. The teacher then explains that there are three kinds of Antagonists and gives an example of each to illustrate:
    Person vs. Person—e.g., a bank robber versus the police
    Person vs. Environment—e.g., a boat captain versus a squall or a burglar versus an alarm system
    Person vs. Self—e.g., a teenager versus her/his own shyness

3. The teacher points out that it is not only possible but also desirable to pit a Protagonist against all three kinds of Antagonists in a single conflict. The resulting story will be complex and realistic and therefore even more interesting for the reader. To illustrate, the teacher tells the story of the Protagonist below and fills in the appropriate columns on the chart on the board:
    PROTAGONIST: a high school athlete
    GOAL: to get an athletic scholarship

29

MOTIVATION: Parents can't afford college tuition. Older brother failed to earn a scholarship and is now unemployed—protagonist doesn't want to end up like him. Wants to be first in his family to go to college, make his parents proud, etc.

ANTAGONISTS: A coach who keeps him on the bench (PERSON). Has to keep his part-time job to help support his family, so he can't practice much (ENVIRONMENT). His own self-doubts—is he really good enough? (SELF).

Guided Practice

The teacher and class together chart a second conflict on the board for a different Protagonist, selected by the students.

Practice and Product

1. The class is organized into groups of three, and each student receives a copy of the THREE TYPES OF CONFLICT WORKSHEET.

2. Each group chooses three different Protagonists and builds a dramatic conflict for each one, being sure to give each Protagonist all three kinds of Antagonists to deal with. The details of each conflict discussed by the group are recorded by group members on their individual worksheets.

3. Working independently, each student then selects her/his favorite conflict, from the two charted on the board and the three on her/his worksheet, and first-drafts the story it suggests.
   Students should be advised that their first drafts will be read by other students to help them glean ideas.

4. Students get into four or five groups (up to six students per group) to share their completed stories. The stories are passed to the right within each group, silently read by the receiving students, and then passed along once more. This continues until each student has read the work of every other group member and has received her/his own writing back.

5. After taking several minutes to incorporate the changes and additions suggested by reading the work of the others, each student places her/his chart and first-draft story in her/his Ideas File.

EXTENSIONS

To help students become sensitized to the dramatic conflicts in other people's stories, hand out extra copies of the worksheet and assign for analysis and charting:

- an episode of a dramatic television show;
- a remembered incident as told by a friend or family member; and
- a movie

THREE TYPES OF CONFLICT

	PROTAGONIST	GOAL	MOTIVATION	ANTAGONISTS (vs Person/Environment/Self)
1				1) 2) 3)
2				1) 2) 3)
3				1) 2) 3)

GSR 9

Getting Started: Skill Set 6

Understanding Story and Scene Structure

✍️ **YOU WILL NEED:**

- GSR 10—STORY OUTLINE SHEET—1 per student (Skill 1)
- GSR 11—STORY EVENT SHEET (Skill 1)—6 copies, photocopied and cut into strips
- 6 containers to hold Story Event slips (Skill 1)
- GSR 12—A SCENE FROM A SHORT STORY to be read aloud—1 per student (Skill 2)

PURPOSE

In order to create a successful work of fiction, an author has to be competent first at constructing scenes and then at using them to build a story. Young authors need to work at developing these essential skills. As well, authors understand that stories are about the changes or problems that occur in people's lives. As students learn to recognize how dealing with change and resolving problems form the basis for interesting fiction, they will also begin to realize that real people are constantly learning from and being changed by their experiences, whether they are successful or not.

SKILL 1: UNDERSTANDING STORY STRUCTURE

Introduction and Modeling

1. The teacher draws the following story outline chart on the board (or puts it up on the screen):

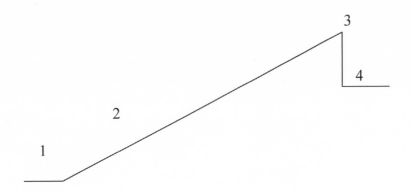

2. The teacher now proceeds to tell the class about a movie s/he recently saw or a book s/he recently read, in which the main character encountered a problem or a change in her/his life and had to deal with it. (e.g., In *The Hobbit*, Bilbo Baggins is dragged away from his safe, predictable life in the Shire by the wizard Gandalf to go on an adventure. In the movie *Speed*, there's a bomb planted on a city bus and set to detonate if the bus slows down below 50 miles per hour.) While describing the problem/change, the teacher labels the part of the chart numbered 1 *problem/change/ challenge*.

3. The teacher goes on to explain that the character tried very hard to solve the problem or deal with the problems arising from the change or overcome the challenge. While describing what actions the character took to deal with her/his situation and whether each one was successful, the teacher labels the part of the chart numbered 2 *attempts to deal with situation*.

4. Finally, the character did solve the problem or adjust to the change or overcome the challenge. While describing the climactic scene in which this happened, the teacher labels the part of the chart numbered 3 *problem is solved, challenge is met, change is accepted*.

5. Following the climax, the main character's life went back to normal, but it was a different normal than before. While describing this part of the story, the teacher labels the part of the chart numbered 4 *life returns to normal*.

Guided Practice

1. Each student pairs up with a partner, and each pair of students designate themselves as Student A and Student B. The teacher asks Student A of each pair to describe to Student B the plot of a movie s/he has just seen or a book s/he has just finished reading, using the same structure as the teacher has put up on the board.

2. The teacher now leads the class in a discussion to identify and label the parts of the chart with the following terms: *Story Event*, *Rising Action*, *Climax*, and *Resolution*.

3. The teacher summarizes what is on the chart:

    The Story Event (1) can be a problem, a challenge, or a change that disrupts the normalcy of the hero/ine's life. If it is a problem, then the Rising Action (2) will be about the hero/ine's repeated (and unsuccessful) attempts to resolve it. If it is a change or a challenge, then the Rising Action (2) will be about the hero/ine's attempts to deal with all the problems that arise from the change or that stand in the way of her/his meeting the challenge. In all these cases, the hero/ine wishes only to get past the Story Event and return to living a normal life. In the Climax (3), the hero/ine finally resolves the problem, overcomes the challenge, or accepts and adapts to the change. In the Resolution or Denouement (4), we see that the hero/ine's life has returned to a different kind of normalcy, but it is a normalcy that the character can live with because s/he has changed as well.

4. Student B of each pair now tells Student A the plot of a story that Student B has just finished reading or viewing, identifying each part of the story using the labels on the STORY OUTLINE SHEET.

Practice

1. The class is organized into six groups. Each group is given a container holding a number of STORY EVENT slips. Each group member selects a slip from the container and receives a copy of the STORY OUTLINE SHEET from the teacher.

2. Working independently, each student uses the Question and Answer technique to imagine *what happens next* in order to generate ideas to develop her/his story.

3. The student then selects three or four possible actions by the Protagonist and arranges them in the most effective order for telling the story before entering them on her/his worksheet.

Students should be reminded that in order to create suspense, each problem on the rising action should be worse than the previous one, and each action taken by the Protagonist should make her/his situation more difficult than it was before. At the climax, the Protagonist should be facing the worst problem or be in the most difficult situation of the entire story.

4. The worksheet is completed with a brief description of the Protagonist's life after the climax and how dealing with the Story Event has changed her/him.

Product

1. Each student first-drafts the story s/he has just finished charting.

2. The class organizes into groups, each containing authors whose stories begin with the same Story Event. Each group member shares her/his story by reading it aloud to the rest of the group.

3. Each student's first-draft story should be placed in her/his Ideas File.

SKILL 2: UNDERSTANDING SCENE STRUCTURE

Introduction and Modeling

1. The teacher reads aloud A SCENE FROM A SHORT STORY to the class.

2. The teacher elicits answers from the students to the following questions:
    - *Who is the main character in this scene?*
    - *What is the character's goal in this scene?*
    - *What action does the character take to achieve her/his goal?*
    - *Is the character successful? If not, why not?*
    - *What is the character's reaction to her/his success or failure?*
    - *What does the character decide to do next?*

3. The teacher then draws on the board the Scene Structure diagram below, and explains that every scene in a story, including the one just read, has these five parts: Purpose, Action, Reaction, Peak, and Decision.

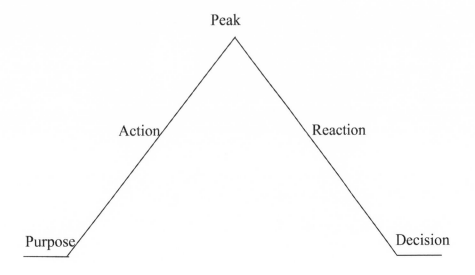

Referring to the scene read in Step 1, the teacher and class work together to place the various parts of the scene on the diagram.

It should be pointed out that there are three types of Peaks for a scene and that the students will need to learn these terms:

ACHIEVEMENT—the character achieves her/his goal in the scene

CONFRONTATION—the character is prevented from achieving her/his goal in the scene

REVELATION—the character learns something that renders her/his goal invalid or unimportant, forcing her/him to choose a different goal

4. Referring to the scene that was read in Step 1, the teacher and class discuss which type of Peak it has and what might have happened if the scene had peaked differently.

Practice and Product

1. The teacher draws a fresh Scene Structure diagram on the board and writes in the following:

    Purpose—a teen has decided to ask her/his uncle for a summer job

    Action—s/he goes to the uncle's workplace and talks to him

2. The class is organized into three groups. Members of Group A will complete the scene by having it peak with ACHIEVEMENT, Group B will have it peak with REVELATION, and Group C will have it peak with CONFRONTATION.

3. Working independently within her/his group, each student then completes the scene chart and writes the resulting scene.

    Students may need to be reminded that they are writing a scene, not an entire story. Scenes can be very short—some are just a paragraph long.

4. The class is organized into groups of three, each containing one student from Group A, one from Group B, and one from Group C. Each student author in a group reads her/his completed scene aloud to the other two.

5. Each student's scene should be placed in her/his Ideas File.

EXTENSIONS

Now would be a good time to stop and review with your students the steps involved in generating and developing story ideas:

Wonder about everything you see, hear, or experience. Brainstorm questions that begin with WHO, WHERE, WHY, and HOW, and let your imagination answer them.

"What-if" to come up with an intriguing situation, then put a main character into that situation and use the Question and Answer technique to imagine what happened before and what happens next.

Construct a strong Dramatic Conflict for your story, being sure to give the Protagonist all three kinds of Antagonists to deal with.

Think carefully about the superficial and underlying themes of your story and establish what these are before you begin to write.

STORY OUTLINE CHART

Clarify your story idea by filling in
this diagram:

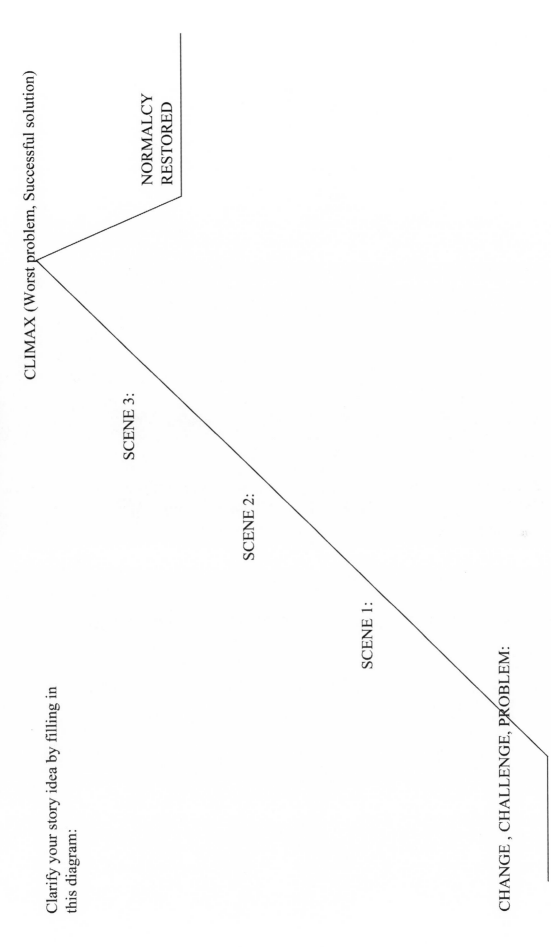

CLIMAX (Worst problem, Successful solution)

NORMALCY
RESTORED

SCENE 3:

SCENE 2:

SCENE 1:

CHANGE , CHALLENGE, PROBLEM:

STORY EVENTS

1. After being independent all his/her life, an ailing grandparent or other elderly relative is no longer able to care for her/himself and is forced to move in with the protagonist's family. Financially and emotionally, the family has been under a strain lately, even without this new responsibility. What happens next?

2. The protagonist's parent or guardian announces that in order to make ends meet, she will have to turn their home into a day care center. There haven't been small children in the house for years. Suddenly there are five. What happens next?

3. After writing an article for the school newspaper about teen gangs, the protagonist receives a death threat. What happens next?

4. The protagonist's best friend has had a few drinks at a party, and the protagonist refuses to let him/her drive him/herself home. While driving the friend's car, the protagonist is involved in a minor traffic accident which is not his/her fault. The car is damaged. What happens next?

5. A lottery ticket which the protagonist received as a birthday gift is a big winner. The protagonist appears in person to collect his/her winnings and that same day has his/her name and picture in the paper. What happens next?

6. The protagonist wins a school election s/he entered as a joke. The principal has made it clear that s/he expects the protagonist to either fail miserably or admit that s/he can't do the job and bow out. What happens next?

7. The protagonist receives a phone call in the middle of the night from his/her best friend. The friend sounds drunk, is obviously frightened, and can't tell the protagonist where s/he is. What happens next?

8. The protagonist is falsely accused of theft and loses his/her job. What happens next?

SCENE FROM A SHORT STORY

Vijay peered over the top of the brick wall around Old Man Zielinski's yard. The ground was littered with leaves and broken twigs. And there was his ball, tucked between the roots of an old maple tree in the middle of the yard. Nimbly, Vijay swung himself over the top of the wall and dropped down onto the bed of dry leaves with a muted crunch. He wasn't about to leave his ball on somebody else's property, no matter what stupid stories were being whispered about.

However, two steps into the yard, he heard something that stopped him in mid-stride. Frowning uneasily, Vijay struggled to identify the sound. It was close, somewhere to his left, and it reminded him of someone shaking an almost-empty box of cereal, or a baby's rattle. . . .

Rattle! Now he saw it, the tail of a large snake sticking out of a pile of leaves not two feet away from him. Vijay's eyes widened in horror. He tried to shout, but all that came out was a choked squeal. The rhythmic twitching of the rattler's tail was almost hypnotic—Vijay couldn't stop staring at it as he backed, ever so slowly, away from the snake, closer and closer to the wall.

The moment he felt his hand touch rough bricks behind him, Vijay whirled and flung himself up and over the wall. He fell down on the other side, still flushed and panting with terror. Snakes! Zielinski's yard was crawling with poisonous snakes. Vijay could have been killed. He had to tell someone, had to warn everyone to stay away from the old man's yard.

After reading the above scene, can you answer the following questions?

1. Who is the main character in this scene?

2. What is the character's **purpose** in the scene?

3. What **action** does the character take to achieve the goal?

4. Is the character successful? If not, why not?

5. What is the character's **reaction** to his/her success or failure?

6. What does the character **decide** to do next?

Getting Started: Skill Set 7

Writing Descriptively: Wake Up Your Senses

✍ **YOU WILL NEED:**

- For Station 1 (Sense of Smell):
  - 10 plastic containers with lids, numbered consecutively
  - 10 interesting aromatic things or substances put inside the containers
  - GSR 13—SENSE OF SMELL CHART—class set
- For Station 2 (Sense of Hearing):
  - A playback device and headset
  - 10 interesting sounds, each recorded for about 5 seconds
  - GSR 14—SENSE OF HEARING CHART—class set
- For Station 3 (Sense of Touch):
  - 10 numbered containers (must be opaque)
  - 10 items with interesting textures
  - GSR 15—SENSE OF TOUCH CHART—class set
- For Station 4 (Sense of Sight):
  - 10–12 small everyday items arranged on a tabletop
  - A cloth to cover the tabletop
  - Plain paper—1 piece per student
- GSR 16—DESCRIPTIVE WRITING WORKSHEET—1 per student (Skill 2)

PURPOSE

In order to give a reader the illusion of being in an actual place at an actual time, the author must provide descriptive details that stimulate the reader's senses in her/his imagination. In order to describe sensory details convincingly, an author needs to have experienced them her/himself. It is important, therefore, that young authors reawaken their senses and establish a growing vocabulary of sensory words and phrases to enhance their reality as well as their writing.

SKILL 1: AWAKEN YOUR SENSES

Introduction: The Day before Guided Practice

The teacher explains that in the next two class periods the students will be rotating through four stations. Each station will focus on one of the senses and will present a number of items to be smelled or touched, a series of sounds to be listened to, or observation exercises to be performed. If a chart is supplied at the station, each student is to take one and fill it out without conferring with others.

Charts that have already been completed can be discussed and compared after the rotation part of the period.

The students will be rotating in groups at regular intervals, half the class covering Stations 1 and 2 and the other half covering Stations 3 and 4 on the first day, then switching for Day 2 to ensure that each student has rotated through all 4 stations. If the class period is one hour long, rotation should be at the twenty-minute mark, leaving twenty minutes for first-drafting. In a forty-minute period, rotation should be at the fifteen-minute mark, leaving ten minutes for first-drafting. *The class should be organized into four roughly equal-sized groups at this time.*

Guided Practice

The students assemble in their groups and begin rotating through the stations. Each student experiences the sensory activities planned for the various areas and fills in the appropriate charts. (These are supplied at each station.)

First half of class: At Station 1, students are to take turns cracking open the lids on each of the plastic containers one at a time, smelling what is inside and reclosing the container before filling in the corresponding numbered line on the chart.

At Station 2, they are to listen to the recorded sounds one at a time and fill in a line of the chart for each.

Following the rotation part of the period, each student then selects her/his favorite line from each of the charts and writes a first-draft paragraph combining the information on the two lines. If there is time, students may pair up and read their paragraphs aloud to each other.

Second half of class: At Station 3, students are to take turns reaching a hand into each of the numbered containers one at a time, fingering the item inside, and reclosing the container before filling in the corresponding numbered line on the chart.

At Station 4, the teacher leads each group in one of the following exercises to test students' powers of observation:

1. The students have two minutes to study the items on the tabletop. Then they turn their backs to the table for fifteen seconds and close their eyes. During this time, the teacher removes some items and rearranges the rest. When the students look at the table again, they are to determine from visual memory which items have been removed.

2. The students study the tabletop for two minutes, after which the teacher covers up the display with the cloth. Each student then takes a piece of paper and begins writing as detailed a description as possible of what s/he saw on the tabletop, including information about colors, shapes, size, position relative to other objects, and so on. After several minutes, the teacher uncovers the items once more to let students compare their descriptions from memory with the actual items.

Following the rotation part of the period, each student selects her/his favorite line from the chart, matches it up with one of the items on the table, and first-drafts a paragraph that includes both visual and tactile sensory descriptions. If there is time, students may pair up and read their paragraphs aloud to each other.

Practice and Product (Optional)

1. Each student chooses one of the items on the table to write about in a paragraph incorporating one line from each of the three charts found at Stations 1 through 3.

2. These first-draft paragraphs should be attached to the three charts and placed in the students' Ideas Files for possible further development.

SKILL 2: EXPLORE DIFFERENT SENSES

Introduction

1. The teacher reviews briefly with the students what happened in the previous classes at each of the sensory stations. Were students able to focus on one sense only, when asked to? What happened to the other senses then? Our senses

help us to define reality. What happens to reality if one sense becomes much more acute than the others? Or if we are robbed of one or more of our senses?

2. The students count off from one to four. The teacher explains that for today's exercise, each student who said the number 1 will be a specialist in the sense of sight, each student who said number 2 will specialize in the sense of hearing, each number 3 will focus on the sense of smell, and each number 4 on the sense of touch. Everything they write today will be from the point of view of a person who only has one sense, the one in which they now specialize.

Guided Practice

1. Each student receives a copy of the DESCRIPTIVE WRITING WORKSHEET. On the worksheet, each student independently writes a single descriptive sentence about each of the ten listed situations while the teacher circulates, offering assistance where necessary.

2. The class is now organized into groups of four, each containing one number 1 (sight specialist), one number 2 (hearing specialist), one number 3 (smell specialist), and one number 4 (touch specialist).

3. Each group's members now put their sentences together to create ten short descriptive paragraphs. Additional detail may be added to make the paragraphs read more smoothly and feel more complete, but they should still retain details pertaining to all four of the senses.

4. Each group can select its favorite paragraph to read aloud to the rest of the class.
   Each student should ensure that s/he has a personal copy of all the paragraphs completed by her/his group.

Practice and Product

1. Working independently, each student selects one of the ten short paragraphs produced by her/his group in the previous part of the activity and rewrites it two different ways:
   1—from the point of view of a blind person
   2—from the point of view of a hearing-impaired person
   Students should be reminded that when one sense is taken away, the remaining senses become more acute. Additional sensory detail will therefore need to be added to each situation.

2. Students can be organized into groups of three or four to share their paragraphs with one another.

3. Each student's completed paragraphs should be placed in her/his Ideas File.

EXTENSIONS

Tell your class the story of the five blind men who encountered an elephant and used their other senses in an attempt to identify it. "It is a snake," declared the first blind man, who was holding the elephant's trunk. "It is a huge bird," said the second blind man, who was standing near the elephant's large, flapping ear. "It is a tree," said the third blind man, and "It is a forest of trees," said the fourth. (They were touching the elephant's legs.) The fifth blind man was standing near the elephant's rear end. "I don't know what it is," he said, "but it has terrible bad breath."

Challenge your students to write a description of the following things as it might be given by one of these blind men:

a traffic intersection | an airport
a hospital emergency room | a shopping mall at Christmas
their backyard | the school cafeteria
a public library | a children's playground

THE SENSE OF SMELL

Smell #	Words to Describe It	Pleasant or Unpleasant?	What Image(s) or Memory does it bring to mind?	What do you think it is?
1				
2				
3				
4				
5				
6				
7				
8				
9				
10				

THE SENSE OF HEARING

SOUND	DESCRIPTION OF SOUND	POSSIBLE SETTING FOR THIS SOUND
1.		
2.		
3.		
4.		
5.		
6.		
7.		
8.		
9.		
10.		

THE SENSE OF TOUCH

Item #	Words to Describe How It Feels	Pleasant or Unpleasant?	What Color, Image(s) or Memory does it bring to mind?	What Setting does it bring to mind?
1				
2				
3				
4				
5				
6				
7				
8				
9				
10				

DESCRIPTIVE WRITING WORKSHEET

Write a single sentence using only one of your senses to describe each of the following:

1. You are inside the house, and it is raining outside.

2. There is a cat curled up beside you on the sofa.

3. You are sitting at the kitchen table while someone prepares breakfast.

4. You are in the living room, and there is a fire in the fireplace.

5. You are walking and take a shortcut through a children's playground.

6. You pass by a school building just as it lets out.

7. You are at a shopping mall on a busy Saturday afternoon.

8. You are at a service station waiting for your car to be repaired.

9. You are visiting someone at the hospital.

10. You are at an amusement park.

Getting Started: Skill Set 8

Writing Descriptively: Use Figurative Language

✍ **YOU WILL NEED:**

- GSR 17—QUESTIONNAIRE—1 per student (handed out the day before, to be completed for homework)
- GSR 18—METAPHOR WORKSHEET #1—1 per student (Skill 2)
- GSR 19—METAPHOR WORKSHEET #2—1 per student (Skill 3)
- GSR 20—ASSESSMENT SHEET—enough for class (Skill 3)

PURPOSE

Authors frequently use similes and metaphors to make their descriptive writing more evocative. It is important that students understand and learn how to use these powerful writing tools.

SKILL 1: UNDERSTANDING SIMILES

Introduction and Modeling

1. The teacher takes up the first question on the QUESTIONNAIRE with the class: *If you were a kind of tree, what kind would you be?* The teacher writes some of the students' answers on the board, along with a descriptive word that could apply to each tree, and turns each answer into a simile. For example:
    Joan is an oak. (strong) Joan is as strong as an oak.
    Jonathan is a poplar. (tall) Jonathan stands as tall as a poplar.

2. The teacher then points out that there are two kinds of comparisons, *literal* and *figurative*, and the ones on the board are figurative. (Joan isn't really as strong as an oak, nor is Jonathan really as tall as a poplar. All these sentences are saying is that Joan is *very* strong and Jonathan is *very* tall.) Figurative comparisons that use "as . . . as" or "like" are called *similes*. *(This word should be written on the board.)*

3. The teacher then supplies examples of literal comparison, writing them alongside the similes on the board:
    Denim is as strong as sailcloth.
    My younger brother is now as tall as I am.

4. The teacher and class discuss and establish the difference between a figurative and a literal comparison: In a literal comparison, the similarity or difference is measurable, and the two things being compared can be placed side by side. In fact, without both halves of the comparison being mentioned, the sentence loses its meaning. *My younger brother is now as tall as I am* is not the same thing as *My brother is now very tall.*

49

5. The teacher points out that each of the similes can be rewritten using the word *very* because the purpose of the comparison is to *emphasize* whatever quality is shared by the two items being compared. That is why authors often use similes and other figures of speech to make their descriptions more lively and interesting.

Practice and Product

1. The class is organized into groups of three or four.

2. Together, the students in each group share their answers to the rest of the questions on the QUESTIONNAIRE sheet and help one another to turn each answer into a simile.
   Students should test whether each comparison is a true simile by rewriting it, as above, to see if it still makes sense.

SKILL 2: UNDERSTANDING METAPHORS

Introduction

1. The teacher reviews with the class that a simile is a one-point comparison and puts a couple of examples on the board to illustrate:

   > *Harry runs like the wind. (i.e., very <u>fast</u>)*
   > *Monica is as <u>graceful</u> as a gazelle.*

2. The teacher then explains that there is a figure of speech that will let you compare several points at once:

   > *For example, let's think of a woman, perhaps your grandmother or someone else's grandmother. She's strong. And she's stubborn. Once she makes up her mind, she can't be budged. But she is the center of her family. She keeps it steady and gives it a solid foundation. What does she remind you of (a rock, an anchor, etc.)? Therefore, in describing her, you could say: Grandma was the rock (or the anchor, etc.) of her family.*

3. The teacher explains that this is a figure of speech called a *metaphor*, and that the words "as . . . as" and "like" are not found in a metaphor.

Modeling

1. The teacher now asks the students to think for a moment about a large city. What have they heard about the core of the city? What kind of people would they find there? The students jot down in point form all the things that the city brings to their minds. The students are then asked to think of something they would compare it to, something that also brings those same thoughts or images to mind, and to create a sentence that will express this comparison as a metaphor.

2. On the board, the teacher writes one of the students' metaphors and beneath it, three points of similarity (expressed as similes) elicited from the students to support the metaphor. For example:

   > *M: The city is a jungle.*
   > *S: It's as full of predators as a jungle.*
   > *S: You can lose your way in the city as easily as in a jungle.*
   > *S: The city has as many strange noises as a jungle.*

Practice and Product

The class is organized into working groups of four or five. Each student receives a copy of METAPHOR WORKSHEET #1, and each group of students works together to complete it.
   Students should be instructed to save these sheets, as they are part of the next skill activity's writing assignment.

SKILL 3: EXTENDING METAPHORS

Introduction and Modeling

1. The teacher reviews with the class the definition of a metaphor. The teacher then points out that metaphors can be either *revealed* or *subtle*. "The city was a jungle" is an example of a *revealed* metaphor because both halves of the comparison are provided by the writer. In a *subtle* metaphor, the author wouldn't tell the reader what the city was being compared to but would instead describe it using words and images that would also make the reader think of a jungle. As well, because there is no limit to the number of points of similarity in a metaphor, that single comparison could be extended through an entire story or poem, just by the writer's continuing to add more descriptive details. The teacher writes an example of a subtle metaphor on the board:

    Silent and alert, Maury prowled the night streets, looking for unwary tourists carrying wads of cash.

2. The teacher asks the students to imagine, *What prowls at night looking for unwary victims?* (A big cat—Maury is being compared to a panther or a tiger.) What are the descriptive details or images that establish the comparison? (The silent alertness of a hunter, the action of prowling at night, and the word "unwary" to describe the tourist who will be his prey.) These are written down in a list on the board.

3. The teacher then asks the students to add further details to the list. What other resemblances might there be between a man like Maury and a big cat? ("Sinking his claws" into someone, dressing all in black or in a black-and-orange striped T-shirt, speaking in a growling voice, etc.) Students should be told that when these descriptions are added, later in the story, they are still part of the same metaphor—Maury as a big cat. The metaphor has been *extended* with further detail. You cannot do this with a simile.

Practice

1. Each student receives a copy of METAPHOR WORKSHEET #2, and students organize into groups of three to discuss and develop the possibilities on the worksheet.

2. Each student then chooses one of the questions on either of the metaphor worksheets and uses it as the basis for a descriptive paragraph containing an extended metaphor.
    If this writing activity is being done as a summative assignment to be handed in for evaluation, the paragraph should also contain at least one simile and a variety of sensory details.

Product (if being evaluated)

1. When the students have completed their first-draft versions, the teacher hands out copies of the ASSESSMENT SHEET, to be used as a guideline for author revision and editing of the paragraphs.

2. Final-draft versions of student work should be handed in as part of a package that includes the edited first-draft copy and evaluation sheet.

EXTENSIONS

This would be a good time to reinforce the students' understanding of simile and metaphor with a poetry mini-unit.

The class can be organized into groups of five, with each group receiving a selection of poems written by a single poet. (Robert Frost, E. J. Pratt, and Carl Sandburg would be good poets to include in this exercise.) Group members can take turns reading each poem aloud to the rest of the group, who can identify various examples of simile and metaphor and discuss how their use has made the poem more effective.

QUESTIONNAIRE

1. If you were a kind of tree, what kind would you be? Think of a word that would describe both you and the tree.

2. If you were a kind of breakfast cereal, what kind would you be? Make up a list of ingredients that would appear on the outside of the box.

3. If you were a piece of furniture in your home, what piece would you be? Think of two words that would describe you.

4. If you were an animal in the zoo, what animal would you be? Would you be happy there?

5. If you were a method of transportation, what would you be? What would your favorite destination be?

6. If you were a fiction book in the library, which genre would you be? Would you have a happy or a sad ending?

7. If you were a plant in your backyard, which plant would you be? Describe your leaves and flowers, if any.

8. If you were a kind of footwear, what kind would you be? Think of words that would describe both you and the footwear.

METAPHORS—PART 1

Explain the metaphor in each of the following sentences and record three similes that support it:

1. His <u>rough</u>, <u>scratchy</u> voice <u>grated</u> on my nerves.
   M:

   S:

   S:

   S:

2. The <u>stealthy</u> assassin <u>stalked</u> his victim <u>relentlessly</u> through the night.
   M:

   S:

   S:

   S:

NOW TRY INVENTING SOME METAPHORS OF YOUR OWN. Be sure to write down the points of comparison that support each one.

1. Compare an unlikable person to an animal, plant, or insect:

2. Compare a family gathering to a rock concert, a wake, or the Olympics:

3. Compare a messy bedroom to the aftermath of a natural disaster (a tornado, an earthquake, etc.)

METAPHORS—PART 2

1. Compare an unlikable person to a fish. Decide which fish to use and then list as many points of similarity as you can think of.

2. Compare someone to a musical instrument. Think of three ways you could compare this person to one of the following: a piano, a guitar, a drum, a tuba.

3. Compare someone's means of transportation to an animal, wild or domesticated. Think of at least two points of comparison.

4. List four ways in which a room in your house can be compared to a public place (such as a zoo, a museum, a department store, etc.).

5. How many different things can you compare an umbrella to? Think of the umbrella open and closed, moving and still, striped, colored and black, and used in different kinds of weather.

WRITING A DESCRIPTIVE PARAGRAPH
ASSESSMENT SHEET

Student Author's Name: _____

SCORING		
3 = EXCELLENT 2 = SATISFACTORY 1 = NEEDS IMPROVEMENT		

HAS THIS AUTHOR:	3	2	1
1. selected a strong metaphor to develop?			
2. extended the metaphor with appropriate details?			
3. added similes that create pictures in the reader's mind?			
4. made effective use of sensory details?			
5. created interesting opening and closing sentences?			
Column totals:			

TOTAL SCORE =   /15

Comments:

WRITING A DESCRIPTIVE PARAGRAPH
ASSESSMENT SHEET

Student Author's Name: _____

SCORING		
3 = EXCELLENT 2 = SATISFACTORY 1 = NEEDS IMPROVEMENT		

HAS THIS AUTHOR:	3	2	1
1. selected a strong metaphor to develop?			
2. extended the metaphor with appropriate details?			
3. added similes that create pictures in the reader's mind?			
4. made effective use of sensory details?			
5. created interesting opening and closing sentences?			
Column totals:			

TOTAL SCORE =   /15

Comments:

Getting Started: Skill Set 9

Writing Descriptively: Use Descriptive Language

✍ **YOU WILL NEED**

- GSR 21—DESCRIPTIVE ACTION WORDS WORKSHEET—1 per student (Skill 1)
- Thesauri and dictionaries—class set of each (Skill 1)
- Two lists of short sentences on the board but concealed (Skill 2):

A	B
Her/his eyes flashed angrily.	She/He raced away.
Her/his coat hung in tatters.	She/He dropped the vase.
She/He wore a sly grin.	She/He picked up the letter.
Color drained from her/his face.	She/He punched the pillow.
Her/his heart was pounding.	She/He lifted the child.

PURPOSE

Authors understand that the connotations of words can make them more descriptive and therefore more powerful. Students need to learn to recognize and use words with specific connotations in order to make their writing more effective.

SKILL 1: USE DESCRIPTIVE ACTION WORDS

Introduction

1. The teacher explains to the class that descriptive writing also includes action words. An author must be able to describe people's actions in colorful, interesting ways, and that means using a variety of "flavorful" verbs. The teacher writes an example on the board:

   The boy ran down the street.

   The teacher explains that the verb "ran" is not terribly descriptive. It doesn't describe how the boy ran, and it gives no hint as to why the boy was running. In the world of ice cream, this would be vanilla. Vanilla verbs are boring.

2. The teacher changes the verb in the example to "jogged." What does this tell the reader about how the boy is running? What does this suggest as his probable reason for running? "Jogged" is obviously a much more descriptive verb than "ran," and therefore much more flavorful. *(Chocolate crunch. Delicious.)*

3. The teacher changes the example again, substituting the verb "fled." Now how is he running? Now why is he running? Either of these two flavorful verbs tells you much more about the boy than the verb "ran," making them much better choices for a piece of descriptive writing.

Guided Practice

1. The teacher distributes thesauri and dictionaries and explains that whenever the students want to find more flavorful alternatives to any kind of vanilla word, they can find them in the thesaurus. A thesaurus is a collection of synonyms and related words, sort of a menu of different flavors. The dictionary is used to verify the meaning of any synonym the student plans to use, to ensure that it will communicate correctly what the student wants to say (i.e., that the word means what the student thinks it does).

2. Each student receives a copy of the DESCRIPTIVE ACTION WORDS WORKSHEET. The teacher and students together complete the first question on the worksheet to ensure that everyone understands how to use the thesaurus and dictionary to finish the assignment:
   - First, look up the vanilla word in the thesaurus and choose three promising-tasting synonyms to fill in the blanks in the three sentences given.
   - Then look up each synonym in the dictionary to discover exactly what it means and get a mental picture of how the subject of the sentence is acting or moving.
   - Finally, deduce why s/he might be acting or moving that way and write a brief explanation in parentheses following each sentence. For example:
        The boy raced down the street. (He was late.)
        The boy scurried down the street. (He was loaded down with books.)

Practice and Product

1. Students can pair up with working partners to complete this assignment in class.

2. Each pair of students can share their most exciting verb with the rest of the class.

3. Each student's completed worksheet should be placed in her/his Ideas File.

SKILL 2: PUT DESCRIPTION AND ACTION TOGETHER

Introduction and Modeling

1. The teacher explains to the students that authors need to be able to describe a character while the character is involved in an action. The author cannot freeze the action of a story and describe the character standing still. The action must continue. There are two common sentence patterns that combine both character description and action description, and learning to use these in their writing will greatly improve the pacing and effectiveness of the students' work.

2. The teacher writes an example of the first sentence pattern on the board:
        Andrea's back and legs glistened as she slid through the water like a dolphin.
   The teacher points out that in this one sentence there are two separate descriptions—one of Andrea and one of her action, each contained in a separate clause. The students supply a couple more examples of this same pattern, and the teacher writes them on the board.

3. The teacher points out that there is a second pattern authors can use and writes an example on the board:
        Grinning fiendishly, he drew his dagger.
   Once again, there are two descriptions—one of the character and one of the action he is performing. This time, one of them has been summed up in a participial phrase. The teacher should underline the "-ing" and "-ly" in the sentence and elicit several more examples of this pattern from the students.

4. It should be emphasized to the students that either pattern could be used for any of the examples on the board. To demonstrate, the teacher can have students convert each of the examples from Step 2 into the participial phrase pattern and each of the examples from Step 3 into a complex sentence. Each pair of examples should now be compared to determine which of the two alternatives makes a better-sounding sentence.

Guided Practice

1. The teacher reveals the two lists, A and B, written on the board.

2. Together, the teacher and students find different ways to combine a character description from column A with an action description from column B, using the two sentence patterns illustrated earlier. These sentences are written on a section of the board, one below the other.

Practice and Product

1. Working independently, each student selects her/his favorite sentence from the lists on the board and develops it into the outline for a story.

   If students have practiced Skill Sets 1 and 2, they can do this by asking Who, Where, Why, and How to expand the sentence into an intriguing situation and then using the Question and Answer technique to imagine *what happened before* and *what happens next* scenarios.

   If they have practiced Skill Set 3: After choosing one of the scenarios for her/his story, each student can then formulate a superficial theme and a list of possible underlying themes. Finally, the student should settle on one underlying theme from her/his list and write it down.

2. Students can assemble in groups of four for sharing. Each group member can describe her/his story to the other three.

3. Each student's outline should be written up as a first-draft story for homework. Completed homework can either be shared in class with listening partners or handed in for formative assessment by the teacher.

DESCRIPTIVE ACTION WORDS WORKSHEET

Fill in the blanks with a more descriptive synonym for the verb in brackets to tell HOW the character performed the action, and then explain briefly WHY s/he did it that way:

(RAN)   The boy _____ down the street.

                  The boy _____ down the street.

                  The boy _____ down the street.

(WALKED)   Elizabeth _____ out to the corner.

                  Elizabeth _____ out to the corner.

                  Elizabeth _____ out to the corner.

(JUMPED)   Ken _____ over the fence.

                  Ken _____ over the fence.

                  Ken _____ over the fence.

(TALKING)   Rose couldn't stop herself from _____.

                  Rose couldn't stop herself from _____.

                  Rose couldn't stop herself from _____.

(CRIED)   Daniel _____ all night.

                  Daniel _____ all night.

                  Daniel _____ all night.

(SHAKING)   She stood _____ in the doorway.

                  She stood _____ in the doorway.

                  She stood _____ in the doorway.

Getting Started: Skill Set 10

Putting Everything Together

✍ **YOU WILL NEED:**

- Each student's Ideas File
- GSR 22—CREATING THE FIRST DRAFT—1 per student
- GSR 9—THREE TYPES OF CONFLICT SHEET—1 per student
- GSR 10—STORY OUTLINE SHEET—1 per student
- GSR 23—PROOFREAD WITH A PARTNER CHECKLIST—1 per student
- GSR 24—ASSESSMENT SHEET—1 per student

PURPOSE

As students take a story through the entire process from outlining to final draft, they will begin to understand how all the steps fit together to ensure the success of their writing.

WEEK 1: CREATE THE FIRST DRAFT

1. The teacher explains to the students that they will be completing a major writing assignment to be handed in for evaluation and that over the next two weeks they will be expected to go through all the steps in the writing process.

2. The teacher hands out copies of CREATING THE FIRST DRAFT for students to use as a reference. These steps should be reviewed and discussed with the class:

   1. *Go through your Ideas File to find a sentence, paragraph, or outline that twigs your imagination. This will be the starting point for your story.*
   2. *Ask Who, Where, Why, and How to develop the idea into an intriguing situation. Then use the Question and Answer technique to generate possible "what happened before" and "what happens next" scenarios. Select the most promising scenario to develop into a story outline.*
   3. *Establish the superficial theme of the story and write it down. List some possible underlying themes that might be appropriate for this story.*
   4. *Identify the protagonist and use the THREE TYPES OF CONFLICT Chart to outline the dramatic conflict of your story. Be sure to give the hero/ine all three kinds of antagonists to deal with.*
   5. *Decide what the change or problem will be that disrupts the normality of your hero/ine's life and list all the problems that will arise from the change or all the ways your hero/ine can attempt to solve the problem. Select the most interesting possibilities and arrange them for increasing dramatic effect. Remember that in a problem story, all attempts must be unsuccessful until the climax, when the problem is finally resolved, and in a change story, the worst problem must be kept for the climax, when the hero/ine finally accepts and adjusts to the change. Diagram your story on the STORY OUTLINE Sheet.*

 6. *Now go back to the list of underlying themes and select the one that fits best with the story you've outlined. Bear this underlying theme in mind as you diagram the structure of each scene of your story. Remember to link each scene to the one before it by making the character's decision in the preceding scene her/his intent in the current one.*

 7. *Once you are satisfied with the story you've outlined, write it in first-draft form.*

3. Each student is given the rest of the week to follow these steps and produce a completed first draft. This may be done in class, as homework, or both. An abbreviated version of the above list can remain on the board for reference as the students work.

WEEK 2: REVISE, EDIT, AND POLISH

1. The teacher hands out copies of the PROOFREAD WITH A PARTNER CHECKLIST. Using this as a guide, students revise their first-draft work and produce a second draft of their stories.

2. The teacher then puts up on the board (or on an overhead screen) the following guidelines for peer-assisted editing and goes over them with the class:

 1. *Editing partners are to work together, first on one author's story and then on the other author's story, discussing areas where improvements can be made. Editing partners are not to trade stories and work independently.*

 2. *Editing partners are to check off each criterion on the author's sheet as soon as it has been discussed, using the left-hand column of the checklist. Authors will use the right-hand column while editing their second drafts to check off that each criterion has been considered and necessary improvements have been made. A checklist without check marks down both sides will be considered incomplete.*

 3. *Editing partners may suggest improvements but are not allowed to make changes to an author's work. Authors are the owners of their work. Therefore, if changes are necessary, the author must be the one to make them.*

 4. *Remember that the job of an editing partner is to help the author improve. All criticism of another writer's work must therefore be constructive (i.e., suggesting ways to make it better).*

3. Students then pair up with editing partners and work together to improve both their stories, following the instructions on the board or screen. Once the editing partner has signed off on her/his side of the sheet, each student author is responsible for making the necessary improvements to her/his second-draft work, checking off the other side of the sheet. The student then rewrites the story as a third draft.

4. The teacher hands out copies of the ASSESSMENT SHEET for students to use as reference while polishing their completed third drafts.

5. Polished work is then recopied in final-draft form, formatted in accordance with the teacher's instructions, and packaged together with the student author's planning materials, edited previous drafts, peer-editing checklist, and ASSESSMENT SHEET. The entire package is submitted to the teacher for summative assessment.

TEACHING TIP

I recommend against setting a length for student fiction-writing assignments. When a student author resorts to padding or cutting a story to fit a specific number of words, s/he frequently ends up destroying the charm or the effect of the tale. Some stories are perfectly told in five hundred words or less, while others won't unfold properly in fewer than five thousand. Each student should be permitted to tell the tale that is inside her/him, without having to worry about word counts; nonetheless, students need to take all writing assignments seriously, treating each one like a contract with an editor and respecting deadlines.

 Time management is important. Show your students how to work backwards from the specified deadline to determine when their first, second, and third drafts must be completed in order to have the final product ready to hand in on schedule.

CREATING THE FIRST DRAFT

1. Go through your Ideas File to find a sentence, paragraph, or outline that twigs your imagination. This will be the starting point for your story.

2. Ask *Who*, *Where*, *Why*, and *How* to develop the idea into an intriguing situation. Then use the Question and Answer technique to generate possible *what happened before* and *what happens next* scenarios. Select the most promising scenario to develop into a story outline.

3. Establish the *superficial theme* of the story and write it down. List some possible *underlying themes* that might be appropriate for this story.

4. Identify the protagonist and use the THREE TYPES OF CONFLICT Chart to outline the *dramatic conflict* of your story. Be sure to give the hero/ine all three kinds of antagonists to deal with.

5. Decide what the *change or problem* will be that disrupts the normality of your hero/ine's life and list all the problems that will arise from the change or all the ways your hero/ine can attempt to solve the problem. Select the most interesting possibilities and arrange them for increasing dramatic effect. Remember that in a problem story, all attempts must be unsuccessful until the climax, when the problem is finally resolved; and in a change story, the worst problem must be kept for the climax, when the hero/ine finally accepts and adjusts to the change. Diagram your story on a STORY OUTLINE Sheet.

6. Now go back to the list of underlying themes and select the one that fits best with the story you've outlined. Bear this underlying theme in mind as you diagram the structure of each scene of your story. Remember to link each scene to the one before it by making the character's decision from a preceding scene her/his purpose or intent in the current one.

7. Once you are satisfied with the story you've outlined, write it in first-draft form.

GETTING STARTED: SHORT STORY CHECKLIST
REVISE, EDIT AND PROOFREAD WITH A PARTNER

AUTHOR'S NAME: _____

EDITING PARTNER'S NAME: _____

Partner has checked	Editing and Proofreading Criteria	Author has improved
	1. The story has an interesting title.	
	2. The story is built around a strong and textured dramatic conflict: (a) with multiple antagonists (vs person, vs environment, vs self); (b) with a powerful motivation for pursuing the story goal.	
	3. Characters are shown reacting realistically to their settings and to one another.	
	4. The story is revealed to the reader as a series of scenes, each structured to make best use of the five scene elements: purpose, action, peak, reaction, decision.	
	5. The rising action leads to a decisive and emotionally satisfying climax (i.e., the problem is solved, the challenge is overcome, the change is finally accepted).	
	6. The Illusion of Reality has been successfully created: characters, settings and plot events all influence and impact upon one another.	
	7. The story contains sensory details to make the descriptions more interesting and realistic.	
	8. The author has made effective use of at least one simile or metaphor to underline or reinforce the theme of the story.	
	9. Actions are described using 'flavorful' verbs that paint pictures in the reader's head.	
	10. The story is interesting to read.	
	11. The author has shown respect and consideration to the reader by making the story as well-written as possible: (a) spelling has been checked (not just on the computer); (b) there are no run-on sentences; (c) there is correct use of capital letters, commas and apostrophes; (d) there is agreement of subject and verb (i.e., both are either singular or plural).	

Remember to attach this checklist (completed by both editing partner and author) to the back of your edited second draft when assembling your package for submission.

RUBRIC: GETTING STARTED SHORT STORY

STUDENT NAME: _____

CRITERIA	LEVEL 1 (below grade level) (Student shows limited ability.)	LEVEL 2 (approaching grade level) (Student shows moderate ability.)	LEVEL 3 (at grade level) (Student shows considerable ability.)	LEVEL 4 (above grade level) (Student shows exceptional ability.)
THEME	Theme is superficial only, hasn't been thought through.	Both superficial and underlying themes are present but could be better integrated into the story.	Underlying theme is present throughout the story and demonstrates an appropriate level of thought.	Underlying theme underpins the entire story and demonstrates a sophisticated level of thought.
DRAMATIC CONFLICT	Conflict is incomplete. Protagonist lacks a believable goal and/or sufficient motivation. Only one antagonist.	Conflict is complete but weak. Antagonists present no real obstacles or goal is relatively unimportant.	Conflict is complete and strong, with at least 2 antagonists.	Conflict is complete and textured, with 3 or more antagonists.
STORY STRUCTURE	Story is incomplete. Story event is not a problem, change or challenge and/or does not lead to a rising action/climax. Author has written a plot summary rather than a series of scenes.	Story is complete but weak. Story event is relatively unimportant to protagonist. Climax is indecisive or emotionally flat. Scenes could be more firmly linked to each other.	Story is complete and well-structured. Scenes are firmly linked to one another and effectively sequenced from story event to climax. Climax is both logical and decisive.	Story is well and thoughtfully organized. Scenes flow seamlessly from story event to climax and resolution. Climax is both inevitable and emotionally satisfying for the reader.
ILLUSION OF REALITY	Weak. Characters do not react to their settings or to one another in realistic ways. Reader keeps getting jarred out of the story.	Moderate. Character reactions are generally realistic. Plot, character and setting need to interact more.	Strong. Plot, character and setting impact on one another. Character reactions are generally realistic.	Utterly convincing. Character reactions are completely natural and realistic. Plot, character and setting are interdependent.
DESCRIPTIVE LANGUAGE	Student has not included any similes or metaphors in the story. Little or no sensory detail. Few to no descriptive word choices.	Student has included similes and/or metaphors in the story but sensory detail and descriptive word choices could be stronger.	Student has included similes and metaphors in the story, along with some interesting sensory detail and descriptive action words.	Student has made interesting and effective descriptive writing choices. Similes and metaphors are original, description is vivid.
GRAMMAR, SPELLING, PUNCTUATION	Limited effectiveness: 10 or more major and minor errors, sometimes affecting meaning.	Moderate effectiveness: 8 or more major and minor errors but meaning is not affected.	Considerable effectiveness: 5 to 8 major and/or minor errors but reader is not distracted from the story.	Transparent writing: Fewer than 5 errors in total.

Part II

WRITING THE SHORT STORY

GRADE 10 (15 YEARS) AND UP

Story writing is both an art and a science. Having captured and developed a story idea, the author must then use written language to create a bridge between her/his own mind and that of the reader. If the bridge is well built, then the scenes, images, and characters that cross it may carry with them not only a story, but also powerful truths and emotions that will move and change the reader.

This module is about writing a complete short story, from opening scene to denouement. Here your students will learn how to organize and put together a compelling tale that will immediately draw the reader in and make her/him care about the main characters. Along the way, students will also gain valuable practice in story planning and in using a wide variety of writing techniques.

AIMS AND OBJECTIVES

Aims:

In this module and the next, students will have the opportunity to:

1. continue to engage in interactive learning;
2. deepen their understanding of both the creative process and the writing process;
3. understand the importance of each stage in the writing process;
4. gain a better understanding of human motivations and behavior;
5. further explore and appreciate the nature of personal reality;
6. enhance their decision-making and problem-solving skills; and
7. strengthen their confidence in their own opinions and writing.

Objectives:

Students will be encouraged to:

1. find and develop believable characters for their stories;
2. explore and appreciate the relationship between people and places, in real life and in fiction;
3. further develop their group-learning skills;
4. practice analyzing causes and predicting outcomes of imagined events;
5. practice organizing and outlining stories before writing;
6. increase their familiarity with the revising, editing, and polishing process; and
7. develop a "critical eye" as they practice evaluating the quality of their own writing and that of others.

	SKILL SET	DESCRIPTION	NCCS ANCHORS ADDRESSED
1	Building a strong main character	Students practice the techniques that authors use to bring fictional personalities to life on the page.	R.1, R.3, R.10, W.4, W.5, W.10
2	Constructing a solid dramatic conflict	Dramatic conflict is the backbone of any story. Student authors practice building and developing the strongest possible level of dramatic conflict in their stories.	R.1, R.3, R.6, R.8, R.9, W.3, W.4, W.5, W.10, L.6
3	Creating an interesting setting	Students practice developing and using realistic, well-written settings to strengthen and deepen every element of their stories.	W.2, W.3, W.4, W.5, W.7, W.8, W.10, L.3, L.5
4	Structuring a story effectively in scenes	Students learn how to make their stories flow interestingly from beginning to end.	R.1, R.2, R.3, R.5, W.3, W.4, W.5, W.10
5	Setting up the story	As student authors practice techniques for laying a strong story foundation, they will come to appreciate the importance of good beginnings.	R.5, W.3, W.4, W.5, W.10
6	Hooking the reader	Students practice creating story openings that will 'hook' the reader's attention from the very beginning of a tale.	R.5, W.3, W.10
7	Putting it all together	Students are now ready to put together all the writing skills they have learned in a story-writing assignment which will be revised, edited and polished and handed in for evaluation.	W.3, W.4, W.5, W.6, W.10, L.1, L.2, L.3, L.5

Writing the Short Story: Skill Set 1
Building a Strong Main Character

✍️ **YOU WILL NEED:**

- Students' Ideas Files
- WSR 1—CHARACTER BIO SHEET: PRESENT SITUATION—2 per student (Skill 1)
- WSR 2—CHARACTER BIO SHEET: PAST CIRCUMSTANCES—2 per student (Skill 1)
- WSR 3—CHARACTER BIO SHEET: FUTURE GOALS—2 per student (Skill 1)
- WSR 4—PREDICTING CHARACTER REACTIONS SHEET—1 per student (Skill 1)
- A short-short story (to be read aloud)—(Skill 2)
- WSR 5—DIMENSIONS OF LIFE CHART—1 per student (Skill 2)—1 per student (Skill 3)

PURPOSE

Authors know that the key to a successful story is strong characterization—making the reader believe in and care about the main character(s). While practicing the techniques that authors use to bring fictional personalities to life on the page, students will also gain a deeper understanding of the principal characters in their own real-life story.

SKILL 1: DETERMINE WHO THE MAIN CHARACTER IS

Introduction

1. The teacher asks the class: *How do you know who the main character of a story is?* Referring to books, television programs, and movies that students have read or viewed, the teacher and class then discuss ways for a reader/viewer to identify the main character or protagonist of a story. This discussion should lead to a list of "identifying characteristics" written on the board:

   The main character is:

   1. *the one whose goal is most important in the story.*
   2. *the one the reader/viewer cares about the most.*
   3. *the one we learn the most about in the course of the story.*
   4. *the one whose point of view dominates the story.*
   5. *the one who has learned and/or changed by the end of the story.*

2. The teacher observes that in order to present a convincing main character to the reader, an author needs to get to know the character very well. Many authors won't even begin writing until they "have a handle" on the protagonist of their story.

   A good place to start is with a character biography. And because every person is the protagonist of her/his own life story, a good way to practice filling out a bio on a main character is to do it first on oneself.

Guided Practice

1. Each student receives a copy of each of the three CHARACTER BIO SHEETS: PRESENT SITUATION, PAST CIRCUMSTANCES, and FUTURE GOALS. Each student then fills in the three charts with factual (i.e., not imagined) information about her/his own life and personality.

   Students should understand that it is not necessary for them to fill every space on the charts. Blanks may be left if information is unknown or too personal to reveal.

2. When done, each student can pair up with a partner, and they will discuss their two sets of bio sheets. In particular, students should notice how past circumstances have contributed to each partner's present situation and what connections may exist between the plans outlined on each student's goals sheet and the information recorded on her/his other two charts.

   To facilitate the discussion between partnered students, the teacher may wish to write some questions on the board:

   Which aspects of your present life are the direct result of events in your past?
   To what extent are your plans for the future determined by your life so far?
   If you could go back in time and change any one thing in your past, what would that be and why?
   What effect would the change have on both your present choices and your future plans?

Practice

1. Each student now looks through her/his Ideas File for an interesting character to be the protagonist in a story that the student will write.

   Students need to realize that not all characters have the "right stuff" to be heroes/heroines. Possible protagonists should therefore be measured against the list of identifiers written on the board to rule out those characters that are not deep enough or strong enough to play the main role in a story.

2. Each student receives a second copy of each of the three bio sheets and proceeds to fill these out for her/his selected character. *Allow about twenty to twenty-five minutes for this activity.*

   Students will need to make sure that all the facts recorded on the sheets are compatible with a realistic character. In other words, there should be a cause-and-effect relationship between the character's past and present circumstances, as well as a logical connection between the character's life so far and her/his goals and aspirations, *just as if the character were a real-life person.*

3. After working independently for the pre-set period of time, students should be instructed to get into pairs or groups of three to "bounce ideas off one another." Group mates can thus help one another to complete the three sheets with realistic information.

Product

1. Students remain in their groups of three while the teacher hands out copies of the PREDICTING CHARACTER REACTIONS SHEETS. Each group proceeds to discuss what each of their three main characters would do in each situation and why.

   A character's behavior should follow naturally from his or her past experiences and current circumstances. Students should be instructed to ensure that each character's reactions jibe with the information recorded on the three bio sheets.

2. Each student chooses one of the situations on the handout and works independently to first-draft a paragraph describing her/his main character's reactions to it. The character will need to react in at least two of the following ways: by taking action, by experiencing an emotion, by thinking about what is happening.

3. If there is time, students can get back into their groups of three and share their paragraphs before putting them into their Ideas Files.

SKILL 2: EXPLORE THE CHARACTER'S DIMENSIONS

Modeling and Guided Practice

1. The teacher reads a short-short story aloud to the class. The teacher and students discuss the characters in the story to determine which one is the protagonist.

2. A copy of the top half of the DIMENSIONS OF LIFE CHART is drawn on the blackboard. The teacher and students discuss the chart headings and the story just read and together fill in the chart on the board for the protagonist of the story.

3. The teacher then explains the difference between character *description* and character *dimension*. (A character being described means the author is *telling* the reader about the character—"Sally was feeling very happy." However, a character with dimension *shows* the reader who and what s/he is through the character's speech, thoughts, and actions—"Grinning from ear to ear, Sally danced out the door.")

4. The bottom half of the DIMENSIONS OF LIFE CHART is added to the board, and the teacher and class fill it in together while further discussing the main character in the short-short story.

Practice

1. Each student receives a copy of the DIMENSIONS OF LIFE CHART.

2. Each student's homework for the next day is to read a short story of his or her choice and fill in the chart for the protagonist of the story.

Product (if the class will not be continuing on to Skill #3)

Students can form groups of three and take turns telling one another about the protagonists they charted for homework. Members of each group can select their favorite of the three characters to share with the rest of the class, either as a straightforward oral presentation or by writing up a profile of the character for an imaginary matchmaking Web site and posting it on the bulletin board.

SKILL 3: MAKE THE READER CARE

Introduction

1. Students form groups of four and proceed to share the information they recorded for homework on their DIMENSIONS OF LIFE CHARTS. Members of each group discuss which of their four protagonists they would most like to read about in a novel or see in a movie and why.

2. In whole-class discussion, student groups share their favorite protagonist and their reasons for choosing this character (*e.g., interesting personality, funny, character shares similarities with the reader, character has many good qualities, etc.*).

3. The teacher lists these reasons on the board and points out that even without having read the story, students have already started to like and care about the main character. As authors, the students should strive to create a main character that the reader will like and care about right from the beginning of the story.

4. Together, the teacher and class brainstorm all the things that people do and say that make other people like them: *they make people smile, they're truthful without hurting people's feelings, they're willing to share their belongings, and so on.* (This list should be recorded on the board for student reference during the next steps.)

Practice

1. Each student takes out the three bio sheets filled out earlier for the protagonist of her/his story and reads them over to refresh her/his memory. Students may wish to make additions or changes to these sheets before going on to the next step.

2. Each student then receives a blank DIMENSIONS OF LIFE CHART and proceeds to fill in the top half of the chart for the protagonist of her/his story.
    Students should be encouraged to consider all the ways in which their characters might have been affected by past experiences, how they might be influenced by their present situation, and what they might have been thinking when they formulated their goals. The more points that are written onto the chart, the wider and more interesting the author's storytelling choices will be.

3. Referring to the list of characteristics on the board, each student then brainstorms and records possible ways in which her/his specific story character might demonstrate these qualities in order to make the reader like and care about her or him.

Product

1. Each student writes three short descriptive paragraphs about her/his character, each revealing one of the character's DIMENSIONS OF LIFE along with one or more of her/his positive qualities.

2. If there is time, students can pair up to share their paragraphs with a partner.

3. These paragraphs, along with the DIMENSIONS OF LIFE CHART, should be placed in each student's Ideas File.

EXTENSIONS

The dimensions of a character can be revealed not only by what s/he wears, says, and does, but also by where s/he lives, where s/he likes to spend time, and what s/he owns. Challenge your students to describe what is revealed about a character who:

> has never lived in a house s/he didn't build entirely with her/his own hands
> recently emptied her/his bank account to purchase a racehorse
> refuses to own a computer or television set
> spends most of her/his spare time window-shopping in malls
> speaks fluent Klingon and goes to sci-fi conventions all over the country
> spends every spare minute playing video games
> collects and restores old musical instruments

CHARACTER BIO SHEET: PRESENT SITUATION

AGE: BIRTHDATE:

FAMILY (both by blood and by marriage):

OCCUPATION: HAPPY AT HER/HIS JOB?

PLACE OF RESIDENCE (i.e., type of building, what street, which city, which country):

(PREFERRED) MODE OF TRANSPORTATION:

SPECIAL TALENTS/SKILLS:

HOBBIES/INTERESTS:

MEDICAL SITUATION (Any problems?):

FEARS:

WEAKNESSES/BAD HABITS:

FAVORITE FOOD:

FAVORITE SPORT (Does s/he play or watch?):

PET PEEVES:

POLITICAL LEANINGS:

OTHER (e.g., Dreamer, doer, or talker? Optimist or pessimist? Leader, follower, or loner? Innocent or cynical? Strong or weak?):

CHARACTER BIO SHEET: PAST CIRCUMSTANCES
(which have helped to create the character's present personality and situation)

FAMILY MEMORIES:

CHILDHOOD ILLNESSES:

EDUCATION HISTORY (e.g., List schools attended and where. Was each year completed successfully? Areas of interest? Any honors or scholarships? Favorite subject and favorite teacher? Most vivid school memory?):

EARLIER TRAUMATIC EXPERIENCE (Any external scars?):

VACATIONS TAKEN (Where? With whom? Did they have fun?):

ACHIEVEMENTS, AWARDS, AND TROPHIES:

FAILURES/DEFEATS:

OTHER:

CHARACTER BIO SHEET: FUTURE GOALS
(dreams, hopes, and aspirations)

WHAT WILL THIS CHARACTER BE DOING IN FIVE YEARS?

MARRIAGE/CHILDREARING PLANS:

CAREER PLANS:

DREAM RESIDENCE (What kind of house and where situated?):

NEXT VACATION (Where and with whom?):

NEW HOBBIES:

PROGNOSIS OF MEDICAL SITUATION:

PROJECTED AWARDS OR ACHIEVEMENTS:

WHAT DOES THIS CHARACTER WANT MORE THAN ANYTHING IN THE WORLD?

PREDICTING CHARACTER REACTIONS

What would your character do, say, and think in each of the following situations?

1. The character is at a movie theater, and sitting behind her/him are a mother and her very young child. Eventually, the child becomes bored and cranky and starts to whine and complain rather loudly. The mother tells the child, also rather loudly, to be quiet and let her enjoy the movie. She clearly has no intention of taking the child outside and letting everybody else enjoy the movie.

2. The character has just returned from a long and tiring shopping trip. While putting away groceries, s/he discovers that s/he left one bag behind at the store. It only contained a few items, easily replaceable, but at the store the character just left the items came to five dollars, and at the local food market the same items would cost eight dollars.

3. The character is wakened in the middle of the night by the doorbell ringing. When s/he calls out, "Who's there?" through the locked door, there is no reply, just the muttering sound of male voices. The character is not expecting visitors at this hour, and the people at her/his door refuse to identify themselves.

4. While dining at a restaurant, the character notices that a man at the next table is choking. Quickly, the character goes to his assistance and administers the Heimlich maneuver, saving the man's life. "I must reward you," says the man, pulling out his wallet.

5. The character is on her/his way to an important job interview. S/He steps into the elevator and stands directly in front of a fast-food delivery person. After entering the personnel office and announcing her/himself to the receptionist, the character notices that there is a rather large food stain on her/his jacket.

THE DIMENSIONS OF LIFE

CHARACTER IS: _____

PHYSICAL DESCRIPTION The character's appearance.	EMOTIONAL DESCRIPTION The character's feelings.	PSYCHOLOGICAL DESCRIPTION The character's thoughts.
PHYSICAL DIMENSION: The character influences her/his surroundings.	EMOTIONAL DIMENSION: The character demonstrates her/his feelings.	PSYCHOLOGICAL DIMENSION: The character reveals her/his thoughts.

Writing the Short Story: Skill Set 2
Constructing a Solid Dramatic Conflict

✏️ **YOU WILL NEED:**

- A two- to three-page short story or children's picture book (to be read aloud)—(Skill 1)
- WSR 6—SHORT STORY CONFLICT CHART A—class set
- Copy of Chart A on the board (Skill 1)
- WSR 7—DRAMATIC CONFLICT CHART B—on the board (Skill 2)
- WSR 8—DEVELOPING ANTAGONISTS SHEET—class set (Skill 2)
- A different two- to three-page short story (Skill 3)
- WSR 9—KNOW YOUR CHARACTER'S GOAL WORKSHEET—class set (Skill 3)
- WSR 10—REAL GOALS AND STATED GOALS WORKSHEET—class set (Skill 3)

PURPOSE

Dramatic conflict is the backbone of any story. Authors know that the reader of a fiction tale is most interested in seeing how a character with a burning need or desire to achieve a particular goal will overcome obstacles, solve problems, and finally reach the goal. This is what makes life interesting and dramatic and also what creates a solid work of fiction. Young authors, therefore, need to practice building and developing dramatic conflict in their stories.

SKILL 1: BUILD CONFLICT AROUND STORY GOALS

Introduction and Modeling

1. The teacher reads aloud to the class either a children's picture book or a short-short story of about two or three pages. *(There should be at least three or four characters in the story, and these should be listed on the board at some point before or during the reading.)*

2. Using the SHORT STORY CONFLICT CHART A on the board with reference to the story just read, teacher and class discuss what should be filled in on the chart by asking and answering the following questions:

   1. Who is the main character in this story?
   2. What does s/he want more than anything in the world?
   3. Why does s/he want it?
   4. What does s/he do to achieve it?
   5. Who or what gets in the way?

Practice

1. Each student receives a copy of the SHORT STORY CONFLICT CHART A and then pairs up with a working partner.

2. Each pair of students selects any character from the story just read by the teacher, makes that character the hero/ine of her or his own story, and comes up with three different goals for the character (one for each line of the chart).

3. Students then work together with their partners to fill in their charts, developing each goal into the outline for a separate story.

Product

1. Working individually, each student selects her/his favorite line of the chart and writes it up as a first-draft story.

2. For sharing, the teacher may divide the room into areas, assigning one to each character from the original story and instructing students to gather there with others who have written about the same selected character. Within each character group, students can pair up with a different partner than before and read their stories aloud to each other.

3. Each student should keep her/his completed chart for further development in Skill 2.

SKILL 2: INCLUDE THREE TYPES OF ANTAGONISTS

Introduction and Guided Practice

1. The headings from DRAMATIC CONFLICT CHART B are written across the board. Teacher and students review the meanings of the terms *protagonist*, *goal*, *motivation*, and *antagonist*.

2. Each student receives a copy of the DEVELOPING ANTAGONISTS SHEET. The teacher reads aloud the first excerpt on the page, and the teacher and students fill in the chart on the board together, discussing and noting the type of antagonist with which the main character is involved *(e.g., Person vs. Person, Person vs. Environment, Person vs. Self)*.

3. Step 2 is repeated for the second excerpt (in which there are two antagonists) and the third (in which there are three antagonists). In each case, the teacher and students discuss and note whether the hero/ine is opposed by another person, by the environment, or by some aspect of her/himself.

   It should be pointed out to students that any kind of being or animal would fall under the heading of "person vs. person," and that an environment can be artificial (an automated security system) as well as natural (a weather pattern).

4. Together, the students and teacher discuss which of the three excerpts presents the most interesting story and why this excerpt is so effective.

   Through discussion, the students should also come to realize that with each additional antagonist, the suspense level increases. In the first scene, Yana seems to succeed very easily; in the second, she makes it to the island but only after an intense struggle; in the third, we see her apparently fighting a losing battle.

Practice

Each student working individually now refers to the SHORT STORY CONFLICT CHART A, which s/he filled out in Skill 1, and develops additional antagonists (if needed to total three different ones) for each line of the chart.

Product

1. The student then selects her/his favorite line from the chart and writes up the story in first-draft form, adding two or three interesting character traits to the protagonist.

   Students should ensure that the three antagonists are included in the story in appropriate (i.e., logical and believable) ways.

2. The class is organized into groups of three for sharing. Students can read their stories to one another, in order to appreciate the narrative texture they have created.

SKILL 3: UNDERSTAND REAL AND STATED GOALS (PART 1)

Introduction

1. The teacher writes the headings for DRAMATIC CONFLICT CHART B across the board:

PROTAGONIST   GOAL   MOTIVATION   ANTAGONIST(S)

2. The teacher then tells the class about a protagonist who used to be an avid mountain climber. One year ago, this person had a fall while climbing a peak. He wasn't badly injured, but since then, he has been "too busy" to go climbing with his friends, and they are beginning to think he's lost his nerve. At the beginning of this story, he is on his way with two buddies to tackle a very dangerous mountain. Teacher and students fill in the chart together:

   Protagonist: mountain climber
   Goal: to climb the mountain
   Motivation: to prove that he hasn't lost his nerve
   Antagonists: the mountain, the weather, etc.

3. The teacher now explains that the protagonist in any dramatic conflict actually has two goals, not one. For example, this mountain climber's stated goal is to climb the mountain . . . but what does he really want? *(To prove that he hasn't lost his nerve.)* Can he achieve his real goal without reaching his stated goal? *(Yes—by taking a risk to help one of his buddies who gets in trouble during the climb or by performing some other feat of courage and strength while on the mountainside.)* As long as he reaches his real goal, will the protagonist be satisfied? *(Yes.)* Will the reader be satisfied? *(Let's find out . . .)*

Guided Practice

1. The teacher asks the class, "What if you could get somebody to think that his real goal was the same as something you wanted him to do?"

2. The teacher then tells the story of the yacht owner whose deodorant doesn't work. *(This was an actual television commercial for a real product years ago.)* She invites a crowd of guests to a party on her yacht, but because she has body odor, the guests mutiny. They put her into a dinghy and tow her a hundred yards behind the boat. Then they offer to take her back aboard if she'll use a particular deodorant powder. She agrees, and at the end of the story, everyone is happily together on the yacht, singing an advertising jingle.

3. To determine what this television commercial is really about, teacher and class together fill in a line of the dramatic conflict chart on the board for the example of the yacht-owner protagonist: Goal—*to rejoin her guests on the yacht*; Motivation—*to end her loneliness and embarrassment*; Antagonists—*her body odor and her guests' refusal to be around her because she smells bad.*

At this point, the students should realize that in both examples so far, the goal of the dramatic conflict is the stated goal, and the character's motivation is her/his real goal.

4. The teacher then changes the chart headings on the board from Goal to Stated Goal, and from Motivation to Real Goal.

5. The teacher points out that if the mountain climber believes that the only way to prove he hasn't lost his nerve is to climb a really dangerous peak, then he has confused his real goal with his stated goal; and if the yacht owner believes that the only way to end her loneliness and embarrassment is to use a particular brand of deodorant powder, then she has confused her real goal with somebody else's goal, namely, the advertiser's.

   The teacher explains that what the yacht owner has done is precisely what the people who sell the deodorant powder want the television viewer to do: to confuse her/his real goal of avoiding loneliness and embarrassment with the stated goal of using their product. That is how advertising works.

6. Teacher and students now brainstorm various strategies that advertisers use to break down the viewer's defenses, and these are listed on the board.

   Teacher's information: Advertising strategies can be boiled down to:
   a. *Verbal associations (jingles, catchy slogans, identifying phrases to help the reader/viewer to remember the product)*
   b. *Carefully chosen spokespersons (suggestions carry extra weight coming from someone who is well known and highly regarded)*
   c. *Images associated with the product (symbols of whatever the viewer/reader is looking for in life—fun, power, freedom)*
   d. *Mini-dramas (the viewer identifies with the protagonist in the scene—as in the deodorant powder commercial)*
   e. *Music (usually with a compelling, urgent beat to grab/hold your attention)*
   f. *Humor (tends to disarm the viewer, catch her/him off guard)*

7. The teacher writes the headings from the KNOW YOUR CHARACTER'S GOAL WORKSHEET across the board, and together the teacher and students proceed to fill in one line of the chart for a product or service currently being advertised that is of interest to the class.

Practice

1. The teacher hands out copies of the KNOW YOUR CHARACTER'S GOAL WORKSHEET and organizes the class into groups of three or four students.

2. Each group is now an advertising agency planning television commercials for three very different products of their own choosing: one food or food product, one item of clothing, and one personal hygiene product (such as toothpaste or acne cream). Each group discusses and records on their charts information about the targeted viewer (age, gender, lifestyle), the product being promoted, what the viewer's real goal might be, and strategies that might work in a commercial aimed at the viewer.

   Each student should be sure to make a personal copy of the chart produced by her/his group.

Product

1. When the charts are completed, each group member selects her/his favorite product and, working independently, outlines a commercial for it, being sure to use at least two of the advertising strategies listed on her/his chart.

2. The students reassemble in their "ad agency" groups and "pitch" their finished commercials to their group mates.

3. Each group then picks its favorite commercial, prepares a thirty-second improvisation based on the outline, and presents it to the rest of the class.

SKILL 4: UNDERSTAND REAL AND STATED GOALS (PART 2)

Introduction and Modeling

1. The teacher explains that sometimes a character does not attain her/his *stated* goal at the end of a story; however, the reader will be satisfied so long as the character achieves her/his *real* goal.

2. The teacher writes the headings from the REAL GOALS AND STATED GOALS WORKSHEET across the blackboard. Teacher and class then discuss the plots of several current movies, identifying in each case what the protagonist's stated and real goals are. They select one of the films to use as an example and together fill in the first line of the chart on the board.

Guided Practice

The teacher now either reads aloud a short-short (two- to three-page) story or reminds the students of a story recently read in class. Teacher and students fill in a second line of the chart for this story, in the process discussing:

> *What were the protagonist's real and stated goals?*
> *Were they both reached at the end?*
> *If only one, which one?*
> *Was the ending of the story emotionally satisfying for the reader?*

Practice

1. The teacher hands out a copy of the REAL GOALS AND STATED GOALS WORKSHEET to each student and organizes the class into groups of three students.

2. Each group then creates and charts three stories, each having three antagonists.
   Each student in a group should be sure to make a personal copy of the group's chart.

Product

1. The groups dissolve. Each student then takes or is assigned a number 1, 2, or 3 and works independently to write up the corresponding numbered line from her/his REAL GOALS AND STATED GOALS WORKSHEET as a first-draft story.

2. The students reassemble in their groups of three and share their stories with their group mates.

EXTENSIONS

Here are some storytelling games that will stretch your students' plotting muscles by letting them explore a variety of dramatic conflict possibilities. Try challenging your students to:

- plot and write a story in which each antagonist is associated with a different geometric shape, a different country, a different color, a different food, a different texture, a different piece of clothing, a different state of matter, a different smell . . . the possibilities are endless.
- create a story about a protagonist who cannot or does not move, but who still encounters all three types of antagonists.
- list all the different ways in which a common household item might become an antagonist in a dramatic conflict, then incorporate the three most interesting uses for the item into a story.
- discover how it might be possible for a single antagonist to fulfill all three roles in a story—person, environment, self—and write the story in which this happens.

- write duet or trio stories—the same plot events unfolding in two or three separate stories, each from the point of view of a different main character with a different goal and therefore developing a different dramatic conflict.
- create a choose-your-own-adventure-style story for readers in a younger grade. (This is not as easy as students might think!)
- write a cliffhanger, in which a protagonist trying to accomplish something quite ordinary encounters antagonist after antagonist. How many obstacles can your students conjure up to plague a teenager trying to get to school on time or an office worker trying to take a quiet lunch break?

SHORT STORY CONFLICT CHART A

	PROTAGONIST	GOAL	MOTIVATION	ACTIONS TAKEN	ANTAGONISTS
1					
2					
3					

DRAMATIC CONFLICT CHART B

	PROTAGONIST	GOAL	MOTIVATION	ANTAGONISTS (person, environment, self)
1				1) 2) 3)
2				1) 2) 3)
3				1) 2) 3)

DEVELOPING ANTAGONISTS

1. Yana stood on the muddy bank and stared across the water. The river had to be a mile wide at this point. The island looked like a speck in the distance. But she could swim there. She'd done it before.

   She took off her clothes, all but her underwear, and tucked them behind a bush. Then she dashed to the water and waded in. Shivering with cold and feeling the current tug at her knees, Yana focused stubbornly on the island.

   She pushed off and began stroking steadily across the river, across the current and then against it as it tried to force her downstream. She pumped her arms, dragging herself determinedly through the water, drawing closer to the island with each stubborn thrust of arms and legs.

   At last, she staggered out of the water and dropped, gasping, onto the stone-strewn beach.

2. Yana stood on the muddy bank and stared across the water. The river had to be a mile wide at this point. The island was a speck in the distance. She had swum a mile before—it was seventy lengths of the pool. But she could tell just by looking that this swim would be far, far different.

   Quickly, before she could lose her nerve, Yana took off her clothes, all but her underwear, and tucked them behind a bush. Then she dashed to the water and waded in. Shivering with cold and feeling the current tug at her knees, Yana focused her thoughts on the island. She tried to visualize herself arriving on the beach, but all she could see was dark, rushing water. Mark should be here, she thought, fighting down a wave of panic. Mark was the one who kept telling her what a great swimmer she was.

   Yana pushed off and began stroking steadily across the river, across the current and then, suddenly, against it as it forced her slowly downstream. *Keep calm*, she commanded herself. *Keep calm and keep stroking. Kick!* But her rhythm faltered as she saw the island slip past her, and then the current had her in its icy grip and was pulling her under. Desperately, Yana pumped her arms and legs, knowing that if she let the current win she would drown. Fear sent strength surging into her weary limbs as she dragged herself through the water, cold and aching but determined not to die without a fight.

   Hours later, it seemed, she staggered out of the water and dropped, gasping and sobbing, onto the stone-strewn beach of the island.

3. Yana stood on the muddy bank and stared across the water. The river had to be a mile wide at this point. The island was a speck in the distance. She had swum a mile before—it was seventy lengths of the pool. But she could tell just by looking that this swim would be far, far different.

   Suddenly, from behind the trees, she heard the growl of a car engine and a man's shout. Grayson had followed her. Quickly, before he could reach her, Yana took off her shoes and flung them behind a bush. Then she dashed into the river. The current tugged at her knees almost immediately, but Yana focused her thoughts on the island. She had to get there!

   Yana pushed off and began stroking steadily across the river, across the current and then, suddenly, against it as it forced her slowly downstream. *Keep calm*, she commanded herself. *Keep calm and keep stroking. Kick!* But suddenly she heard the distant buzzing of a motorboat, coming downstream toward her. It had to be Grayson's boat. Yana's rhythm faltered, and then the current had her in its icy grip and was pulling her under. Desperately, Yana pumped her arms and legs, knowing that if she let the current win she would drown. And if she stayed on the surface of the water Grayson would scoop her up. She was dead either way. A swimmer couldn't outrace a motorboat. Nonetheless, she decided grimly, she would rather die fighting.

   Fear sent strength surging into her weary limbs as she dragged herself stubbornly through the water, cold and aching but determined not to let the river or Grayson win without a struggle.

KNOW YOUR CHARACTER'S GOAL

VIEWER	STATED GOAL: BUY...	REAL GOAL	STRATEGIES USED
1			1) 2) 3)
2			1) 2) 3)
3			1) 2) 3)

REAL GOALS AND STATED GOALS

	PROTAGONIST	STATED GOAL	REAL GOAL	ANTAGONIST OVERCOME (and how overcome)	CONCLUSION (and what was learned)
1					
2					
3					

Writing the Short Story: Skill Set 3
Creating an Interesting Setting

✍ **YOU WILL NEED:**

- A container to hold slips of paper (Skill 1)
- Slips of paper containing new room uses (Skill 1)—see Practice Step 1
- WSR 11—MAKING SETTINGS EXCITING WORKSHEET—1 per student (Skill 2)
- WSR 12—GEOGRAPHICAL SETTINGS SHEET (Skill 4)—photocopied and cut into slips of paper
- 4 containers, one per season group (Skill 7)
- 8 slips of paper for each container, as follows:
  - Sunrise, good weather
  - Sunrise, bad weather
  - Midday, good weather
  - Midday, bad weather
  - Dusk, good weather
  - Dusk, bad weather
  - Midnight, good weather
  - Midnight, bad weather

PURPOSE

Authors are aware that a realistic, well-written setting can strengthen and deepen every element of a story. As students practice developing and using settings both familiar and surmised, they will also increase their awareness of their surroundings and their understanding of how people and events interact with time and place in the real world.

SKILL 1: BECOMING AWARE OF FAMILIAR SETTINGS

Introduction and Guided Practice

1. Together, the teacher and class create on the board a floor plan drawing of the classroom (not necessarily to scale), including all important items *(e.g., the furniture, the clock, the windows, the doorway, etc.)*.

2. The teacher then leads a discussion of how the classroom could be rearranged and adapted to suit a different purpose *(for example, to serve as a backstage room for the school play)*. Which items could be used as is? Which ones would

have to be moved, removed, or disguised? This information is listed on the board in point form to serve as a reference during the next step.

3. A second floor plan is now drawn on the board, showing the modifications discussed by the class and bearing appropriate labels.

Practice

1. The teacher organizes the class into groups of three or four students. Slips of paper have been placed into a container, each denoting a different possible use for the classroom. *(For example: a court trial, a labor union meeting, a dental clinic, a daycare center, a military headquarters, a Red Cross first-aid station, a newspaper office, a haunted house for a Halloween party, etc.)* Each student group selects one situation from the container.

2. The teacher explains that each group is to discuss how the classroom space and furnishings might be turned to the purpose they have drawn from the container. Each group is then to prepare a point-form list describing the conversion, along with a floor plan drawing as in Step 3 (Introduction), illustrating the conversion. The list and drawing will be shared with the rest of the class at the end of the period, and a vote will be taken to determine how successful the students feel the conversion would be.

   A good way to conduct the vote would be to ask groups to post their work along one wall of the classroom, creating a gallery. The teacher would then hand out three different-colored sticky dots to each student—blue for the student's first choice, red for the second choice, and yellow or green for the third choice. As students walk along the gallery, they select the three conversions they feel would be most successful, rank them 1-2-3, and place their sticky dots accordingly to indicate their choices. A pair of students can then tabulate the results to arrive at a winner, assigning three points for each blue dot, two points for each red dot, and one point for each yellow or green dot.

Product

1. Working independently, each student now selects one of the conversions posted on the wall and writes a first-draft paragraph beginning with the sentence: *We had just one evening to transform our classroom into* _____. The paragraph should describe in detail how the transformation was accomplished.

2. Each student's completed paragraph can be read aloud to a partner before being placed in the student's Ideas File.

SKILL 2: MAKING FAMILIAR SETTINGS EXCITING

Introduction and Modeling

1. Each student receives a copy of the MAKING SETTINGS EXCITING WORKSHEET. The teacher explains that in each paragraph on the sheet, the author has made a familiar setting more exciting by pulling selected setting elements into the foreground and giving them a twist.

2. The teacher reads aloud the first paragraph, then leads a whole-class discussion to determine:
   a. which setting elements have been singled out for attention;
   b. why these elements are important to the story; and
   c. how the author has connected them to the story being told.

Practice

1. Students form working groups of three and proceed to repeat Step 2 (above) for each of the other three paragraphs on the handout.

   A group member should be designated as the secretary, responsible for recording on a sheet of paper the group's answers to the three discussion questions.

2. In a whole-class discussion, groups share their findings for each paragraph in turn as the teacher summarizes on the board the four ways in which an author can make a familiar setting more exciting:

    a. Personify elements of the setting—give them emotions, motives

    b. Have certain items conjure up memories

    c. Have characters in a particular frame of mind notice aspects of the setting they would otherwise ignore

    d. Make the setting an antagonist in the dramatic conflict

Product

1. Working independently, each student selects a setting that is familiar to her/him, matches it with one of the writing techniques listed above, and writes a first-person story in which the setting is made interesting and exciting.

    Students who are having difficulty getting started may be provided with two or three opening sentences to choose from: for example, *It was the worst day of my life* or *Really, officer, I'm telling you the truth* or *Things weren't supposed to happen this way.*

2. If there is time, students can pair up and read their stories to each other.

SKILL 3: EFFECTIVE USE OF SENSORY DETAIL

Introduction and Guided Practice

1. The teacher explains to the students that a younger brother has misbehaved badly and has been grounded for a week. His response to being told this is to trash his bedroom. Mother waits until his tantrum is over and then goes to survey the damage. What is she going to find? Specifically, *What will she see, hear, smell, feel, and taste?*

2. The teacher writes these five sensory headings across the blackboard. As the students brainstorm sensory details to include in the scene, the teacher (or a student secretary) records them on the board under the appropriate headings.

3. The teacher then asks: How do you suppose Mother feels as she looks around her son's bedroom *(saddened, disgusted, shocked, angry, helpless, etc.)*? This brainstormed information is listed on the board as well.

4. The students are now organized into groups of three or four. The teacher explains that when Mother looked at what her son had done to his room, she was completely *disgusted*. Selecting sensory details from the chart on the board, each group is to first-draft a paragraph describing the trashed bedroom as vividly as possible.

    It should be emphasized to students that the purpose of this activity is to try to make the reader feel as disgusted as Mother was when she stepped into her son's room. Completed paragraphs will be shared with the whole class and voted on to determine which is the most disgust-inspiring description of a trashed bedroom.

    (Students may need to be reminded to use similes and metaphors, "flavorful" language, and a thesaurus.)

5. Each group's completed paragraph is read aloud to the class. Students can raise their hands to vote for the most *yech*-ful description.

Product

1. Working independently, each student now selects one of the other emotions from the list on the board and proceeds to first-draft a paragraph describing the trashed bedroom in a way that will inspire this new emotion in the reader.

    The description can be written from the point of view of someone other than Mother, if this will make the paragraph more powerful.

2. If there is time, students can pair up and share their first-draft stories with a partner. Partners may offer suggestions for additional sensory details to improve the effectiveness of each other's stories.

SKILL 4: RESEARCHING UNFAMILIAR SETTINGS

Introduction

The teacher has cut a photocopy of the GEOGRAPHICAL SETTINGS SHEET into slips of paper, each one naming a different geographical location, and has placed these in a container. Each student begins by drawing a setting slip from the container.

Guided Practice

1. Students now go to the library/resource center to conduct preliminary research on their assigned locations, using both print and electronic sources. Specifically, students will need to find out where in the world these places are situated and what they look like, both inside and (from) outside. Students can print out images for future reference or can make drawn or written notes. The teacher circulates while students are working, providing assistance where needed.
   NOTE TO TEACHER: In some cases, a location may need to be made more specific before it can be researched (e.g., an Olympic Village, a European castle—there are many of these).

2. Based on the results of their preliminary research, students should narrow their focus, first to either the interior or the exterior of the location (if it is a building) and then to a particular part of the location. The narrower the focus, the more easily manageable the rest of the research assignment will be.
   A maximum of one class period should be sufficient for preliminary research and an additional one or two periods for the completion of the research portion of the assignment.

3. The students continue to search for images and written descriptions of their specific locations, printing out information or making notes/drawings for future reference. Students should be instructed to look not only online, but also in print media such as encyclopedias, back issues of *National Geographic* magazines, and so on.
   It should be explained to the students that even if they are unable to find the full range of sensory detail in the resources of the school library, visual information about a place can often provide clues regarding what a visitor would probably see, hear, smell, taste, and/or feel while there.

Practice

1. Based on the research s/he has done, each student draws a detailed map or diagram of her/his assigned setting and places her/himself somewhere on it, either mentally or literally (with an arrow and "I am here").

2. Each student then makes a list of the sensory details that he or she would notice in that location, ensuring that as many of the five senses as possible are included.

Product

1. Each student now decides on an emotion that s/he wants the reader to feel and selects two or three significant aspects of the setting that should evoke this emotion.

2. The student writes a descriptive paragraph, focusing on the selected aspects of the setting, including at least three kinds of sensory detail, and using one of the strategies listed in Skill 2 to make this location "come alive" for the reader.
   The teacher may wish to collect this piece of writing for formative assessment.

3. For sharing, the class can be organized into groups of four. Students can pass their written work around for silent reading by other members of their group.

SKILL 5: BUILDING HISTORICAL SETTINGS

Introduction and Guided Practice

1. The teacher and class brainstorm a list of eight to ten historical settings *(e.g., the court of Elizabeth I, the maiden voyage of the Titanic, winter in Valley Forge, a pirate ship in the Caribbean, the site of gladiatorial combat in the Roman Coliseum)*, and these are written on the board.

2. The students then assemble in groups of four. Each group selects or is assigned a different historical setting and goes to the library/resource center to research it, using both print and electronic sources. Specifically, students need to find out what it would have been like to be there, experiencing the setting. What would they have seen, heard, smelled, tasted, and/or felt?

    The teacher should instruct students to search for drawings and old photographs as well as written descriptions of their selected/assigned locations. Valuable information can be found in encyclopedias, in back issues of National Geographic *magazines, and so on. Information can be printed out for students' reference, or they can make notes. In most cases, a location may need to be made more specific before it can be researched (e.g., the court of Elizabeth I was a large place with many corners. Do preliminary research and pick one room.).*

    HINT: An effective way to expedite the research process is by dividing the work among the members of each group and then having them pool their findings. In a group of four, for example, one person could browse Web sites or online databases, a second could check out back issues of periodical magazines, a third could delve into print encyclopedias, and a fourth could mine the circulating bookshelves.

    Each student should be instructed to ensure that s/he has a personal copy of her/his research group's findings.

Practice and Product

1. After the time allotted for research is over, each student working independently first-drafts a descriptive paragraph about the group's setting. Each paragraph should try to evoke a particular emotion in the reader. Each paragraph should contain plenty of realistic sensory detail, as in Skill 4, and should also make use of one of the strategies listed in Skill 2 to bring the setting to life for the reader.

2. The research groups reassemble. Each student reads her/his paragraph aloud to the other group members, who may offer suggestions for improvement.

SKILL 6: BUILDING FUTURISTIC SETTINGS

Introduction and Modeling

1. The teacher and class brainstorm a list of eight to ten common settings in the present. These should be places most students can visualize without having to do research *(e.g., a hospital, a movie theater, a race track, a prison, a factory warehouse, a shopping center, etc.)*. The settings are listed on the board.

2. The teacher leads a class discussion on the changes taking place in education due to the rapid advancement of technology *(e.g., online sources for research, the electronic publication and distribution of textbooks, virtual learning, voice-controlled computer programs that compensate for students' physical and learning challenges, etc.)*. During the discussion, the teacher or a student secretary records these changes on the board.

3. The teacher then asks: If changes continue at this rate, do you think there will still be schools as we know them two hundred years from now? If so, what do you think they'll look, sound, smell, feel, and taste like? If not, what do you think will replace them, and what will *those* settings look, sound, smell, feel, and taste like?

    As students brainstorm answers to these questions, the information is recorded in point-form notes jotted on the board.

4. The teacher explains that s/he and the class will now work together to compose a descriptive paragraph, written from the point of view of a time traveler who has just returned from the future and is reporting what s/he has seen there. This person is experiencing an emotion (sadness, alarm, optimism, etc.) and wants the reader to feel the same way s/he does about the future of education. Before beginning the first draft, therefore, the author must choose which details to include in order to achieve this purpose.

5. Together, teacher and class identify three or four details from the list on the board and first-draft a paragraph, being sure to include plenty of sensory detail. The completed paragraph is then read aloud to the class and its emotional impact scored on a scale of 1 to 5.

Practice and Product

1. Each student selects one setting from the list on the board and follows the process modeled in Steps 2, 3, 4, and 5 (above).

   The student begins by considering how advancing technology is already changing the activities that usually go on in her/his selected setting and jots down a list of the changes in point form.

2. The student then brainstorms and records answers to the questions: If changes continue, will there still be _____ two hundred years from now? If so, what will they look, smell, sound, feel, and taste like? If not, what will replace them, and what will *those* settings look, smell, sound, feel, and taste like?

3. Students should be reminded that they will be composing a descriptive paragraph, written from the point of view of a time traveler who has just returned from the future. This person is experiencing an emotion (sadness, alarm, optimism, etc.) and wants the reader to feel the same way about the future of (health care, shopping, or whatever). Before beginning the first draft, therefore, each student must choose from her/his brainstormed list those details that will inspire the desired emotion in the reader.

4. Using this information, each student now writes up a first-draft descriptive paragraph containing plenty of realistic sensory detail, as in Skill 4, and including the details selected in Step 3 (above).

   If time and interest permit, students may follow up this exercise by doing one of the following:

   > *creating a mural that includes all the selected settings*
   > *improvising a drama that takes place in one or more of these settings*
   > *exchanging paragraphs and drawing pictures of one another's settings*

SKILL 7: ADDING IN WEATHER AND TIME OF DAY

Introduction and Modeling

1. The teacher asks the class, "How do you know when it's about to rain?" *(For example, the air feels heavy, there's a damp smell in the air, dark clouds overhead block the sun, there's a sudden drop in air temperature, the birds stop singing, you can hear thunder rumbling far away, the wind suddenly comes up, etc.)* Students' responses are listed on the board.

2. The teacher then asks, "How can you tell what time of day it is without looking at a clock?" *(For example, length of shadows, direction of shadows, location of sun in the sky, quality of light, temperature of the air, amount of traffic in the street, whether stores are open or closed, etc.)*

   Again, students' responses are listed on the board.

3. The teacher points out that we live in a world with regular patterns of weather and time of day. A setting that lacks patterns of change will not seem realistic to the reader of a story, so it is important for authors of fiction to include weather and time-of-day details in setting descriptions.

Practice

1. The teacher leads the class in brainstorming all the items to be found in a particular outdoor setting, such as a local park or playground. Details should be listed on the board for student reference later on.

2. The class is then organized into four groups, one for each season of the year, and the members of each group brainstorm and record all the possible descriptive/sensory details that characterize the park or playground during their assigned season. *Each group member should ensure that s/he has a personal copy of this list.*

3. Each season group receives a container holding eight slips of paper, each specifying a time of day and either good or bad weather. Each group member selects a slip of paper from the container and will be writing a detailed description of the park or playground at the time of day and in the kind of weather specified.

Product

1. Working independently, each student proceeds to first-draft her/his descriptive paragraph, taking care to include a variety of sensory details in order to create a realistic setting for the reader.

2. When finished, students assemble in four different groups, one for each time of day specified on the slips of paper. Each time-of-day group then divides into a good-weather subgroup and a bad-weather subgroup.

3. Members of each subgroup organize their paragraphs in sequence according to seasons and take turns reading them aloud to the rest of the group.

EXTENSIONS

Some settings naturally seem to lend themselves to certain kinds of stories. For example, the jungle is dangerous, making it the perfect setting for a suspenseful contest between predator and prey. A decrepit old mansion is spooky, making it the perfect place for a hair-raising confrontation with the supernatural. Writers have chosen "perfect settings" for their stories often enough that many readers now automatically expect danger to be lurking in the jungle and ghosts to emerge from the inky shadows of the cemetery. In order to surprise a reader, an author needs to turn such expectations on their heads by setting a tale in an unlikely time and place. As an exercise in creating surprise, challenge your students to write:

- a love story that takes place in a haunted castle, in a cemetery, or in a prison;
- a hair-raising adventure that takes place in their own homes, in a public library, or in a museum;
- a tale of the supernatural that takes place in school, at the supermarket, or at the dentist's office; or
- a mystery that unfolds and is resolved in broad daylight in a restaurant, at a playground, or in a department store.

MAKING SETTINGS EXCITING

1. Scarcely had I announced that child number two was on the way when the 32" flat-screen TV in the living room began throwing tantrums. We were already dealing with sibling rivalry, but our toddler's behavior was angelic compared with the ill temper displayed by that television set. It would wait for the climax of a dramatic show, for the thirty-yard touchdown pass, for the crucial closeup of the villain's face and then spin the picture like a roulette wheel, or replace it with hissing zigzag lines. Naturally, the color reverted to its wild state. Faces, when discernible, were green or purple, sometimes both at once. We debated at length about replacing the TV. We couldn't continue to watch it, and yet with the baby coming we couldn't really afford to buy a new one. My suggestion that we do without was met with an incredulous stare.

2. Maurine dreaded the thought of returning to the apartment, but it had to be done. Terry had left instructions for disposing of his things after the funeral, and the responsibility for carrying out his wishes naturally fell to her. Mothers shouldn't have to bury their children, she thought as the door to his little flat swung silently open. The place was warm, filled with sunlight and neat as a pin. Just the way he always was, right up to the end, she thought with a stab of renewed loss. Tears welled in her eyes as she entered the bedroom, the row of swimming trophies on the dresser top a further painful reminder of the strength and energy she had had to watch ebb away over the months of his illness.

3. Johnson slowly closed the door behind him and stared all around his office, the enormity of his task sinking in for the first time. He had spent years giving this room a comfortably lived-in look, amused and even proud to be nicknamed "Junkman" by the office cleaning staff. Now, with his life on the line, he had to find something out of place in a cluttered mess in which virtually everything was out of place. He had never actually seen a plastique bomb, only knew that it was small and—Lord help him—easy to conceal. Could there be a tiny digital timer blinking away somewhere among the hundreds of files and documents loosely stacked on the floor and the credenza? Stuck to the back of the air conditioner access panel? Buried in the middle of the executive sandbox on his desktop? Tucked behind one of the walls of catalogues on the shelf unit? He would have to search absolutely everything in the room.

4. The plan had looked terrific on paper. Get up onto the roof, ungrate a ventilation shaft, and slide down. Just one detail that louse Murray had failed to mention—that the ventilation ducts narrowed. Now, barely ten yards from her target, Celeste was having to turn her head sideways in order to keep moving, and she could feel the ductwork compressing her hips like a girdle. She would have to turn back.

GEOGRAPHICAL SETTINGS

Eiffel Tower (Paris)	CN Tower (Toronto)	Victoria Falls (Africa)
Red Square (Moscow)	a Shinto temple	an Inuit settlement (Northern Canada)
Tiananmen Square (China)	Great Wall of China	a Dutch windmill
Valley of the Kings (Egypt)	Hadrian's Wall (England)	Grand Canyon
Diamond Head (Hawaii)	Stonehenge (England)	English moors
Acropolis (Greece)	Sydney Opera House (Australia)	an Alaskan glacier
Coliseum (Rome)	Argentinean Pampas	a South African diamond mine
Tower of London	Panama Canal	Taj Mahal (India)
a film studio	The Alamo (Texas)	a theme park
Wailing Wall (Jerusalem)	a European Castle	a fishing village (Newfoundland, Canada)
an Olympic Village	Loch Ness (Scotland)	a Near-Eastern bazaar
an Alpine village (Switzerland)	an Andean village (South America)	an oasis in the Sahara Desert

Writing the Short Story: Skill Set 4

Structuring a Story Effectively in Scenes

✍️ **YOU WILL NEED:**

- File cards (at least 200) and colored pens—1 set of 4 per student
- Students' Ideas Files
- A short story (2–3 pages) that the class has read before—class set (Skill 1)
- WSR 13—SCENE DEVELOPMENT CHART (Skill 2)—1 per student, photocopied on both sides

---

PURPOSE

Authors know that the success of a story depends on how well it is organized for presentation. Scenes must fulfill a variety of story purposes. They must also be firmly linked, to the story theme and to one another, by a cause-and-effect chain of events and character decisions. As students learn how to make their stories flow interestingly from beginning to end, they will become more aware of the differences between real life and fiction.

SKILL 1: STRINGING SCENES TOGETHER

Introduction and Modeling

1. The teacher explains to the class that the scenes of a story are like the beads of a necklace. Just as beads are strung on a wire or cord in a visually pleasing pattern, scenes are strung on a plotline in a logical sequence of cause and effect. Just as some bead arrangements are more visually attractive than others, some scene arrangements are more effective than others for telling a story.

2. The teacher points out that every scene in a story must fulfill at least one, and preferably more than one, of the following scene purposes:

   Advance the plot—the protagonist does something to try to achieve her/his story goal, or the antagonist does something to prevent her/him from achieving it
   Introduce or reveal a character—by her/his words, deeds, or thoughts
   Establish or enhance a setting or mood—including suspense
   Introduce Important Background Information (IBI)

These should be written on the board in different colors of chalk or on a blank transparency using different colors of marker (e.g., green for plot, orange for character, and so on).

3. The teacher hands out a copy of the short story to each student and provides time for the class to reread the story silently.

4. Together, teacher and class then identify the first scene in the story and give it a name or a number, which is recorded on the board. Teacher and class then discuss what happens in that scene and compose a one-sentence summary, which is written on the board beneath its name/number *(e.g., Scene 1: Jack is sitting in the school office waiting to be picked up by his stepfather and wondering what the big emergency is.).*

5. Referring to the list of scene purposes, the teacher and class discuss which of them this opening scene fulfills and how, and this further information is added below the one-sentence summary on the board *(e.g., IBI—the stepfather is a police officer).*

Guided Practice

1. The class is then organized into working groups of four. Each group is instructed to follow the process modeled on the board for the remaining scenes in the story. Group members are to draw up a list of all the scenes in the story, provide a one-sentence summary of each scene, note which of the purposes on the board each scene fulfills, and briefly describe how it fulfills them.

    HINT: Scenes are easier to find if one looks for the decision made at the end of each one by the main character in the scene. At this point, the teacher may wish to review Skill Set 6, Skill 2 from Part I: Getting Started.

2. The teacher and class together discuss and list on the board the order of scenes in the story and their various purposes. Students should note that every scene in the story has at least one (and usually more than one) purpose.

    As well, by using the four different colors of chalk, the teacher can provide a visual demonstration of the necessary *balance and variety of purposes* in an effective story, as each color should appear to be evenly distributed throughout. If there are noticeable clumps and gaps, these should be pointed out and discussed as storytelling weaknesses.

Practice

1. Each student selects a first-draft story or story outline from her/his Ideas File to develop further.

2. The student then takes two file cards, one for the opening scene and one for the closing scene (resolution or denouement). On the closing scene card, s/he summarizes in a sentence or two what happens in the scene, then writes (in the appropriate colored pens), *Plot Purpose: Show that protagonist has achieved goal and normalcy is restored. Character Purpose: Show how main character has changed since beginning of story.* Finally, the student briefly notes on the card how the scene either fulfills or will fulfill these two purposes.

3. The teacher reviews briefly with the class the five important functions of an opening scene, recording them on the board using the appropriately colored chalk (or on a blank transparency using different colored markers):

    > *Establish the setting*
    > *Introduce a main character*
    > *Launch the dramatic conflict (plot)*
    > *Present any IBI*
    > *Grab the reader's interest.*

4. After briefly summarizing what happens in the opening scene of her/his story, each student then copies the five purposes from the board onto the second card (in the appropriate colored pens), noting also how the scene fulfills or will fulfill each of these purposes.

Product

1. Using colored pens and however many file cards are necessary to link up the opening and closing scenes of her/his story, each student first summarizes each additional scene, then lists the purposes that it will fulfill.
   Students should ensure that when the completed cards are laid out in sequence before them, a balanced variety of colors appears.

2. Students reassemble in their earlier groups of four. Standing in front of the story cards of each member in turn, each group is to offer encouragement and suggestions for improvement *(e.g., ways to balance scenes by having them fulfill additional purposes or ways to combine scenes with only one purpose each into stronger, multipurpose scenes, and so on).*
   Students should be advised to hang on to their story cards, as they will be using them for the next two skills.

SKILL 2: PLANNING SCENE DEVELOPMENT

Practice

1. The students get out their story cards and arrange them in order on their desks. Each student reviews the outline of her/his story by reading over the cards, making any adjustments that seem appropriate in order to improve the flow or logic of the story.

2. The teacher hands out a SCENE DEVELOPMENT CHART to each student. The student proceeds to chart her/his story by copying the information from the story cards.

3. When finished, each student pairs up with a partner, to review and improve each other's work. It is important that students check carefully to make sure each scene is firmly linked to the next by a *Decision = Purpose* bond. This keeps the necklace from falling apart.

SKILL 3: STRENGTHENING THE STORY STRUCTURE

Introduction 1

1. The teacher explains that if the scenes of a story are like beads on a string, then the string must be strong enough to hold them all together and in order. In a story, the string is made up of two separate strands: *Dramatic Conflict* and *Theme*. It is important that each of these be established in the opening scene and carried all the way through to the conclusion of the story.

2. Students take out their completed SCENE DEVELOPMENT CHARTS and look at the first scene. The teacher reviews with the class the parts of a dramatic conflict *(Protagonist, Goal, Motivation, Antagonists)*, and teacher and class together discuss different ways to introduce each part at the beginning of a story. For example:
   • *open with action: the protagonist trying to achieve the goal or the antagonist trying to prevent her/him*
   • *open with dialogue: the protagonist identifying the goal and/or motivation or the protagonist and antagonist arguing*
   • *open with description (only if the setting is going to be an antagonist in the conflict)*

Practice 1

1. Students pair up with different partners than in the previous skill activity. The students examine each other's opening scenes, looking for the beginning of the conflict in each story.

2. Student partners then continue tracing the conflict through each of the scenes on the chart, identifying the climax and the resolution of each author's story and discussing ways to strengthen the climax and tie up loose ends in the resolution.

Introduction 2

1. The teacher discusses with the class the various ways for a theme to be delivered to the reader of a story:

   A character can *embody* the theme by her/his actions, words, thoughts, personality or nature.
   A plot event can *enact* the theme by showing the reader what it looks like in action.
   A setting can *reflect* the theme by its nature or the way it is described.
   An author's choice of similes, metaphors, or descriptive language can *reinforce* the theme by bringing it to the reader's mind.

   These 4 ways are listed on the board for student reference.

2. The students now brainstorm examples to go with each item on the list, and the best one or two are recorded on the board as well.

3. The teacher reminds the class how important it is that the theme of a story be delivered in some way in every scene, as this is really the cord that holds the "necklace" together.

Practice 2

1. In pairs once again, the students go over each other's SCENE DEVELOPMENT CHARTS and work together to identify and state the underlying themes of both their stories.

2. Student partners trace the development of the theme in each other's stories and discuss ways to ensure that the theme has been delivered in every charted scene.

Product

Student authors can now proceed to write up their stories, paying special attention to the structuring of their narrative in a "necklace" of scenes.

   At the teacher's discretion, these drafts may be collected for formative assessment or can be revised, edited, and polished for submission and summative evaluation.

EXTENSIONS

Many professional writers use file cards to organize the scenes of a story, among other things. Encourage your students to do as the pros do by:

- filing thumbnail character sketches and postcard plot summaries they might like to develop into a story sometime, each on its own card;
- filing interesting quotations they run across that they might like to use in an article later on (noting on the card the necessary footnote or bibliography information, so they won't have to go hunting for the source a second time);
- building an index of printed resource material, allotting one card per reference book used (including name of article or project, bibliography information, and library identification to make it easy to find again);
- creating a "human resources" file of experts (or people with particular experience/expertise) who can be called upon to provide information that will make a story authentic and believable (name, area of expertise, e-mail address, phone number, how s/he was originally reached); and
- for serious writers, keeping track of manuscripts completed and sent out, using one card per story to show where sent, name of editor, date sent, and date returned or sold.

SCENE DEVELOPMENT CHART

	PURPOSE (Intent)	ACTION TAKEN TO ACHIEVE IT (antagonists encountered)	OUTCOME OF SCENE (peak)	REACTION	DECISION
1					
2					
3					
4					

Writing the Short Story: Skill Set 5

Setting Up the Story

✍ **YOU WILL NEED**

- A list of the four criteria for opening scenes, on the board:
  - Introduce a main character
  - Introduce the conflict
  - Establish the setting (place and time)
  - Provide Important Background Information (IBI)
- Thesauri and dictionaries—one for every 3 or 4 students
- Students' Ideas Files

PURPOSE

Authors are aware that the setup is the most important part of a story, requiring the most care and effort to write. As students practice techniques for laying a story foundation, they will come to appreciate the importance of good beginnings, both in fiction and in real life.

SKILL 1: KEEPING IT SHORT AND SWEET

Introduction

1. The teacher reminds the students of a time when they were watching a television show and a family member who had missed the first five minutes came into the room and asked, "What did I miss?" Now the information must be given quickly so that the person who was there from the beginning doesn't miss the next five minutes.

2. The teacher explains to the students that, as authors, they have the responsibility of telling the reader "what s/he missed" at the beginning of a short story as quickly as possible. Referring to the list on the board, the teacher defines "what s/he missed" as a series of questions:

   Who is the main character?
   Where and when is the story set?
   What is the character's goal and why is s/he trying to achieve it?
   What other information will help me to understand what's going on?

Guided Practice and Practice

1. The teacher and class begin by discussing the various ways in which a character can be introduced—*by word, by deed, by setting or belongings, by what others say about her/him*—and should conclude that the most efficient and effective way is to let the character walk onstage, doing something that reveals the kind of person s/he is.

    Therefore, when the hero/ine of the story is being introduced in the opening scene, there should be some description of how s/he is *moving* and what s/he is *doing*, not just of what s/he *looks like*.

2. Together, teacher and students brainstorm words that describe how people move, matching each word up with an emotion and recording the information on the blackboard. For example, an angry person might *storm* into a room. A very determined person might *stride* through the door. A proud person might *strut* around. A happy person might *skip* or *dance* along the street. A fearful person might *scurry* or *creep* away.

    Students should be encouraged to use thesauri and dictionaries to find descriptive words to add to the list on the board.

3. Each student is asked to select a first draft or outline of a story from her/his Ideas File (this may be the same one used in Skill Set 4) and visualize the opening scene of the story, in which the protagonist is introduced. Each student then "writes the protagonist onstage" in one or two sentences, ensuring that the character's actions reveal as much as possible about her/him *(e.g., Emmett raced home from school, checking his watch as he ran through the playground and across the street.)*.

4. The teacher next points out that another story element the reader needs to know about right away is the dramatic conflict—*what does the protagonist want to achieve, why, and who or what is standing in the way?*

    The teacher explains that the most effective way to reveal what the conflict is about is by overhearing the character's thoughts *(e.g., Emmett raced home from school, checking his watch as he ran through the playground and across the street. Baseball tryouts would be starting in less than ten minutes. If only his English teacher hadn't made him stay to finish that stupid essay!)*.

5. Each student now adds a sentence or two relating what the protagonist is thinking as s/he enters the scene—why s/he is performing this action in this place, and what precautions s/he must take in order to avoid failure.

6. Referring to the list on the board, the teacher explains that in order for a reader to "get into" a story, s/he needs to know where and when it is taking place. Setting details should be added coincidentally with the action to establish time and place.

    In the example above, for instance, we know that it's around 4:00 p.m. on a weekday because Emmett had to stay after school to finish an essay and is now going to be late for baseball tryouts. Unless told otherwise, the reader will assume that this story takes place somewhere in North America. If necessary, an additional sentence could include the name of a city or town.

7. Each student now examines her/his opening paragraph(s) to see how incidental information that will establish for the reader the time and the place of the story can be added. The paragraph(s) are then revised to include this setting information.

8. The teacher and students discuss what is meant by IBI.

    Everything that happens later in the story must be traceable backward through a chain of logical cause and effect to the opening scene(s). If the hero is going to defeat his antagonist by using karate, for example, his ability to do that must be hinted at in the introduction to the story. If a tiger that has escaped from the zoo is going to figure in the climax of the story, the escape must be mentioned much earlier on.

    Readers don't like it when important information is withheld and then sprung on them in the climactic scene.

    Teacher and students can discuss Emmett's story, identifying one or two important pieces of information that need to be introduced at the beginning. *(For example: Emmett is the son of a retired Major League Baseball player. Even though Emmett is the opposite of athletic, he is determined to make his dad proud of him. Emmett doesn't make the team, but he gets to use his first-aid training when there is an accident at a team practice, and this is how he makes his own parents proud and another boy's parents grateful. IBI to be introduced in the opening scene: Emmett's skill at first aid and his father's pro baseball career. He'll demonstrate his lack of athletic ability at the tryouts.)*

9. The teacher and students now brainstorm and list on the board some of the ways to include IBI coincidentally in a scene: *a brief mention in character dialogue, a memory inserted in the character's thoughts, a newspaper headline, a wall poster, a note from one character to another, and so on.*

   Teacher and students refer to the IBI to be introduced in the opening scene of Emmett's story and discuss which method(s) would work best.

10. Each student refers to the first draft or outline of her/his story, reading it all the way through to see what IBI needs to be added to the opening scene. The student then rereads her/his opening paragraphs, looking for a way to introduce that information indirectly or coincidentally, and revises accordingly.

Product

1. Students pair up and read their opening paragraphs aloud to each other. The listening partner should be instructed to determine whether the other author has included all the items listed on the board. If any are missing, both partners should discuss ways to add them.

2. Each student's completed first-draft paragraphs should be clipped to the story they introduce and saved in her/his Ideas File for possible further development.

SKILL 2: TRYING DIFFERENT OPENINGS

Introduction

Reviewing the list of four criteria and what was done in the previous skill activity, the teacher explains that introducing the protagonist is only one possible way to begin a story. There are other ways and, depending on the kind of story being told, each one can be very effective. These ways are discussed and then listed on the board:

  * *introduce the hero or villain first*
  * *begin with the IBI*
  * *start with a line of dialogue*
  * *start with a detail of the setting*
  * *start in the middle of an action*

Modeling and Guided Practice

1. The teacher tells the students about a story s/he is writing, about two teens who get separated from their class on a field trip to a state park. Night is falling, and even though these two students have never liked each other and have even avoided each other in the past, they now have to work together to survive until the park rangers can find and rescue them. At the end of the story, both teens are found alive, although one of them is seriously injured. Forced to depend on each other, the teens have learned to accept their differences and respect each other. The teacher asks: *What would be the best way to begin this story?*

2. In a whole-class discussion, teacher and students go down the list, considering and discussing what each type of opening scene would look like if it were to be used for this story.

3. The class is organized into five groups, and each group chooses or is assigned a different type of story opening from the list on the board.

4. Each group now proceeds to first-draft its assigned type of opening scene for the teacher's story.

5. When done, each group can select a reader to share its opening scene with the rest of the class. After all the scenes have been heard, students can vote by a show of hands for the type of scene they consider to be most effective.

   The teacher should collect these first drafts for use in the next Skill Set.

Practice and Product

1. Each student selects a first draft or story outline from her/his Ideas File (this may be the same one used in Skill 1) and proceeds to write a number of original opening scenes for the story, trying all the different types of openings listed on the board in the Introduction. Students should be sure that they have included all four of the criteria listed in Skill 1.

2. Once finished, each author should read over all the scenes s/he has written and determine which story opening s/he likes best for this particular story.

3. Each student then finds a partner and asks her/him to decide which opening s/he prefers and why. *(It may not be the same opening. If not, the author will have a decision to make when the time comes to finish writing the story.)*

4. Each student's selected opening(s) should be clipped to the story being introduced and saved in the student's Ideas File for possible further development.

EXTENSIONS

Encourage your students to notice which story elements are being emphasized in the introductory scenes of a variety of television programs. Students can get into groups to discuss the kinds of openings they have found being used for:

police shows	soap operas
science fiction shows	reality shows
supernatural/horror shows	sitcoms

Writing the Short Story: Skill Set 6

Hooking the Reader

✍ **YOU WILL NEED:**

- Each student's chosen story opening from Skill Set 5
- Story openings for the teacher's example in Skill Set 5
- List of story hooks on the board (see Introduction, Step 1)

PURPOSE

Authors understand how important it is to "hook" the reader's attention from the very beginning of a story. As students practice creating effective story openings, they will become more aware of the techniques used by the media to "hook" viewers and listeners and reel them in.

SKILL 1: TRYING DIFFERENT HOOKS

Introduction and Modeling

1. The teacher asks students to recall stories they've read or movies they've seen that "grabbed" them right from the beginning and drew them into the story. Referring to these remembered stories, teacher and students discuss what about their opening scenes the students found so compelling.

    As students identify the following strategies, the teacher records them in a list on the board:

    - *mystery—raise intriguing questions to be answered later*
    - *open with a provocative/unusual statement or situation (e.g., "When I asked the bartender for a zombie, I wasn't expecting it to be six feet tall.")*
    - *action—people doing things, a storm at sea, etc. (no static description)*
    - *change—describe something in the process of becoming something else, something in motion (almost as good as action)*
    - *immediate identification with a character (why stories for teens have teenaged protagonists)—first-person narrative, especially, is an invitation to get closer and find out more about the character*
    - *introduction of an unconventional character—someone radically different from the reader's norm can be fascinating*

    It should be pointed out to students that a well-written opening scene can contain several of these techniques, all operating at the same time.

2. The teacher reminds students of the story about the two teens surviving the night in a state park and asks, *How could the opening of that story become a "hook" to grab the reader's attention and draw her/him into the narrative?*

3. Teacher and class together consider the list of strategies on the board, discussing which of them would be appropriate and effective for this type of story.

4. The teacher organizes the class into five groups and gives each group one of the openings written in Skill Set 5 (Skill 2) for the story in Step 2. Each group then chooses or is assigned one of the first five strategies listed on the board.

5. Each group proceeds to rewrite its assigned opening scene, incorporating the selected "hook." *It should be pointed out to students that depending on how the scene was originally written, making this change could be as simple as adding a sentence, or it could entail a complete rewrite. Students will need to decide as a group what would be the best way to do this.*

6. When done, each group can choose a reader to share its rewritten scene with the rest of the class.

Practice and Product

1. Each student now takes out the story opening s/he wrote for her/his own story in the previous Skill Set and, working independently, tries rewriting it with each of the "hooks" listed on the board.

2. The student then reads over all the scenes s/he has revised and selects the combination s/he feels is most effective.

3. If there is time, each student can find a different partner from last time and ask the partner to decide which opening s/he thinks is most effective and why. (If the partner's choice is different from the author's, then the student pair should discuss the reasons why.)

4. The finished story openings should be clipped to the stories they introduce and saved in the authors' Ideas Files for possible further development.

Writing the Short Story: Skill Set 7

Major Writing Assignment (2 Weeks)

✍ **YOU WILL NEED:**

- WSR 14—AUTHORS NEED A WRITING PLAN—class set
- WSR 15—STEPS FOR STORY COMPLETION HANDOUT—class set
- WSR 16—PROOFREAD WITH A PARTNER CHECKLIST—class set
- All the rough materials developed so far for the students' short stories
- Students' Ideas Files
- Copies of planning charts used in previous skills activities
- A collection of revising and editing checklists from the Writing Process Module
- WSR 17—SHORT STORY ASSESSMENT RUBRIC—1 per student

PURPOSE

Students are now ready to put together all the writing skills they have learned in a story-writing assignment, which will be revised, edited, polished, and handed in for evaluation.

WEEK 1: COMPLETE THE FIRST DRAFT

1. The teacher explains to the students that over the next two weeks they are going to be producing a final-draft short story and handing it in for summative evaluation. Students may choose to work with a first draft or story outline from their Ideas Files, or they may decide to start from scratch with a fresh story idea. Regardless, there will be deadlines set that students will be expected to meet.

2. The teacher hands out copies of the AUTHORS NEED A WRITING PLAN and goes over with the class the steps in the writing process. Students are to keep this sheet handy to use as reference later on.

3. Referring to the writing plan handout, the teacher and class work backwards from the final deadline to establish due dates for the various steps in the process: second-draft revision, proofreading with a partner, third-draft text editing, and submission of the final draft for evaluation. Students should write these due dates on their handouts to serve as a reminder.

     NOTE TO TEACHER: Students who are starting over from scratch will require more time to plan and produce their first-draft stories. This should be taken into account when planning final deadlines.

4. Next, the teacher hands out copies of STEPS FOR STORY COMPLETION and goes over the first part (Prepare Your First Draft) with the class.

5. Each student works independently to complete the first draft of her/his story by the due date. This may be done in class, as homework, or both. The teacher should make available to those students who require them copies of any story-planning charts used in previous Skill Sets (e.g., DRAMATIC CONFLICT CHART B, STORY OUTLINE SHEET, SCENE DEVELOPMENT CHART, and so on).

WEEK 2: REVISE, EDIT, AND POLISH

1. The teacher refers each student who has completed her/his first-draft story to the self-editing criteria on the STEPS FOR STORY COMPLETION HANDOUT. Using these criteria as a guide, students are to revise their first-draft work and produce a clean second draft of their stories by the due date established earlier.

2. On the due date, the teacher hands out copies of the PROOFREAD WITH A PARTNER CHECKLIST and puts up on the board (or on an overhead screen) the following guidelines for peer-assisted editing, going over them one at a time with the class:

   a. *Editing partners are to work together, first on one author's story and then on the other author's story, discussing areas where improvements can be made. Editing partners are not to trade stories and work independently.*
   b. *Editing partners are to check off each criterion on the author's sheet as soon as it has been discussed, using the left-hand column of the checklist. Authors will use the right-hand column while revising and editing their second drafts, to check off that each criterion has been considered and necessary improvements have been made. A checklist without check marks down both sides will be considered incomplete.*
   c. *Editing partners may suggest improvements but are not allowed to make changes to an author's work. Authors are the owners of their work. Therefore, if changes are necessary, the author must be the one to make them.*
   d. *Remember that the job of an editing partner is to help the author improve. All criticism of another writer's work must therefore be constructive (i.e., suggesting ways to make it better).*

3. Students then pair up with editing partners and work together to improve both their stories, following the instructions on the board or screen. Once the editing partner has signed off on her/his side of the sheet, each student author is responsible for making the necessary improvements to her/his second-draft work, checking off the other side of the sheet. The student then rewrites the story as a third draft.

4. The teacher hands out copies of the SHORT STORY ASSESSMENT RUBRIC for students to use as a reference while polishing their completed third drafts.

5. Polished work is then recopied in final-draft form, formatted in accordance with the teacher's instructions, and packaged together with the student author's planning materials, edited previous drafts, peer-editing checklist, and assessment rubric. The entire package is submitted to the teacher for summative assessment.

   NOTE TO TEACHER: The attached rubric is meant to be a starting point for your own customized evaluation tool. Select those aspects of the assignment that you wish to emphasize and import the descriptors into an appropriately formatted marking checklist or rubric. I have found that trying to grade every aspect of every assignment is both time-consuming and unnecessarily onerous.

AUTHORS
NEED A WRITING PLAN

FIRST DRAFT—Get the ideas down on paper.

SECOND DRAFT

    (1) Personal revision to improve story flow, logic
        - Plot, characters, setting, theme/structure, style
           -Evaluate for interest, believability.
        -How can this story be improved in any or all of the above areas?

    (2) Share with a peer (using a checklist)
        Ask your peer the above question and discuss.

THIRD DRAFT

    -Text editing for clarity and impact
        -Trim the fat, sharpen the focus, smooth the read, etc.
        -Correct spelling, grammar, punctuation, word repetition,
        verb tenses, pronoun references, etc.

FINAL DRAFT

    -Perfect form for sharing with the teacher and/or chosen audience.

STEPS FOR STORY COMPLETION

1. **Prepare your first draft:** If you haven't already done so, diagram your story first on the STORY OUTLINE SHEET and the SCENE DEVELOPMENT CHART. Then write each charted scene in paragraph form, paying special attention to your opening scene. Write, type, or print the story out, double-spaced on one side of the page only. This is your first draft.

2. **Self-edit:** Reread your story as often as necessary, watching for and correcting the following:

   a. Theme: Is your story theme carried through from beginning to end? (If not, this usually means that a scene has become too involved with character, setting, or plot and has lost track of the main idea of the story. Once you have located the scene where the story began going off track, identify which element dominates the scene and remove the colorful but irrelevant details that have overshadowed the theme.)

   b. Transitions: Is there a smooth transition from one scene to the next? (Check to be sure that the character's intent in each scene is the result of a decision s/he made in a previous scene.)

   c. Conflict: Is there a strong dramatic conflict in your story? (Remember, the backbone of your story must be clearly defined, and the more serious the problem, the more exciting your story will be.)

   d. Protagonist: Have you created a strong, realistic main character? (Be sure that s/he shows the reader all three Dimensions of Life.)

   e. Setting: Does the setting of your story help develop the conflict? (Setting can be a background but also an antagonist. As an antagonist, it is more interesting.)

   f. Opening Scene: Does the opening of your story "hook" the reader, introduce a main character, establish the setting, provide Important Background Information (IBI), and launch into the action?

   g. Closing Scene: Have you tied up all loose ends?

REVISE, EDIT AND PROOFREAD WITH A PARTNER
CHECKLIST: THE SHORT STORY

AUTHOR'S NAME: _____

EDITING PARTNER: _____

Checked by editor	Editing Criteria	Improved by author
	1. The story has an apt and intriguing title.	
	2. The opening scene draws the reader into the story by: (a) introducing a main character right away; (b) coincidentally establishing the setting of the story; (c) providing important background information; (d) quickly launching the dramatic conflict.	
	3. There is a realistic, multi-dimensional Protagonist: (a) whose goal is the most important in the story; (b) whose point of view dominates the story; (c) who learns and/or changes by the end of the story; (d) whom the reader cares about and wants to see succeed.	
	4. The story has been developed around a strong and textured Dramatic Conflict: (a) with all 3 Antagonists (vs person, environment, self); (b) with a powerful Motivation for pursuing the story Goal; (c) with both Real and Stated Goals; (d) with a decisive and emotionally satisfying Climax.	
	5. The setting is interesting and supports the unfolding of the story: (a) with sensory detail that creates the illusion of reality; (b) by being an antagonist in the dramatic conflict; (c) by reflecting the emotional state of the character(s); (d) by including details of weather and time of day.	
	6. The story flows smoothly in scenes from start to finish: (a) each scene delivers the theme in some way; (b) each scene fulfils multiple storytelling purposes; (c) all scenes are linked by the Decision=Purpose bond; (d) each scene advances the dramatic conflict.	
	7. The author has been considerate to the reader by making the story as well-written as possible: (a) spelling and grammar have been checked (not just on the computer); (b) there are no run-on sentences; (c) there is correct use of capital letters, commas and apostrophes; (d) there is agreement of subject and verb (both either singular or plural).	

RUBRIC: WRITING THE SHORT STORY

STUDENT NAME: _____

CRITERIA	LEVEL 1 (below grade level) (Student shows limited ability.)	LEVEL 2 (approaching grade level) (Student shows moderate ability.)	LEVEL 3 (at grade level) (Student shows considerable ability.)	LEVEL 4 (above grade level) (Student shows exceptional ability.)
MAIN CHARACTER (PROTAGONIST)	Protagonist is flat, lacking dimension and believability. Arouses little sympathy in the reader.	Protagonist shows physical dimension and hints at thoughts and emotions. Arouses some sympathy in the reader.	Protagonist shows all 3 dimensions but thoughts and emotions could be more realistic. Arouses considerable sympathy in the reader.	Protagonist 'comes alive' for the reader. Fully-dimensional and completely believable. Arouses total sympathy in the reader.
DRAMATIC CONFLICT	Conflict is incomplete. Protagonist lacks a believable goal and/or sufficient motivation. Only one antagonist.	Conflict is complete but weak. Antagonists present no real obstacles or goal is relatively unimportant to the protagonist.	Conflict is complete and strong, with at least 2 antagonists. Protagonist has strong motivation to pursue the stated goal.	Conflict is complete and textured, with 3 or more antagonists. Protagonist's motivation is his/her real goal, which is achieved at end.
STORY STRUCTURE	Story is incomplete, lacking an opening scene, a story event, a rising action and/or a climax. OR Author has written a plot summary rather than showing the story to the reader as a series of scenes.	Story is complete but weak. Opening scene fulfils 1 or 2 story purposes, tries with limited success to 'hook' the reader. Climax is indecisive or emotionally flat. Scenes could be more firmly linked to each other.	Story is complete and well-structured. Opening scene successfully fulfils all 4 story purposes. Scenes are firmly linked to one another and effectively sequenced from story event to climax. Climax is both logical and decisive.	Story is well and thoughtfully organized. Opening scene is compelling. Scenes flow seamlessly from story event to climax and resolution. Climax is both inevitable and emotionally satisfying for the reader.
ILLUSION OF REALITY	Weak. Characters do not react to their settings or to one another in realistic ways. There is very little sensory detail.	Moderate. Character reactions are generally realistic. There is some sensory detail.	Strong. Plot logic is sound. Character reactions are realistic. Considerable sensory detail.	Utterly convincing. Character reactions are completely natural and realistic. Vivid sensory detail makes the setting come to life.
SETTING	Setting is flat or vague, not really described. Occasional mention of weather or time of day.	Setting is an antagonist in the dramatic conflict. There is some descriptive detail of time and place.	Setting contributes to dramatic conflict and setting description reflects the emotions of the main character.	The setting is interesting and realistically described. It both supports and plays a part in the unfolding of the story.
GRAMMAR, SPELLING, PUNCTUATION	Limited effectiveness: 10 or more major and minor errors, sometimes affecting meaning.	Moderate effectiveness: 8 or more major and minor errors but meaning is not affected.	Considerable effectiveness: 5 to 8 major and/or minor errors but reader is not distracted from the story.	Transparent writing: Fewer than 5 errors in total.

Part III

WRITING LONGER FICTION

GRADE 11 (16 YEARS) AND UP

Fiction is an organic creature—once a story has taken root in an author's fertile mind, the tale can take on a life of its own, sprouting new characters and revealing unsuspected aspects of old ones, branching and intertwining plotlines, and stubbornly refusing to be resolved in one thousand or even five thousand words. That is when a student finds her/himself writing a novelette—or even a novel—instead of a short story.

This Writing Longer Fiction module is meant to provide additional writing skills for those students who have undertaken the challenge of creating longer fiction. Here they will learn how to deepen and strengthen characterizations, how to make optimum use of minor characters, how to weave in subplots, how to put settings to work, and how to build dramatic tension. In the process, they will also increase their literary and media awareness as they practice molding language into the most effective vehicle for their storytelling.

STORY LENGTHS

Short-short story—200 to 1,200 words (1 to 5 manuscript pages)
Short story—1,200 to 7,500 words (5 to 30 manuscript pages)
Novelette—7,500 to 20,000 words (30 to 80 manuscript pages)
Novella—20,000 to 35,000 words (80 to 140 manuscript pages)
Novel (hardcover)—35,000 to 100,000 words (140 to 400 manuscript pages)
Novel (softcover)—50,000 to 150,000 words (200 to 600 manuscript pages)
Novel for preteens—18,000 to about 35,000 words (72 to 140 manuscript pages)

A manuscript page is here considered to be typed or printed out on every second line, with an inch (2.54 cm) of margin all around, using a non-proportional typeface such as Courier or Pica (10 characters per inch).

Students who are interested in submitting material to a specific publication or publishing house should be encouraged to research that publisher's guidelines, which should indicate the manuscript lengths required.

	SKILL SET	DESCRIPTION	NCCS ANCHORS ADDRESSED
1	Adding minor characters to the cast	Young authors learn and practice how to put minor characters to work in their stories, ensuring that every character pulls his/her weight.	R.3, R.9, W.3, W.4, W.5, W.6, W.10, L.1, L.2, L.3, L.5
2	Giving characters more depth	Students practice building more realistic characters that readers will identify with and care about.	R.3, W.3, W.4, W.5, W.10, L.1, L.2, L.3, L.5
3	Adding a subplot	Student authors learn how to deepen and enrich their stories by adding well-integrated subplots.	R.3, R.5, W.3, W.4, W.5, W.10, L.1, L.2, L.3, L.5
4	Working with settings	Young authors practice putting their story settings to work in various ways, making their stories more engaging for the reader.	R.3, W.3, W.4, W.5, W.10, L.1, L.2, L.3, L.5
5	Step-building dramatic tension	In longer fiction, dramatic tension keeps readers turning pages. Students learn and practice how to build tension using a tested story structure.	R.3, R.5, W.3, W.4, W.5, W.10, L.1, L.2, L.3, L.5
6	Putting it all together	Students are now ready to put together all the longer fiction writing skills they have learned in a story-writing assignment which will be revised, edited and polished and handed in for evaluation.	W.3, W.4, W.5, W.10, L.1, L.2, L.3, L.5

Writing Longer Fiction: Skill Set 1

Adding Minor Characters to the Cast

✍ **YOU WILL NEED:**

- 2 sections of a novel, introducing a major and a minor character (Skill 1)
- LSR 1—CHARACTER SKETCHES SHEET—photocopied and cut into slips of paper (Skill 1)
- Container—to hold the character sketches slips (Skill 1)
- Clip of a scene from a TV or movie showing comic relief (Skill 3)
- TV and DVD player to show the clip
- A suspenseful scene from a story to read aloud (Skill 3)
- LSR 2—SCENE PREMISES SHEET—1 per student (Skill 5)
- Students' Ideas Files (Skill 6)
- WSR 14—AUTHORS NEED A WRITING PLAN SHEET (Skill 6)
- LSR 3—PROOFREAD WITH A PARTNER CHECKLIST (Skill 6)
- LSR 4—ASSESSMENT SHEET (Skill 6)

PURPOSE

Authors understand how important it is that every character in a story pull her/his weight. As students practice putting minor characters to work in their own stories, they will become better storytellers, more economical writers, and more critical readers and viewers.

SKILL 1: INTRODUCING MINOR CHARACTERS

Introduction

1. The teacher writes "Major Character" on the board and then reads aloud a section of a novel in which a major character makes her/his first appearance.

2. The teacher and students then discuss all the ways in which the author let the reader know that this was a major character. A point-form list is recorded on the board under the "Major Character" heading *(character is fully named, lots of descriptive details, we get inside the character's head, story is being told from the character's point of view, etc.).*

3. The teacher then reads aloud a section of the novel in which a minor character makes her/his first appearance, without letting the students know that this is a minor character. The teacher asks: Do you think this character is going to play a major role in the story?

4. In class discussion, students compare the character introduction just read to the list of characteristics on the board and should arrive at the conclusion that this is not a major character.

5. The teacher now writes the heading "Minor Character" on the board. Teacher and students discuss and record on the board a list of clues that will let a reader know s/he is being introduced to a minor character *(one name, no name, or a nickname; just a couple of descriptive details; no thoughts or emotions; a single defined purpose in the story; not a point-of-view character, etc.).*

6. The teacher asks: What do you think would happen if a major character were introduced as if he were a minor character (and vice versa)? *(The major character would be flat, two-dimensional, and lack believability. The minor character would create false expectations in the reader, who would feel confused when the character only appeared once or twice in a limited role.)*

Modeling

1. The teacher pulls two slips of paper from the container and tells the class who these characters are. Teacher and class decide which should be the major character in the scene about to be written and which should be the minor character. The character designations are now written on the board over their corresponding headings, and the teacher reminds the class that both these characters will be making their first appearance in the scene being planned and will therefore have to be introduced properly according the criteria listed under those headings.

2. The teacher now reviews with the class the parts of a scene *(purpose, action, peak, reaction, decision)* and asks the students: What will be the major character's purpose in this scene, and what action will he or she take to achieve it? *(For example: an emergency room nurse needs to find out information from a taxi driver about the unconscious woman he just dropped off at the hospital. She will run after him and try to convince him to stay long enough to answer some questions.)* The teacher selects the most interesting answer and records it on the board.

3. The teacher now explains to the class that when the reader gets inside the major character's head, s/he will learn that the character is feeling tired at the end of a long day and just wants to get home and feed her/his cat (or some other thoughts and feelings). What is probably going to happen when these two characters meet? *(Hopefully, a very interesting scene. In fact, the teacher might want to actually write up this scene and share it with the class.)*

Practice and Product

1. The teacher replaces the two slips of paper in the container and instructs students to pair up with partners.

2. Each student pair then draws two slips of paper from the character sketch container. Students should be instructed to record both their own character and that of their partner at the top of a piece of paper.

3. Following the process modeled by the teacher, each student proceeds to plan and write a scene involving the two characters that s/he and her/his partner drew. Student A of each pair makes Character A the major character in her/his scene, while Student B makes the same character the minor one in hers/his.

4. Each student reads her/his finished scene aloud to her/his partner, and the two students can compare and discuss how effectively the characters were introduced in each case.
   Students should be reminded to save all first drafts in their Ideas Files for possible further development as stories.

SKILL 2: MINOR CHARACTERS AS FOILS

Introduction and Modeling

1. The teacher explains that very often, we don't notice certain things until we are presented with their opposite. For example, the sound of a refrigerator motor is usually just part of the background until the fridge turns itself off, and

without a villain to provide evil, we can't really measure the hero/ine's goodness. Sometimes an author who wants us to notice a particular trait in a major character will bring it to our attention with a minor character who is the exact opposite—a *foil*.

2. The teacher asks students to provide a list of at least eight to ten traits that could be given to major characters (such as courage, thrift, compassion, etc.). These are recorded on the board under the heading "Major Character." The students then complete the list by supplying the opposite characteristics that could be given to minor characters acting as foils *(e.g., a naive main character could have a streetwise friend)*. These are recorded under the heading "Minor Character."

3. The teacher reviews with the class the parts of a scene *(purpose, action, peak, reaction, decision)*, then selects a pair of opposite characteristics that suggest a scene to her/him and shares it with the class. *(For example: a shy major character wants to ask a girl to the school dance and his sociable, extroverted friend tries to give him advice.)*

Practice and Product

1. Working independently, each student selects a pair of characteristics that twigs her/his imagination and first-drafts a scene involving a major and a minor character who demonstrate those traits.

2. When done, the students assemble in groups of three for sharing. Each author reads her/his scene aloud to the rest of the group, who can assess the effectiveness of the minor character in the role of foil and offer positive suggestions for improvement.

SKILL 3: MINOR CHARACTERS AS COMIC RELIEF

Introduction

1. The teacher explains that what the students are about to see is called *comic relief*. The teacher then shows a scene from a television show or movie in which a minor character in a comic role provides a release of tension following a scene of heavy drama (for example, Artoo and Threepio bickering in one of the *Star Wars* movies, a Joe Pesci moment in the *Lethal Weapon* sequels, or Falstaff in *Henry IV* or *Henry V*).

2. The teacher explains to the class that *comic relief* is a device often found in drama or suspense stories, where it provides a safety valve to prevent the level of tension from rising too high and too soon in the story. (Tension needs to be at its highest in the climax.)

Guided Practice

1. In class discussion, the teacher and students establish a list of criteria for comic relief scenes, including the following:
   • *They are instigated by a minor character.*
   • *They originate from the personality of the minor character (e.g., Falstaff's drinking, Threepio's fussiness).*
   • *They are short and self-contained.*

2. The teacher reads aloud a tense, suspenseful scene from a story.

3. Students assemble in groups of four to brainstorm and list on paper their ideas for a comic relief scene to follow this one. The lists are all handed to the teacher, who writes the ideas on the board.

Practice and Product

1. Working independently, each student selects her/his favorite idea from the list on the board and first-drafts the scene.

2. When done, students can pair up and exchange scenes with a partner, who can offer positive suggestions for improvement.

SKILL 4: MINOR REACTIVE CHARACTERS

Introduction

1. The teacher asks students to recall and think about a fight scene they have viewed in a TV show or movie. It's a one-on-one confrontation between the good guy and the bad guy, and somewhere in the scene there's a minor character, wide-eyed with fear, watching it happen and wondering who will win. *(Students should be able to identify and describe several different examples.)*

2. The teacher explains that the minor character is there for a reason. The role of the minor character in a scene like this is to *cue the audience* by reacting with the emotion that the scriptwriter and director wish the audience to feel. The teacher asks the class: Why do you suppose it's necessary to add a reactive character to this kind of scene? *(Because the combatants are unable or unwilling to show fear, and somebody in the story has to provide an emotion the audience can identify with.)*

3. The teacher explains that every scene of a story contains a reactive character. Usually, this will be the main character, with whom the reader/viewer should be identifying. Sometimes, however, what the main character is feeling is different from what the author wants the reader/viewer to feel. When that happens, the author must ask her/himself (listed on board or on overhead screen):

    > *a. What emotion do I want the reader to feel?*
    > *b. Of the minor characters who appear in this scene, which one would be best to project this emotion?*
    > *c. If there are no minor characters in this scene, how can one be written in?*
    > *d. What actions would the reactive character take in this scene?*
    > *e. Where would the character be situated in the scene?*

Guided Practice

The teacher writes a list of situations on the board:

> *1. a house fire*
> *2. a high school graduation*
> *3. a wedding ceremony*
> *4. a robbery*
> *5. a basketball finals game*
> *6. an ambulance ride*
> *7. a rock concert*
> *8. the finish line of a grueling race*

Going through the list one situation at a time, the teacher and class discuss what emotion the reader should be feeling and why the main character cannot or will not show that emotion. *(For example, the firefighters at the house fire mustn't show fear, or the people they're saving might panic and make things worse.)*

Practice and Product

1. Each student selects the situation that suggests possibilities to her/him and writes it up as a fully developed scene, including a major character with a purpose who takes action to achieve it, successfully or unsuccessfully, along with a reactive minor character.
    Students should be reminded to ask themselves the questions written on the board in Step 3 (Introduction, above).

2. Students who chose the same situation can get together in a group and share their stories by passing them around for silent reading. Alternatively, students can pair up with partners and read their completed scenes aloud to each other.

SKILL 5: MINOR CHARACTERS AS PLOT FACILITATORS, PLOT COMPLICATORS, AND LOGISTICS CHARACTERS

Introduction and Guided Practice

1. The teacher writes the title of this skill activity on the board and explains to the students what each of the three terms means. *(A plot facilitator helps the protagonist get closer to achieving her/his scene or story goal; a plot complicator hinders the protagonist from achieving her/his scene or story goal; a logistics character moves the other characters or objects necessary to the story from point A to point B—e.g., a taxi driver, a ferry captain.)*

2. In a whole-class discussion, students then brainstorm several examples to illustrate each term and the teacher records them on the board. The teacher points out that in most cases, these truly minor roles will appear only once or twice in a story. That is why authors try to give each of the minor characters in a story more than one job to do.

3. The teacher presents students with two characters (e.g., a taxi driver and his passenger). The class is then divided in half and is instructed that all the students on one side of the room will be working with the taxi driver as the major character and the passenger as the minor character, and the students on the other side of the room will have the passenger as the major character and the taxi driver as the minor character.

4. Within each group, students pair up and work together to imagine two scenes involving these two characters. In one scene, the minor character is a plot facilitator, and in the other s/he is a plot complicator.

   Students should be reminded that the major character in a scene needs to have a purpose (a scene goal) and be taking action to try to achieve it. The plot facilitator or plot complicator may therefore be the factor that determines whether or not the main character is successful in reaching her/his scene goal.

5. Students assemble in groups of four, one pair from each side of the room, and share and compare their imagined scenes. Each group selects its favorite scene to share with the whole class.

Practice and Product

1. The teacher distributes copies of the SCENE PREMISES SHEET. Working independently, each student selects one of the situations, decides which of the two characters will be the minor one, and imagines and writes a scene in which the minor character fulfills two of the above-mentioned roles *(plot facilitator, plot complicator, logistics character)*.

2. When finished, each student can find a partner who selected a different scene premise from her/his own. The partners can share their work by reading each other's scenes.

SKILL 6: WRITING ASSIGNMENT (2 WEEKS)

Introduction

Each student refers back to all the first-draft stories s/he has already written and selects her/his favorite to develop, augment, and/or improve using the techniques learned in this Skill Set.

Week 1: Complete the First Draft

1. The teacher explains to the students that over the next one or two weeks they are going to be producing a final draft story and handing it in for evaluation.

2. Referring to the AUTHORS NEED A WRITING PLAN SHEET, the teacher goes over with the class the steps in the writing process.

   Students should be reminded that although the emphasis in this assignment will be on making effective use of minor characters, the students will still be expected to follow the steps as outlined.

3. Referring to the AUTHORS NEED A WRITING PLAN SHEET, the teacher and class work backwards from the final deadline to establish due dates for the various steps in the process: second-draft revision, proofreading with a partner, third-draft text editing, and submission of the final draft for evaluation. Students should write these due dates on their handouts to serve as a reminder.

4. Each student works independently to complete a revised first draft of her/his story by the due date, incorporating minor characters into the story in appropriate roles. This may be done in class, as homework, or both. The teacher should make available to those students who require them copies of any story-planning charts used in previous Skill Sets (e.g., DRAMATIC CONFLICT CHART B, STORY OUTLINE SHEET, SCENE DEVELOPMENT CHART, and so on).

Week 2: Revise, Edit, and Polish

1. The teacher hands out copies of the PROOFREAD WITH A PARTNER CHECKLIST for students' reference during the revising and editing process. The criteria on the sheet should be reviewed in class.

2. Using these criteria as a guide, students are to revise their first-draft work and produce a clean second draft of their stories by the due date established earlier.

3. On the due date, the teacher refers students to the PROOFREAD WITH A PARTNER CHECKLIST and puts up on the board (or on an overhead screen) the following guidelines for peer-assisted editing, going over them one at a time with the class:

   1. *Editing partners are to work together, first on one author's story and then on the other author's story, discussing areas where improvements can be made. Editing partners are not to trade stories and work independently.*
   2. *Editing partners are to check off each criterion on the author's sheet as soon as it has been discussed, using the left-hand column of the checklist. Authors will use the right-hand column while revising and editing their second drafts, to check off that each criterion has been considered and necessary improvements have been made. A checklist without check marks down both sides will be considered incomplete.*
   3. *Editing partners may suggest improvements but are not allowed to make changes to an author's work. Authors are the owners of their work. Therefore, if changes are necessary, the author must be the one to make them.*
   4. *Remember that the job of an editing partner is to help the author improve. All criticism of another writer's work must therefore be constructive (i.e., suggesting ways to make it better).*

4. Students then pair up with editing partners and work together to improve both their stories, following the instructions on the board or screen. Once the editing partner has signed off on her/his side of the sheet, each student author is responsible for making the necessary improvements to her/his second-draft work, checking off the other side of the sheet. The student then rewrites the story as a third draft.

5. The teacher hands out copies of the ASSESSMENT SHEET for students to use as a reference while polishing their completed third drafts.

6. Polished work is then recopied in final-draft form, formatted in accordance with the teacher's instructions, and packaged together with the student author's planning materials, edited previous drafts, peer-editing checklist, and assessment sheet. The entire package is submitted to the teacher for summative assessment.

CHARACTER SKETCHES SHEET

an undercover police officer	a psychiatric patient
an emergency room nurse	a taxi driver
a real estate salesperson	a runaway teenager
a mime who performs on street corners	a news photographer
a gypsy fortune teller	a soldier gone AWOL
a store clerk/cashier	a sports star
a well-known actor	a firefighter answering a false alarm
an airplane mechanic	a pizza delivery person
a garbage collector	a crazed fan (you decide of what)
a foreign tourist	a vacuum cleaner salesperson
a supermarket clerk	a building-safety inspector
a television weatherperson	a valet parking attendant
a letter carrier	a professional bodybuilder
a musician	a famous author (living or dead)

SCENE PREMISES SHEET

1. A single mother has decided to introduce her teenaged child to the new man in her life at a sit-down dinner for the three of them. As she is rushing to get the meal prepared, the building superintendent arrives to fix the leaky tap in the kitchen. He has just learned that his wife wants a divorce. *(This will be a scene between the mother and the super.)*

2. An assistant high school basketball coach has been informed that his contract will be terminated at the end of the current season due to budget cutbacks. On the day of the final game, the team's star player knocks on the assistant coach's office door, asking to speak with him privately. The player has witnessed a drug deal in the locker room. *(This will be a scene between the assistant coach and the star player.)*

3. A high school guidance counselor has taken a special interest in a talented female student and has been quietly working to get her accepted on a full scholarship to a highly respected college/university program. One month before graduation, the student's parent comes to the guidance office. The parent has been cut back from full-time to part-time work and intends to pull the student out of school so she can help support the family. *(This will be a scene between the guidance counselor and the student's mother or father.)*

REVISE, EDIT AND PROOFREAD WITH A PARTNER
CHECKLIST: ADDING MINOR CHARACTERS

AUTHOR'S NAME: _____

EDITING PARTNER: _____

Checked by editor	Editing Criteria	Improved by author
	1. Major and minor characters have been introduced appropriately.	
	2. The opening scene draws the reader into the story by: (a) introducing a main character right away; (b) coincidentally establishing the setting of the story; (c) providing important background information; (d) quickly launching the dramatic conflict.	
	3. Where appropriate, a minor character has been effectively used as a foil to emphasize a quality of the main character.	
	4. Where appropriate, a minor character has been effectively used to insert comic relief.	
	5. Where appropriate, a minor character has been effectively used in a reactive role.	
	6. Where necessary, a minor character has been effectively used for logistical purposes, moving people and things to where they need to be.	
	7. The story has been developed around a strong and textured Dramatic Conflict: (a) with all 3 Antagonists (vs person, vs environment, vs self); (b) with a powerful Motivation for pursuing the story Goal; (c) with both Real and Stated Goals; (d) with a decisive and emotionally satisfying Climax.	
	8. Where appropriate, minor characters have been effectively used as plot facilitators or complicators.	
	9. Wherever possible, each minor character has been given more than one job to do.	
	10. The author has been considerate to the reader by making the story as well-written as possible: (a) spelling and grammar have been checked (not just on the computer); (b) there are no run-on sentences; (c) there is correct use of capital letters, commas and apostrophes; (d) there is agreement of subject and verb (both either singular or plural).	

ADDING MINOR CHARACTERS
ASSESSMENT SHEET

STUDENT AUTHOR: _____

STORY TITLE: _____

SCORING: 5 = OUTSTANDING   4 = VERY GOOD   3 = GOOD
           2 = YOU CAN DO BETTER   1 = POOR

THIS AUTHOR HAS:	5	4	3	2	1
1. introduced each major character appropriately					
2. introduced each minor character appropriately					
3. made effective use of a minor character as a foil for the main character					
4. where appropriate, made effective use of a minor character in a comic relief role					
5. where appropriate, used a minor character to provide a necessary reactive cue to the reader					
6. where appropriate, used a minor character as a plot facilitator or complicator					
7. where necessary, made effective use of a minor character for logistical purposes					
8. whenever possible, given each minor character more than one job to do in the story					
9. developed the story around a strong dramatic conflict					
10. built the story to a decisive and satisfying conclusion					
COLUMN TOTALS =					

TOTAL SCORE =   /50

COMMENTS:

Writing Longer Fiction: Skill Set 2

Giving Characters More Depth

✍ **YOU WILL NEED:**

- List of characters on the board (see Skill 1, Step 2)
- LSR 5—CHARACTER MOTIVATIONS CHART—1 per student (Skill 2)
- A glass of water and a paper bag (Skill 3)
- A major scene from a classic story or play (Skill 3)
- A colleague to sneak up on you and yell "Boo!" (Skill 3)
- Students' Ideas Files (Skill 5)
- WSR 14—AUTHORS NEED A WRITING PLAN—class set (Skill 5)
- LSR 6—PROOFREAD WITH A PARTNER CHECKLIST (Skill 5)
- LSR 7—ASSESSMENT SHEET (Skill 5)

PURPOSE

Authors work hard to create characters with realistic depth so that readers will find it easier to identify with them and become emotionally involved in their adventures. As students practice building more realistic characters, they will gain a better understanding of what makes people think and behave as they do in real life.

SKILL 1: ORDINARY/EXTRAORDINARY CHARACTERS

Introduction and Guided Practice

1. The teacher tells the class about someone s/he went to school with (or lived next door to or used to work alongside). This person was kind of quiet and seemed to be the most boring, ordinary person on the planet . . . until one day the teacher found out that this individual was a prize-winning poet (or a movie stunt person in her/his spare time or training to be a pilot, and so on). No one had a clue that this person had a secret, interesting side to her/his personality. And once people found out about it, they never thought of her/him as boring or ordinary again.

2. The teacher explains that, just as in real life, every character in a story has different sides or facets, and some of them are hidden. If a character seems boring it's probably because the reader needs to be shown one of the character's more interesting facets. An author can make a character memorable by giving her/him some extraordinary characteristic— just one will do *(e.g., a shy retiring librarian can have a black belt in karate).*

3. The teacher reveals the following list of characters on the board, and the students brainstorm several interesting characteristics for each one, which are recorded as well:

- *an insurance salesman*
- *a bus driver*
- *a secretary*
- *a construction foreman*
- *a kindergarten or nursery school teacher*
- *a short-order cook*
- *a garbage collector*
- *a supermarket cashier*
- *a letter carrier*
- *a dog walker*

4. The teacher reviews with the class the three dimensions of life: physical, emotional, and psychological. Together, teacher and class go over some of the extraordinary characteristics on the board and decide which of these three dimensions—action, emotional reaction, or unspoken thought—should be used to show each one to the reader. *(For example: a bus driver who sings opera could burst into song at odd moments (action), or he could be feeling elated because he just landed a role in a local production of* La Traviata *(thought and emotion).)*

Practice and Product

1. Each student selects one of the characters on the board and one of the extraordinary characteristics. The student then works independently to plan and first-draft a scene in which the character reveals this hitherto unsuspected trait or ability, thus deepening one of her/his dimensions of life.

2. If there is time, students can volunteer to read their scenes aloud to the rest of the class.

SKILL 2: BASIC AND SECONDARY MOTIVATIONS

Introduction and Guided Practice

1. The teacher presents the class with a scenario:

   A man comes racing out of an apartment building, dashes across the road dodging traffic, and hurries down the entrance to the subway.

   The teacher then asks the class: What do you suppose made him do that?

2. As the students brainstorm possible reasons for the man's actions, the teacher lists them on the board *(e.g., he's late for work, he left his laptop on the subway and needs to retrieve it, he got a message that a friend is in trouble, etc.)*.

3. Referring to each idea in turn, the teacher first asks the class: What need or desire or fear does this demonstrate? *(The best answer should be recorded beside the idea. For example: If he's running late for work, he might need to be present at an important meeting and/or fear being fired or demoted for being late again.)*
   The teacher then asks for each idea in turn: Can this need or desire be satisfied, or can this fear be set to rest at any point in the foreseeable future?

4. In each case, if the answer is yes, the teacher puts a check mark beside the idea before moving on. At the end, the teacher explains that each idea with a check mark beside it is a Secondary Motivation.

5. The teacher explains that every single individual has some basic need or fear or desire that, because it can never be fulfilled, allayed, or satisfied, drives that person to behave in certain ways, make certain choices, and do certain kinds of things. This is the person's Basic Motivation.

6. For example, the teacher asks the class to consider a student who desperately needs to be liked. What sorts of things might this person do to try to satisfy this need? As the class discusses possibilities, the teacher lists them on the board, creating a chart with the following headings:

Basic Motivations	*Resulting Actions*	*Secondary Motivations*
need to be liked	*smoking with peers*	*to look cool, defy authority, etc.*

It should be explained to the students that the vast majority of people are not aware of the Basic Motivations that drive them. If asked the reason for their actions, they will reply by giving Secondary Motivations instead. For example, on the chart on the board, the student who needs to be liked has taken up smoking in order to have something in common with her/his peers. If asked why s/he smokes, the student will probably answer that s/he does it to look cool or to defy authority. These are Secondary Motivations—needs, fears, and desires that can be fulfilled, allayed, and satisfied.

7. The teacher explains that the major characters in a story must also have Basic and Secondary Motivations if they are to be realistic and consistent in their behavior. The author must therefore know what these motivations are, and must make the characters' speech and actions reflect their motivations in such a way that the reader, with a little thought, can figure out what they are.

Practice

1. The teacher hands out a CHARACTER MOTIVATIONS CHART to each student.

2. The students assemble in groups of three to complete this chart. Each group should be able to come up with three to four actions and corresponding Secondary Motivations for each Basic Motivation indicated.

Product

1. Each student then selects one action and Secondary Motivation from the chart and, working independently, writes a paragraph or two in which the character involved in the action is answering the question "Why are you doing that?" The character's response must also hint at the Basic Motivation behind the action.

2. The students reassemble in their groups of three. Each student reads her/his work aloud to her/his group mates, who try to guess what the character's Basic Motivation is and offer suggestions for improvement.

SKILL 3: USING CHARACTERS' MINOR PROBLEMS

Introduction and Guided Practice

1. The teacher begins to explain to the class how giving a character a minor problem not related to the plot can allow more of the character's personality to be revealed, and thus make her/him more interesting. *(For example, different kinds of people have different ways of dealing with pushy relatives, car troubles, ulcers, etc.)* This also makes the character more realistic, since in real life we generally have to deal with at least one minor problem every day. In a story, however, the minor problem must remain in the background, or it risks overwhelming the main plot.
   To illustrate, the teacher has been hiccupping throughout the above explanation.

2. As the teacher does the following example on the board, s/he also starts trying to cure her/his hiccups, going from drinking some water to holding her/his breath to breathing into a paper bag. The distractions these efforts provide will illustrate to the class how a minor problem given too much attention can take over a story.

The Example: The teacher takes a major scene from a classic story (or a classic play, such as the balcony scene from Romeo and Juliet*) and gives one of the characters hay fever. Together the class discusses how to inject watery eyes and sneezing fits into the story in a way that won't overwhelm the main plot—as the teacher is demonstrating right now.*

The teacher from the room next door can sneak in, stand behind the teacher, and yell, "Boo!", ending the hiccups.

3. The teacher asks the class at what point they switched their attention to the hiccups and away from the lesson on the board. The teacher then explains that this is why authors must maintain control over any minor problems they add to a story.

Practice and Product

1. Each student either finds a character in her/his Ideas File or creates a fresh one, then gives the character a major activity to perform, along with a minor problem from the following list on the board, to add interest to the scene:

compulsive neatness	*itchy nose*
coming down with a cold	*headache*
overdrawn at the bank	*squeaky shoe*
lost her/his keys	*indigestion*
loved one not talking to her/him	*hair keeps falling down onto her/his face*

2. Students may need to be reminded that the character begins the scene with a purpose and takes action to try to achieve that purpose. While the minor problem may interfere with her/his efforts, it should not be the determining factor in the character's success or failure in the scene.

3. The students work independently to first-draft their scenes, making sure that the minor problem adds interest but doesn't take over the plot.

4. Students organize into groups according to which minor problem they selected. Group members can share their work by reading their scenes aloud to one another.

SKILL 4: USING ARCHETYPES

Introduction and Modeling

1. The teacher writes the following words on the board:

red heart	*jack-o'-lanterns*	*dragon parade*

The teacher then asks: What are all the things that we associate with each of these phrases? *(Among other things, they remind us of special holidays—Valentine's Day, Halloween, and the Chinese New Year—which in turn bring other associations to mind.)* As students offer details, the teacher makes a list on the board.

2. The teacher explains that over time, the heart, the glowing pumpkin, and the dragon have become *archetypal images*. Authors use archetypes with their ready-made associations when they want to give instant recognition, added depth, and extra layers of meaning to a story situation.

3. The teacher then explains that characters can be *archetypal* as well and writes the following names on the board:

Judas Iscariot	*Napoleon Bonaparte*	*Ebenezer Scrooge*

The teacher asks: Who are these people, and what do we associate with them? As students offer details, they are recorded beside the corresponding names.

4. The teacher sums up: Judas Iscariot is the archetypal *traitor*, Napoleon Bonaparte is the archetypal *power-hungry leader*, and Ebenezer Scrooge is the archetypal *penny-pinching miser*. The teacher erases the notes previously recorded beside each of these names and replaces them with the corresponding brief summation.

5. Pointing out that Judas is a figure from the Christian Bible, the teacher now asks the class to supply further examples of *religious archetypes* (e.g., Confucius, St. Francis of Assisi, Lucifer, etc.), which are listed on the board beneath Judas Iscariot. The teacher writes the heading "Religious" at the top of the list and discusses with the class the characteristics and actions associated with each listed name. As with Judas, a brief summary note is made beside each name *(e.g., Confucius is the archetypal source of wisdom, St. Francis is the archetypal animal lover, Lucifer is the archetypal fallen one, etc.)*.

6. Step 5 is repeated for Napoleon Bonaparte *(a historical archetype)* and Ebenezer Scrooge *(a literary archetype)*. The teacher then adds a fourth category, "Mythological," and asks students for examples to put under this heading. Here are some names the teacher may wish to ensure are discussed, in order to provide a wide variety of choices later on:

Historical	*Literary*	*Mythological*
Napoleon Bonaparte	*Ebenezer Scrooge*	*Hercules (strong man)*
Joan of Arc (martyr)	*Peter Pan (eternal child)*	*Helen of Troy (beauty)*
Marie Antoinette (self-centered rich girl)	*Pollyanna (optimist)*	*Cupid (matchmaker)*
Capt. Bligh (tyrant)	*Alice (adventurer)*	*the Sirens (deadly lure)*
Columbus (explorer)		*Daedalus (inventor)*

Each archetype should be briefly discussed to establish the sorts of character actions and story events that the reader might expect to see happen *(e.g., a martyr is someone who is killed for refusing to change or betray what s/he believes in and, as a result, becomes an inspiration to others who share the same belief[s])*.

Practice and Product

1. Each student either finds a character in her/his Ideas File or creates a fresh one to write about. The student then selects an archetype from the board whose characteristics and behavior will be displayed by the main character in her/his story.

   It may need to be emphasized to students that by selecting Peter Pan, for example, they are choosing to write about a male character who refuses to grow up and loves to have adventures, NOT simply to retell the story of Peter Pan.

2. Working independently, each student plans and first-drafts a short story featuring the character selected in Step 1 (Practice) as the protagonist. *There should be no mention of the archetype's name in the story (see Step 4, below).*

3. **Homework:** Students are to edit and polish their stories in preparation for reading them aloud to classmates the following day.

4. **The next day:** Depending on the size of the class, each student may read her/his story to a group of four to five classmates or to the whole class. The listening students then try to identify the archetype on which the main character was based.

SKILL 5: WRITING ASSIGNMENT (1–2 WEEKS)

Introduction

Each student refers back to all the first-draft stories s/he has already written and selects her/his favorite to develop, augment, and improve using the character-deepening techniques learned in this Skill Set.

Week 1: Complete the First Draft

1. The teacher explains to the students that over the next one or two weeks they are going to be producing a final-draft story and handing it in for evaluation.

2. Referring to AUTHORS NEED A WRITING PLAN, the teacher goes over with the class the steps in the writing process.

   Students should be reminded that although the emphasis in this assignment will be on deepening major characters, the students will still be expected to follow the steps as outlined.

3. Referring to the AUTHORS NEED A WRITING PLAN handout, the teacher and class work backwards from the final deadline to establish due dates for the various steps in the process: second-draft revision, proofreading with a partner, third-draft text editing, and submission of the final draft for evaluation. Students should write these due dates on their handouts to serve as a reminder.

4. Each student works independently to complete a revised first draft of her/his story by the due date, deepening the main characters by giving them surprising additional facets and minor problems, by hinting at their Basic Motivations, and by making use of archetypes to add layers of association. This work may be done in class, as homework, or both. The teacher should make available to those students who require them copies of any story-planning charts used in previous Skill Sets (e.g., CHARACTER BIO SHEETS, DRAMATIC CONFLICT CHART B, STORY OUTLINE SHEET, SCENE DEVELOPMENT CHART, and so on).

Week 2: Revise, Edit, and Polish

1. The teacher hands out PROOFREAD WITH A PARTNER CHECKLISTS for students' reference during the revising and editing process. The criteria on the sheet should be reviewed in class.

2. Using these criteria as a guide, students are to revise their first-draft work and produce a clean second draft of their stories by the due date established earlier.

3. On the due date, the teacher refers students to the PROOFREAD WITH A PARTNER CHECKLIST and puts up on the board (or on an overhead screen) the following guidelines for peer-assisted editing, going over them one at a time with the class:

   1. *Editing partners are to work together, first on one author's story and then on the other author's story, discussing areas where improvements can be made. Editing partners are not to trade stories and work independently.*
   2. *Editing partners are to check off each criterion on the author's sheet as soon as it has been discussed, using the left-hand column of the checklist. Authors will use the right-hand column while revising and editing their second drafts, to check off that each criterion has been considered and necessary improvements have been made. A checklist without check marks down both sides will be considered incomplete.*
   3. *Editing partners may suggest improvements but are not allowed to make changes to an author's work. Authors are the owners of their work. Therefore, if changes are necessary, the author must be the one to make them.*
   4. *Remember that the job of an editing partner is to help the author improve. All criticism of another writer's work must therefore be constructive (i.e., suggesting ways to make it better).*

4. Students then pair up with editing partners and work together to improve both their stories, following the instructions on the board or screen. Once the editing partner has signed off on her/his side of the sheet, each student author is responsible for making the necessary improvements to her/his second-draft work, checking off the other side of the sheet. The student then rewrites the story as a third draft.

5. The teacher hands out copies of the ASSESSMENT SHEET for students to use as a reference while polishing their completed third drafts.

6. Polished work is then recopied in final-draft form, formatted in accordance with the teacher's instructions, and packaged together with the student author's planning materials, edited previous drafts, peer-editing checklist, and ASSESSMENT SHEET. The entire package is submitted to the teacher for summative assessment.

TEACHING TIPS

Students need regular text-editing practice in order to strengthen their skills. One method that works well is to lift sentences containing writing errors (including spelling and punctuation mistakes) from students' final drafts and compile them into exercises for the entire class to do on a regular basis. As students' skills improve, there will be fewer errors to find in their final drafts. The exercises will therefore become shorter and shorter, thus providing both tangible evidence of improvement and an incentive for further improvement.

Please note: Because it is important for students to realize that editing is the stage in which they are supposed to recognize and correct their own errors and weaknesses, I strongly urge that you use only submitted final drafts as the basis for such exercises.

LSR 5

CHARACTER MOTIVATIONS

BASIC MOTIVATIONS (what drives the character)	RESULTING ACTIONS (what s/he might do)	SECONDARY MOTIVATIONS (reasons s/he might give if asked)
1. Fear of commitment		
2. Thirst for power		
3. Need for acceptance		
4. Need for order		
5. Need to be needed		

REVISE, EDIT AND PROOFREAD WITH A PARTNER
CHECKLIST: GIVING CHARACTERS DEPTH

AUTHOR'S NAME: _____

EDITING PARTNER: _____

Checked by editor	Editing Criteria	Improved by author
	1. Major and minor characters have been introduced in a manner appropriate to each one's role in the story.	
	2. The opening scene hooks the reader right away by: (a) introducing a main character right away; (b) coincidentally establishing the setting of the story; (c) providing important background information; (d) quickly launching the dramatic conflict.	
	3. Minor characters have been effectively used throughout the story.	
	4. Main characters' minor problems have been used to create plot and character interest.	
	5. Protagonist's basic and secondary motivations are demonstrated by his/her words, actions and thoughts.	
	6. Characters have been made interesting with both ordinary and extraordinary characteristics.	
	7. The use of archetypes has added levels of meaning to the story.	
	8. Effective use has been made of descriptive detail and figurative language.	
	9. A compelling main plot has been developed around a strong, textured dramatic conflict.	
	10. The author has been considerate to the reader by making the story as well-written as possible: (a) spelling and grammar have been checked (not just on the computer); (b) there are no run-on sentences; (c) there is correct use of capital letters, commas and apostrophes; (d) there is agreement of subject and verb (both either singular or plural).	

GIVING CHARACTERS DEPTH
ASSESSMENT SHEET

STUDENT AUTHOR: _____

STORY TITLE: _____

SCORING: 5 = OUTSTANDING   4 = VERY GOOD   3 = GOOD
2 = YOU CAN DO BETTER   1 = POOR

THIS AUTHOR HAS:	5	4	3	2	1
1. introduced each major and minor character in a manner appropriate to each one's role in the story					
2. made effective use of the minor characters in the story					
3. developed a compelling main plot around a strong dramatic conflict					
4. given the main character at least one minor problem to create plot and character interest					
5. given the reader insight into the basic and secondary motivations of the protagonist					
6. created interesting characters by giving them both ordinary and extraordinary characteristics					
7. added levels of meaning to the story by the use of archetypes					
8. made effective use of descriptive detail and figurative language to enhance the Illusion of Reality					
9. hooked the reader with an effective opening scene					
10. built the story to a decisive and satisfying conclusion					
COLUMN TOTALS =					

TOTAL SCORE =   **/50**

COMMENTS:

Writing Longer Fiction: Skill Set 3

Adding a Subplot

✍ **YOU WILL NEED:**

- GSR 10—STORY OUTLINE SHEET—1 class set per skill activity
- List of characters on the board (see Skill 4, Step 2)
- Students' Ideas Files (Skill 5)
- Story-planning charts from previous Skill Sets (Skill 5)
- WSR 14—AUTHORS NEED A WRITING PLAN—class set (Skill 5)
- LSR 8—PROOFREAD WITH A PARTNER CHECKLIST (Skill 5)
- LSR 9—ASSESSMENT SHEET (Skill 5)

PURPOSE

Authors of longer fiction understand how a well-integrated subplot can deepen and enrich a story. As students practice adding appropriate subplots to their own stories, they will also become more aware of the ways in which disparate-seeming goals and events can influence one another in real life.

SKILL 1: SUBPLOT AS FOIL FOR MAIN PLOT

Introduction and Modeling

1. The teacher writes the terms "Main Plot" and "Subplot" on the board and asks students to come up with a definition for each one. As students share their ideas, the teacher records them on the board (*e.g., The main plot contains the strongest dramatic conflict of the story and has the most important character as the protagonist. It can stand alone. A Subplot is about a secondary or minor character and may or may not have a dramatic conflict. Its purpose is to add depth and interest to the main plot. It cannot stand alone.*).

2. The teacher then draws the chart of a main plot on the board, to be used as a reference and filled in as the teacher tells the students the story outlined below:

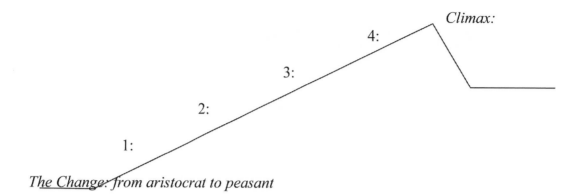

The Change: from aristocrat to peasant

The Story: It is 1789, in France. The protagonist, a spoiled young countess, is living in the family chateau with her personal maid, whom she treats as a possession. The CHANGE that occurs in her life is that the Bastille falls and the Revolution begins.

In the first scene, hearing that the local villagers are on their way to arrest her, the countess forces her maid to trade clothing with her so she can make her escape to England.

In the second scene, en route to the coast, she is weary and tries to get a lift from a fleeing nobleman in a coach. He physically abuses her for speaking to him as an equal, and she begins to realize what life for a servant must be like.

In the third scene, the countess is hungry and can't find any bread, but a poor farmer's wife takes pity on her and gives her half of her own meager loaf.

In the fourth scene, the countess learns that her brother, a court attendant, has been arrested and beheaded.

In the climax, she reaches the coast but discovers that there is a single remaining place in the boat and two people needing to cross over—herself and a mother with a baby. Moved by her newfound compassion for others, the countess gives up her place on the boat and remains behind. Her sacrifice is rewarded when the innkeeper who arranged for the escape boat hires her and gives her a place to stay until the next crossing.

In the denouement, we learn that the countess truly has changed. She has decided to permanently renounce her former privileged station, and hopes the people can make their new Republic work.

The teacher may wish to review at this time the structure of a CHANGE story (see Getting Started, Skill Set 6: Understanding Story and Scene Structure, Skill 1).

3. The teacher explains that just as a character foil emphasizes a particular characteristic of the hero/ine by doing or being the exact opposite, one of the ways a subplot can intensify the main plot is by contrasting with it. The main plot and subplot can develop parallel to each other, but the characters in the subplot do not need to encounter or cross paths with the characters in the main plot.

4. Drawing the students' attention to the chart on the board, the teacher adds the details of the following subplot to each corresponding scene of the main plot:

While the countess is switching clothing with her maid, the brother is at court, meeting with the royal tailor to be measured for a splendid new suit of clothes.

While the foot-weary countess is being slapped hard for daring to request a lift from the fleeing nobleman, the brother is at a ball, slapping a servant for bringing him the wrong drink.

While the hungry countess is greedily devouring a stale crust of bread, the brother is disdainfully surveying a banquet table loaded with delicacies . . . and walking away from it in disgust.

The subplot ends when the countess learns that her brother has been beheaded.

5. The teacher asks the students: How does the reader feel about this news? How do you think the countess feels about it, after all that she has been through to this point? In what way(s) does the presence of this subplot enhance or add to the main plot?

*It should be pointed out to the students that a subplot is like a main plot in that it has a story event, a rising action, and a climax. The students need to be told as well that the climax of a subplot must always occur **before** the climax of the main plot.*

6. The teacher can diagram the relationship between the main plot and the subplot-as-foil, as follows:

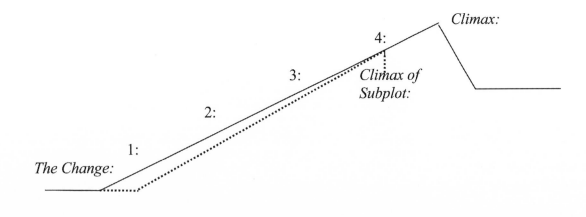

This diagram should be left on the board for reference as students proceed to the next phase of the lesson.

Practice and Product

1. The teacher hands out a copy of the STORY OUTLINE SHEET to each student. Students then number off from 1 to 3.

2. The teacher assigns one of the following main plots to each student, according to number:

    1. When a parent falls ill, a student is forced to get a part-time job to help her/his family make ends meet. This creates problems.
    2. An elderly grandparent is being released from the hospital in five days and will have to move in with the main character's family. There are problems.
    3. A popular teenager falls in love with a person of a different race or religion. They want to be a couple, but there are problems.

3. Each student charts her/his main plot first, in scenes on the STORY OUTLINE SHEET, then creates and charts the contrasting subplot as modeled by the teacher earlier.

4. Working independently, each student then writes up a detailed synopsis of the entire story in sentence and paragraph form.

    Students need to be told that a synopsis is always written in the present tense, that it contains no dialogue, and that a detailed synopsis should also contain information about what the characters are feeling and thinking at important points in the story.
    Students should also be reminded that if they should decide to write a complete first-draft story from this synopsis, they will need to go through the previously taught steps of determining the theme and dramatic conflict and charting the sequence of scenes before they begin writing.

5. **Next day:** The students are organized into groups of three, such that all three of the main plots from Step 2 (above) are represented in each group. The teacher then reveals the following questions (on the board or on an overhead screen)

and goes over them with the class. (These are the questions students should be answering as they share and discuss their work with group mates):

- *Is it clear throughout the story which is the main plot and which is the subplot?*
- *Is the most important plot the one chosen to be the main plot?*
- *Is the subplot resolved before the climax of the main plot?*
- *Does the subplot fulfill its intended role in the story?*
- *Is there a definite contrast between the main plot and the subplot?*
- *Does the subplot add interest to the story?*

6. In each group, one of the authors reads her/his plot synopsis aloud to her/his group mates. Following the reading, the students are allotted a number of minutes in which to discuss the story and offer suggestions for improvement. This is then repeated for the other two authors in each group.

7. When all three stories have been read and discussed in the group, each author should have some time to make the improvements suggested by the audience. *These synopses should then be put in the students' Ideas Files for possible future development.*

SKILL 2: SUBPLOT TO FACILITATE MAIN PLOT

Introduction and Modeling

1. *(If beginning the Skill Set with Skill 2)* The teacher writes the terms "Main Plot" and "Subplot" on the board and asks students to come up with a definition for each one. As students share their ideas, the teacher records them on the board *(e.g., The main plot contains the strongest dramatic conflict of the story and has the most important character as the protagonist. It can stand alone. A subplot is about a secondary or minor character and may or may not have a dramatic conflict. Its purpose is to add depth and interest to the main plot. It cannot stand alone.)*

2. The teacher then draws the chart of a main plot on the board, to be used as a reference and filled in as the teacher tells the students the story outlined below:

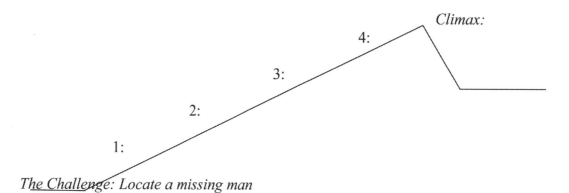

The Plot: A woman hires a private investigator (the protagonist) to find her missing brother. The police are looking for him as well, but only because they want to charge him with robbery. She is certain her brother is innocent and that he has dropped out of sight because he's afraid of the real robbers. She wants to get to him before the police or the criminals do.

In the first scene, the woman visits the investigator at his office to hire him. She explains the situation and gives him enough information about her brother to begin tracking him down.

In the second scene, the private eye arrives at the brother's girlfriend's place and stumbles into a police stakeout. The detective at the scene is a friend of the protagonist. He shares useful information with the private eye before sending him away.

In the third scene, the private eye follows a lead to a cabin outside of town. There's an elderly couple living there that saw and spoke to the brother at about the time the robbery was being committed. He was on the run from someone who wanted him dead. The couple thus gives him an alibi, clearing him of the crime. Just then the police detective arrives on the scene to question the couple. He isn't happy about the private eye meddling in his robbery investigation, but when he hears the elderly couple's story he is forced to agree that the missing brother is probably a frightened witness rather than a suspect.

In the fourth scene, the private eye is at the police precinct when he receives a phone call from the missing brother, begging him to stop looking for him. By now the protagonist and the police are working together, so they are able to locate the source of the phone call.

In the climax, the private eye and the police arrive at the brother's hiding place, just in time to prevent the sister from killing him. She is arrested.

In the denouement it turns out that she was the one who committed the robbery. Her brother's testimony will put her in prison for a long time.

3. The teacher may wish to review at this time the structure of a CHALLENGE story: the story event that disrupts the normalcy of the protagonist's life is not a problem or change at the beginning of the story, but rather an event that causes her/him to set a goal and work toward it. It might be a chance meeting with an old friend that causes the protagonist to regret having dropped out of school. The story goal—the challenge—is to get her/himself back on track to eventually earning her/his high school diploma. In the case of the private eye, the story goal is finding his client's missing brother. The challenge of a challenge story is the goal that the protagonist has set for her/himself. The rising action becomes a series of obstacles that the protagonist must overcome in order to successfully meet the challenge by achieving the story goal.

4. The teacher explains that the subplot in this story is actually serving the same purpose as a minor character who is a plot facilitator. The private detective and the police detective (a secondary character) are working toward the same goal. Sometimes they share information and sometimes they don't. But they keep tripping over each other at moments of crisis and eventually they team up and work together to achieve the goal.

5. The teacher draws the diagram (shown below) for this kind of subplot on the board and explains that the intersections shown are the places in the story where the main plot protagonist and the subplot protagonist trip over each other or meet to compare notes. Unlike a story with a foil subplot, which lets the reader cross back and forth, following both plotlines simultaneously, this kind of story keeps the reader focused on the main plotline, giving glimpses of the subplot only in scenes in which the two protagonists meet.

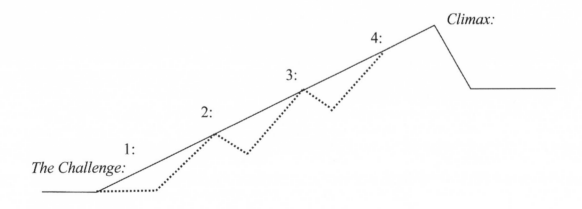

*It should be pointed out to the students that a subplot is like a main plot in that it has a story event, a rising action, and a climax. The students need to be told as well that the climax of a subplot must always occur **before** the climax of the main plot.*

Guided Practice (optional)

Together, the class develops the main plot and facilitating subplot of an original episode for their favorite crime/mystery show. The teacher charts their ideas on the plot diagram on the board.

Practice and Product

1. The teacher hands out a copy of the STORY OUTLINE CHART to each student. Students then pair up with working partners to develop and chart the main plot and facilitating subplot of their own original private detective story, selecting one of the following *subplot protagonists* and one of the listed *story goals* (these can be written on the board or projected onto an overhead screen):

   a police detective   *find a missing person*
   a criminal   *recover a stolen item*
   a social worker   *solve a murder*
   a runaway street kid   *identify someone in a photograph*
   a relative of the person who hired her/him *prevent a crime from happening*

   Each partner will need to have her/his own personal copy of the completed story chart for the next step of the activity.

2. Each student, working independently, writes up a detailed synopsis from the chart developed with her/his partner.
   Students may need to be reminded that a synopsis is always written in the present tense, that it contains no dialogue, and that a detailed synopsis should also contain information about what the characters are feeling and thinking at important points in the story.

   Students should understand as well that if they should decide to write a complete first-draft story from this synopsis, they would need to go through the previously taught steps of determining the theme and dramatic conflict and charting the sequence of scenes before they begin writing.

3. **Next day:** The teacher organizes the class into groups of three, ensuring that three different subplot protagonists are represented in each group. The teacher then goes over with the class the questions they should be answering as they share and discuss their work with group mates (these should be written on the board):

   * *Is there a relationship established between the two protagonists?*
   * *Does the protagonist of the main plot remain dominant in the story?*
   * *Do the two protagonists join forces before the climax of the main plot?*
   * *Does the subplot provide practical support to the main plot?*
   * *Does the subplot add interest to the story?*

4. In each group, one of the authors reads her/his plot synopsis aloud to her/his group mates. Following the reading, the students are allotted a number of minutes in which to discuss the story and offer suggestions for improvement. This is then repeated for the other two authors in each group.

5. When all three stories have been read and discussed in the group, each author should have some time to make the improvements suggested by the audience. *These synopses should then be put in the students' Ideas Files for possible future development.*

SKILL 3: SUBPLOT TO COMPLICATE MAIN PLOT

Introduction and Modeling

1. *(If beginning the Skill Set with Skill 3)* The teacher writes the terms "Main Plot" and "Subplot" on the board and asks students to come up with a definition for each one. As students share their ideas, the teacher records them on the

board *(e.g., The main plot contains the strongest dramatic conflict of the story and has the most important character as the protagonist. It can stand alone. A subplot is about a secondary or minor character and may or may not have a dramatic conflict. Its purpose is to add depth and interest to the main plot. It cannot stand alone.)*

2. The teacher then draws the chart of a main plot on the board, to be used as a reference and filled in as the teacher tells the students the story outlined below:

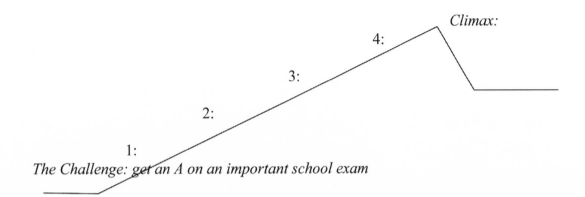

The main plot protagonist is a high school student who must get an A on a final history exam in order to receive the scholarship he needs to go on to college. The subplot protagonist is the jealous ex-boyfriend of a female friend of the student.

    In the first scene, the student is kept after class by his history teacher, who tells him that the only way he's going to get the grade he needs is by earning an A on the final exam next week. The teacher gives him a list of books he should read in preparation for the exam. As the student is leaving the classroom, he receives a text message from the female friend, inviting him to go out clubbing that evening. It's tempting, but he really needs to study. He declines but suggests another day.

    In the second scene, the protagonist is at the library finding the books on the teacher's list and planning in which order to read them. Suddenly the friend rushes up to him, extremely upset because she just learned that her ex-boyfriend hacked into her phone, found the texted invitation and response, and is now talking about beating up the protagonist. In the excitement, the protagonist ends up leaving the library without checking out any books.

    In the third scene, the student is in his bedroom, diligently studying. The exam is in two days, history has never been an easy subject for him, and he's getting nervous. Suddenly he receives a death threat via text message from his friend's ex-boyfriend. This is too much. The protagonist's concentration is destroyed. It's time to involve the adults in his life.

    In the fourth scene, the student and his mother are at the police station watching the ex-boyfriend arrive in handcuffs. He assaulted the officer sent to bring him in and will be facing multiple charges. There should be no further obstacles to the protagonist's preparing for the history exam.

    In the climax, the student enters the room where the exam is being written. He is full of uncertainty, but determined to do his best.

    In the denouement he finds out his final grade in the history course.

3. *(If beginning the Skill Set with Skill 3:)* The teacher may wish to review at this time the structure of a CHALLENGE story: the story event that disrupts the normalcy of the protagonist's life is not a problem or change at the beginning of the story, but rather an event that causes her/him to set a goal and work toward it. It might be a chance meeting with an old friend that causes the protagonist to regret having dropped out of school. The story goal—the challenge—is to get her/himself back on track to eventually earning her/his high school diploma. In the case of the protagonist in Step 2 (above), the story goal is earning an A on the final history exam. The challenge of a challenge story is the goal that the protagonist has set for herself/himself. The rising action becomes a series of obstacles that the protagonist must overcome in order to successfully meet the challenge by achieving the story goal.

4. The teacher explains that the subplot in this story is actually serving the same purpose as a minor character who is a *plot complicator*. The student and the ex-boyfriend (a minor character) are working toward different goals. In his efforts to achieve the subplot goal *(i.e., get back together with his ex-girlfriend)*, the ex-boyfriend keeps interfering with the protagonist's efforts to achieve the main plot goal. Finally, in a scene that comes before the climax of the story, the protagonist puts a stop to the interference, clearing the way for him to achieve the main story goal.

5. The teacher draws the diagram (shown below) for this kind of subplot on the board and explains that the intersections shown are the places in the story where the efforts of the subplot protagonist "throw a grappling hook" onto the main plot. Like a story with a facilitating subplot, this kind of story keeps the reader focused on the main plotline, giving glimpses of the subplot only in scenes in which the two plots collide. Unlike a story with a facilitating subplot, the protagonists of the main plot and subplot are working toward different goals, so joining forces is not a story option.

It should be pointed out to students that, depending on the story, the way to end the interference from the subplot might be to help the subplot protagonist achieve her/his goal.

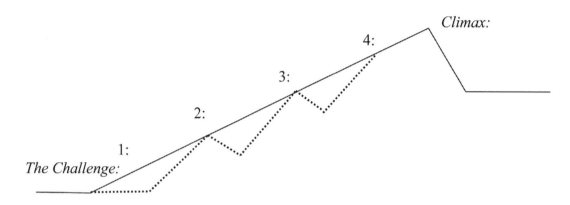

Guided Practice (optional)

The teacher and class together develop the main plot and complicating subplot for the following story:

There is an old unused garage in your backyard that you would like to fix up as a party room. Unbeknownst to you, a family of raccoons has decided to move into the same garage.

The teacher charts the story on the board, using the diagram from Step 5 (above).

*It should be pointed out to the students that a subplot is like a main plot in that it has a story event, a rising action, and a climax. The students need to be told as well that the climax of a subplot must always occur **before** the climax of the main plot.*

Practice and Product

1. The teacher hands out a copy of the STORY OUTLINE SHEET to each student. Students then pair up with working partners to develop and chart the main plot and complicating subplot of their own original story, selecting one of the following pairs of protagonists (these can be written on the board) or coming up with a protagonist pair of their own:

> *a bank robber and an old woman*
> *an undercover police officer and his girlfriend/wife*
> *a tourist and a street kid*
> *a magician and a news reporter*
> *a sales clerk and a spy*

Student pairs will need to determine which of their two characters will be the main protagonist and which will be the subplot protagonist.

Each partner will need to have her/his own personal copy of the completed story chart for the next step of the activity.

2. Each student working independently then writes up a detailed synopsis from the chart developed with her/his partner.

Students may need to be reminded that a synopsis is always written in the present tense, that it contains no dialogue, and that a detailed synopsis should also contain information about what the characters are feeling and thinking at important points in the story.

Students should understand as well that if they should decide to write a complete first-draft story from this synopsis, they would need to go through the previously taught steps of determining the theme and dramatic conflict and charting the sequence of scenes before they begin writing.

3. **Next day:** The teacher organizes the class into groups of three, ensuring that three different pairs of protagonists are represented in each group. The teacher then goes over with the class the questions they should be answering as they share and discuss their work with group mates (these should be written on the board):

   - *Is there a connection established to explain why the two plots keep colliding?*
   - *Does the protagonist of the main plot remain dominant in the story?*
   - *Does the main protagonist end the interference from the subplot before the climax of the main plot?*
   - *Does the subplot truly complicate the main plot?*
   - *Does the subplot add interest to the story?*

4. In each group, one of the authors reads her/his plot synopsis aloud to her/his group mates. Following the reading, the students are allotted a number of minutes in which to discuss the story and offer suggestions for improvement. This is then repeated for the other two authors in each group.

5. When all three stories have been read and discussed in the group, each author should have some time to make the improvements suggested by the audience.
   These synopses should then be put in the students' Ideas Files for possible future development.

SKILL 4: SUBPLOT TO ADD A CHARACTER DIMENSION

Introduction and Modeling

1. *(If beginning the Skill Set with Skill 4)* The teacher writes the terms "Main Plot" and "Subplot" on the board and asks students to come up with a definition for each one. As students share their ideas, the teacher records them on the board *(e.g., The main plot contains the strongest dramatic conflict of the story and has the most important character as the protagonist. It can stand alone. A subplot is about a secondary or minor character and may or may not have a dramatic conflict. Its purpose is to add depth and interest to the main plot. It cannot stand alone.)*

2. The teacher then draws the chart of a main plot on the board, to be used as a reference and filled in as the teacher tells the students the story outlined below:

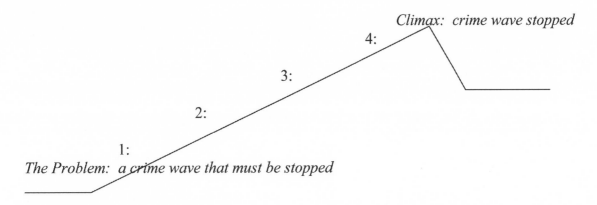

The main character is a police detective in a large city. There has been a rash of break-ins at the homes of wealthy families, who are pressuring the mayor, who is pressuring the police chief, who in turn is pressuring the police department to do something about this right away.

In the story event, the detective is assigned to the case by his precinct commander, who warns him they could both end up directing traffic if an arrest isn't made promptly. The detective gets right to work looking over the files on all the break-ins.
   In the first scene, the detective is interviewing the victims of the latest break-in.
   In the second scene, the detective is interrogating a teen who was caught prowling around the home of a local politician. The detective is certain the kid knows something, but can't break him and has to let him go.
   In the third scene, the detective sets up a stakeout at the home he believes will be the next target. He's wrong. While they're watching this house, another one gets robbed.
   In the fourth scene, the precinct commander calls him into a meeting with a federal agent who has information about a crime organization that might be behind these burglaries. Armed with this new intelligence, the detective is able to set a trap and, in the climax, catch the perpetrators leaving the scene of their latest crime with a van full of stolen goods.

3. The teacher may wish to review at this time the structure of a PROBLEM story (see Getting Started, Skill Set 6: Understanding Story and Scene Structure, Skill 1).

4. The teacher explains that in some stories, it just isn't possible for a character to show all three Dimensions of Life in the main plot. For example, in the police story just told, the detective must be tough and businesslike while conducting the investigation that forms the main plot of the story. However, he is the main character, the one the reader is supposed to care about and be cheering for, and in order for that to happen, he needs to reveal the Emotional Dimension of his personality—evidence that he has recognizable and relatable human feelings.
   A subplot will give her/him that opportunity—perhaps involving her/his family or a love interest or a cherished hobby that reveals an unsuspected talent or facet of her/his personality.
   Drawing the students' attention to the chart on the board, the teacher explains that this detective has a teenaged son who is a pitcher on his school baseball team, and there is a state tournament coming up. The teacher then adds the details of the following subplot to the spaces between pairs of scenes of the main plot:

Between the story event and Scene 1, there is a pleasant family dinner. The detective's teenaged son announces that he will be a starting pitcher for his team at the tournament. Mom and Dad are very proud of him, and Dad promises to help him practice.
   Between Scenes 1 and 2, the detective is at a ball diamond, teaching his son the finer points of throwing a slider.
   Between Scenes 2 and 3, the detective arrives home too late to practice. Wife is annoyed; son is disappointed.
   Between Scenes 3 and 4, the detective arrives at the ball diamond with his glove, but his son is already practicing with somebody else and won't even look in his father's direction. Now Dad is disappointed. He goes home and explains to his wife how frustrating it is when his job interferes with what he really wants to be doing (i.e., helping his son prepare for an important ball game). Wife understands, and tells him Son will too once he cools off.
   After Scene 4 and before the climax, the detective's son asks him to come to the tournament to watch him pitch. The detective replies that nothing will keep him away. (This is the climax of the subplot.)
   In the denouement, the detective slides into a seat in the bleachers in time to watch his son finish striking out the other side. Everybody cheers.

5. The teacher asks the students: How does the reader feel about the main character at this point? In what way(s) does the presence of this subplot change the reader's perception of what is happening in the main plot?
   *It should be pointed out to the students that a subplot is like a main plot in that it has a story event, a rising action, and a climax. The students need to be told as well that the climax of a subplot must always occur **before** the climax of the main plot.*

6. The teacher can diagram the relationship between the main plot and the dimension-adding subplot, as follows:

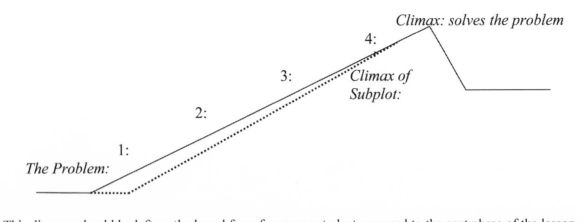

This diagram should be left on the board for reference as students proceed to the next phase of the lesson.

Practice and Product

1. The teacher hands out a copy of the STORY OUTLINE SHEET to each student and reveals the following list of characters on the board:

   - *a school principal*
   - *a professional coach (sports, fitness, life, etc.)*
   - *a judge*
   - *a bus driver*
   - *a (commercial) pilot*
   - *a soldier*
   - *a banker*
   - *a spy*

2. Students pair up with working partners. Together, each pair selects a main character from the list on the board and creates the main plot of a story featuring the character.
   The student authors must then decide which aspect of the character's personality needs to be revealed in order to make the character someone the reader will identify with and care about. The students work together to create the subplot that will accomplish this, and both the main plot and the subplot are charted on the STORY OUTLINE SHEET.
   Each student should ensure that s/he makes a personal copy of the chart produced with her/his partner.

3. Each student working independently then writes a detailed synopsis from the chart developed with her/his partner.
   Students may need to be reminded that a synopsis is always written in the present tense, that it contains no dialogue, and that a detailed synopsis should also contain information about what the characters are feeling and thinking at important points in the story.
   Students should understand as well that if they should decide to write a complete first-draft story from this synopsis, they will need to go through the previously taught steps of determining the theme and dramatic conflict and charting the sequence of scenes before they begin writing.

4. **Next day:** The teacher organizes the class in groups of three, ensuring that three different protagonists are represented in each group. The teacher then goes over with the class the questions they should be answering as they share and discuss their work with group mates (on the board):

   - *Is there a single protagonist with two different goals, one for the main plot and one for the subplot?*
   - *Is there a dimension missing from the character in the main plot, and is it shown to the reader in the subplot?*

- *Does the subplot focus on supplying the missing dimension of the character?*
- *Does the subplot resolve itself before the climax of the main plot?*
- *Does the subplot add interest to the story?*

5. In each group, one of the authors reads her/his plot synopsis aloud to her/his group mates. Following the reading, the students are allotted a number of minutes in which to discuss the story and offer suggestions for improvement. This is then repeated for the other two authors in each group.

6. When all three stories have been read and discussed in the group, each author should have some time to make the improvements suggested by the audience.
   These synopses should then be put in the students' Ideas Files for possible future development.

SKILL 5: WRITING ASSIGNMENT (1–2 WEEKS)

Introduction

Each student refers back to all the detailed synopses written in this Skill Set and selects her/his favorite to develop into a first draft. Students may also refer back to all the first-draft stories already written and select one to develop, augment, and improve using one of the kinds of subplots studied in this Skill Set.

Week 1: Complete the First Draft

1. The teacher explains to the students that over the next one or two weeks they are going to be producing a final-draft story and handing it in for evaluation.

2. Referring to AUTHORS NEED A WRITING PLAN, the teacher goes over with the class the steps in the writing process.
   Students should be reminded that although the emphasis in this assignment will be on effectively using subplots, the students will still be expected to follow the steps as outlined.

3. Referring to the AUTHORS NEED A WRITING PLAN handout, the teacher and class work backwards from the final deadline to establish due dates for the various steps in the process: second-draft revision, proofreading with a partner, third-draft text editing, and submission of the final draft for evaluation. Students should write these due dates on their handouts to serve as a reminder.

4. Each student works independently to complete a revised first draft of her/his story by the due date, enhancing the main plot by adding a subplot that will act as a foil, facilitate or complicate the main plot, or enable the main character to reveal a hidden dimension of her/his personality. This work may be done in class, as homework, or both. The teacher should make available to those students who require them copies of any story-planning charts used in previous Skill Sets (e.g., CHARACTER BIO SHEETS, DRAMATIC CONFLICT CHART B, STORY OUTLINE SHEET, SCENE DEVELOPMENT CHART, and so on).

Week 2: Revise, Edit, and Polish

1. The teacher hands out PROOFREAD WITH A PARTNER CHECKLISTS for students' reference during the revising and editing process. The criteria on the sheet should be reviewed in class.

2. Using these criteria as a guide, students are to revise their first-draft work and produce a clean second draft of their stories by the due date established earlier.

3. On the due date, the teacher refers students to the PROOFREAD WITH A PARTNER CHECKLIST and puts up on the board (or on an overhead screen) the following guidelines for peer-assisted editing, going over them one at a time with the class:

   1. *Editing partners are to work together, first on one author's story and then on the other author's story, discussing areas where improvements can be made. Editing partners are not to trade stories and work independently.*
   2. *Editing partners are to check off each criterion on the author's sheet as soon as it has been discussed, using the left-hand column of the checklist. Authors will use the right-hand column while revising and editing their second drafts, to check off that each criterion has been considered and necessary improvements have been made. A checklist without check marks down both sides will be considered incomplete.*
   3. *Editing partners may suggest improvements but are not allowed to make changes to an author's work. Authors are the owners of their work. Therefore, if changes are necessary, the author must be the one to make them.*
   4. *Remember that the job of an editing partner is to help the author improve. All criticism of another writer's work must therefore be constructive (i.e., suggesting ways to make it better).*

4. Students then pair up with editing partners and work together to improve both their stories, following the instructions on the board or screen. Once the editing partner has signed off on her/his side of the sheet, each student author is responsible for making the necessary improvements to her/his second-draft work, checking off the other side of the sheet. The student then rewrites the story as a third draft.

5. The teacher hands out copies of the ASSESSMENT SHEET for students to use as a reference while polishing their completed third drafts.

6. Polished work is then recopied in final-draft form, formatted in accordance with the teacher's instructions, and packaged together with the student author's planning materials, edited previous drafts, self-evaluation sheet, peer-editing checklist, and ASSESSMENT SHEET. The entire package is submitted to the teacher for summative assessment.

TEACHING TIPS

Students need to practice, not only writing subplots for stories, but also deciding what kind of subplot would be appropriate and what would be the best way to integrate it into the main plot of a story. The strongest main plot–subplot bonds are created when a subplot, like a minor character, is made to serve more than one function. Here are some questions students can ask themselves when considering whether a story needs a subplot:

Is the main plot protagonist a complete, three-dimensional character?
Is there an "opposite side of the coin" to what is happening in the main plot that would heighten and strengthen its impression on the reader?
Is the main plot protagonist receiving assistance throughout the story from a lot of different minor characters?
Is there any reason that the help couldn't come from just one person? (Whether or not s/he becomes the protagonist of a subplot, having a single facilitating minor character will unify and strengthen a story.)
Is there an antagonist who is a constant presence in the story? (If yes, then a subplot is probably not needed.) Am I having to invent a lot of different obstacles to prevent the main plot protagonist from succeeding too easily? Is there any reason that they couldn't be the result of interference from a character with a different but related goal, whose path keeps crossing the main plotline?

REVISE, EDIT AND PROOFREAD WITH A PARTNER
CHECKLIST: USING SUBPLOTS

AUTHOR'S NAME: _____

EDITING PARTNER: _____

Checked by editor	Editing Criteria	Improved by author
	1. The main character is a strong and sympathetic protagonist.	
	2. The opening scene hooks the reader by: (a) introducing a main character right away; (b) coincidentally establishing the setting of the story; (c) providing important background information; (d) quickly launching the dramatic conflict.	
	3. The main plot is compelling and has been developed around a strong and textured dramatic conflict.	
	4. Descriptive detail and figurative language have been effectively used to create the Illusion of Reality	
	5. The subplot effectively fulfils its intended role in the story: facilitating or complicating the main plot, acting as a foil to the main plot, revealing a hidden dimension of the main protagonist.	
	6. The subplot enhances but remains subordinate to the main plot.	
	7. The protagonist of the main plot is the most important character in the story.	
	8. The subplot has been woven meaningfully into the story.	
	9. The climax of the subplot precedes the climax of the main plot.	
	10. The author has been considerate to the reader by making the story as well-written as possible: (a) spelling and grammar have been checked (not just on the computer); (b) there are no run-on sentences; (c) there is correct use of capital letters, commas and apostrophes; (d) there is agreement of subject and verb (both either singular or plural).	

USING SUBPLOTS
ASSESSMENT SHEET

STUDENT AUTHOR: _____

STORY TITLE: _____

**SCORING: 5 = OUTSTANDING   4 = VERY GOOD   3 = GOOD
            2 = YOU CAN DO BETTER   1 = POOR**

THIS AUTHOR HAS:	5	4	3	2	1
1. opened the story with a scene that immediately grabs the reader's interest					
2. developed a strong and sympathetic main character as the protagonist of the story					
3. developed a compelling main plot around a textured dramatic conflict					
4. made effective use of descriptive detail and figurative language to create the Illusion of Reality					
5. created a subplot which enhances but remains subordinate to the main plot					
6. kept the protagonist of the main plot the most important character in the story					
7. included a subplot that effectively fulfils its intended role: facilitator, complicator, foil or character revealer					
8. woven the subplot meaningfully into the story					
9. ensured that the climax of the subplot comes before the climax of the main plot					
10. built the story to a decisive and satisfying conclusion					
COLUMN TOTALS =					

TOTAL SCORE =   /50

COMMENTS:

Writing Longer Fiction: Skill Set 4

Working With Settings

🖎 **YOU WILL NEED:**

- Four two-minute video segments (Skill 1)
- Television and DVD player—for showing the video clips
- Students' Ideas Files (Skills 3 and 5)
- The climactic scene from a short story (Skill 4)
- Story-planning charts from previous Skill Sets (Skill 5)
- WSR 14—AUTHORS NEED A WRITING PLAN—class set (Skill 5)
- LSR 10—PROOFREAD WITH A PARTNER CHECKLIST (Skill 5)
- LSR 11—WORKING WITH SETTINGS ASSESSMENT SHEET (Skill 5)

PURPOSE

Authors of longer fiction must become skilled at using every element of a story to enhance and deepen the others. As students practice putting their story settings to work in various ways, they will become more aware of the extent to which we are all influenced by our real-life surroundings.

SKILL 1: USING SETTING TO ESTABLISH A MOOD

Introduction

1. The teacher and class discuss and define the term *mood. (A mood is the way a person feels. It is also the way a setting/situation feels to a person or makes a person feel.)*

2. *(optional)* Together, the teacher and class brainstorm a list of words that could be used to describe a person's mood *(e.g., happy, sad, angry, fearful, excited, etc.)*. The list is recorded on the board.

3. The teacher then points out that people's moods have always been influenced by their setting. For example, rainy days tend to be depressing no matter where you are. However, a hot sunny day at the beach is quite different from a hot sunny day at the construction site.

4. The class can brainstorm a list of setting factors (e.g., lighting, color, sounds, perception of space, smells, the feel of the air on one's skin—all sensory details) and discuss how changing them tends to change the way we feel.
   Sometimes the change itself creates the mood, as when all birdsong ceases just before a thunderstorm, the sudden silence giving us a sense of foreboding.

157

5. The teacher explains that an author's choice of setting details can create a mood in a scene that echoes or reflects the way a character is feeling . . . or the way the author wants the reader to feel about what is happening or about to happen there.

　　The teacher illustrates the deliberate use of setting detail to create a mood of sadness in a scene: *The day is overcast and dreary, and a light, chilly rain is falling. In the distance can be heard the long, low moan of a foghorn. Except for one anonymous black car that cruises slowly down the block and then disappears, the street is completely empty.*

6. The students now brainstorm a list of different moods that authors might create using setting detail, and these are written on the board. The list should include:

- *foreboding*
- *cheerfulness, optimism*
- *peace, serenity*
- *hospitality, warmth*
- *bleakness, despair*
- *rage*
- *sadness*
- *hostility*
- *awe, reverence*

　　Teacher and class together discuss (and record if desired) a list of places where people might expect to feel particular moods *(e.g., a ski chalet, an abandoned warehouse, a crime scene, a nursery school, a church, etc.)*, as well as the aspects of these locations that can be used to create mood *(e.g., the warmth of the fireplace in the ski chalet, the many dark corners of the warehouse, the smells of a crime scene, the sound of children's laughter at the nursery school, the light filtering through stained-glass windows in the church, etc.).*

　　Students need to understand that by carefully choosing setting details, an author can create virtually any mood in any location. Depending on how a place is described, characters can cheerfully picnic in a graveyard or tremble with fear at a homecoming parade.

Guided Practice

1. The teacher shows four two-minute video segments, each containing a different mood or atmosphere. At the end of each, the students have a couple of minutes to write down the mood they sensed during the scene and the setting elements that combined to create the mood.

　　NOTE TO TEACHER: The production of these video segments would make an excellent assignment for a communications technology class. Interdepartmental collaboration has proven very rewarding for me in the past.

　　After all the video clips have been shown, the teacher and class together share and discuss their findings.

2. Each student selects her/his favorite video clip of the four that were shown and creates a character who will enter that scene with a purpose. The student then plans and charts the scene involving the character, ensuring that the action and reaction of the scene match and are enhanced by the mood created by the setting.

3. Students get together in groups of three or four and share their scene outlines. Group mates can suggest setting details to add in order to deepen the mood.

4. If there is time, each group can select its favorite scene and share it with a larger group or with the rest of the class.

Practice and Product

1. Each student now selects one of the moods from the list on the board and imagines a setting—time, place, and weather—that will be described to create the mood. Each student then brainstorms and records sensory and other details to be included in a scene taking place in that setting.

2. Each student invents a main character and plans and charts a scene from the character's story that will be taking place in the imagined setting. Students should be instructed to ensure that the character's reactions are influenced by the mood created by the author's choice of setting details. *(To preserve the Illusion of Reality, setting influences character.)*

3. Each student proceeds to first-draft the planned scene.

4. The class is organized into groups of three. Without telling her/his group mates which mood was selected from the board, each group member reads her/his scene aloud to the other two, who must identify the mood of the scene based on the setting details that have been included and their influence on the character.

   Students should be encouraged to offer suggestions for additional details to augment or deepen the mood of the piece.

SKILL 2: USING SETTING TO REVEAL CHARACTER

Introduction

1. The teacher asks the students to close their eyes and visualize their bedrooms, as they were left this morning. The teacher then asks: If someone were to enter your bedroom right now, what would they learn about you just from looking around the room?

   The teacher can ask for a show of hands to answer yes to the following questions:

   > *Would they be able to figure out whether you were male or female?*
   > *Would they learn anything about your taste in movies or music?*
   > *Would they learn anything about your plans for the future?*
   > *Would they learn anything about your past achievements?*
   > *Would they learn anything about your ethnic background or heritage?*
   > *Would they learn anything about your interests or hobbies?*
   > *Would they learn which sports teams or players you follow?*
   > *Would they learn anything about your taste in clothes or jewelry?*

2. The teacher then explains to the class that in real life, people tend to imprint themselves on places where they spend a lot of time. Not only bedrooms but also cars and offices will contain information about the persons who "live" there. To make characters more realistic, therefore, authors often use setting details to reveal the interests, talents, tastes, ethnic backgrounds, and personality traits of those characters *(e.g., book titles reveal interests, colors and posters reveal tastes, framed certificates and trophies reveal achievements, etc.).*

Guided Practice

1. The students brainstorm a list of well-known personalities (including fictional characters), and these are written on the board.

2. The teacher selects one of the names and asks students to come up with several characteristics that they would attribute to this person or could imagine the person having *(e.g., sloppy versus neat, athletic versus bookish, quiet versus party-lover, etc.).*

3. Students now brainstorm details that could be included in a description of this person's bedroom, car interior, or office that would reveal these characteristics to the reader, and the teacher records the list of details on the board.

Practice and Product

1. Each student then selects one real or fictional person from the list (not the same name as the teacher chose for Guided Practice) and follows the process demonstrated by the teacher to arrive at a list of characteristics and possible setting details.

2. The student then selects one of bedroom, car interior, or office and first-drafts a description of the chosen person's setting, without mentioning the owner's name.

3. The class is organized into groups of three or four. Each student reads her/his paragraph(s) to her/his group mates, who must determine from the setting details provided which character was chosen and what the setting tells the reader about her/him.

4. Each group then selects its favorite description to share with the rest of the class.

SKILL 3: USING SETTING TO DEEPEN CONFLICT

Introduction and Guided Practice

1. The teacher presents the following scenario to the class: A (wo)man who lives alone is hurrying to get to work on time. Her/His house has other ideas, however.

    The teacher asks: *How many different ways can this person's house interfere with her/his goal of not being late for work?*

2. The students brainstorm a list of ways, and the list is written on the board. It may include:

    > *alarm clock fails to ring, so s/he sleeps in*
    > *wet spot on bathroom floor, so s/he slips (slows her/him down)*
    > *rough edge on countertop snags her/his clothes (forces her/him to change), and so on*

3. The teacher reminds the class that the environment, both natural and artificial, can be an important antagonist in a dramatic conflict.

    The environment of a story may include weather patterns, the layout of a house or an office building, an empty lot, a security system, a city street, the inside of a ship, a state park, and so on.

4. The teacher now draws a dramatic conflict chart on the board and enters the following information under the appropriate headings:

    > *Protagonist: a human space traveler exploring an abandoned alien ship that has entered our solar system*
    > *Goal: return to own ship and signal Earth*
    > *Motivation: self-preservation—alien craft is on a collision course with Earth and will be destroyed at a certain distance from our planet*
    > *Antagonist: the alien ship*

5. The teacher and students together brainstorm ways the alien ship could prevent the spaceman from leaving, and these are listed on the board. *(There should be at least five items in the list [e.g., a door that won't open or won't close, a control board that stuns the space traveler with an energy bolt, etc.])*

6. Students organize into groups of three or four. Each group chooses three of the obstacles listed on the board, ranks them in order of seriousness, and first-drafts a synopsis of a short story in which the space traveler encounters these obstacles one at a time as listed, defeats the worst obstacle last, and is able to return to her/his ship just in time.

7. Each group shares its story synopsis with the rest of the class. Students should be encouraged to offer constructive suggestions for making the setting a stronger antagonist in each story.

Practice and Product

1. Students are instructed to review their Ideas Files and find a story situation and a rich setting that suggest a strong person-versus-environment conflict.

2. Following the process demonstrated by the teacher earlier, each student then builds a short story around that conflict and writes the story in first-draft format.

3. Students who have completed their first-draft stories can pair up with partners for sharing. The student pairs exchange stories, read them, and offer suggestions for improvement.

SKILL 4: USING SETTING FOR FORESHADOWING

Introduction

1. The teacher writes the term "foreshadowing" on the board and discusses with the class what it means: *foreshadowing provides a hint of what is to come without giving away the surprise.*

2. The teacher explains to the students that the opening of a story should always point, directly or indirectly, to future plot events, and in particular to the climax of the story. The setting of an opening scene can be a rich source of foreshadowing details. For example, if a plane crash figured in the climax, the opening setting of the story could foreshadow this in several ways:

The scene could be set at an airport while a safety inspection is in progress.
A cloud in the sky could resemble the front of an airplane, pointed toward the ground.
A television or radio broadcast in the background of the scene could mention an aviation near-disaster.
There could be a book about aviation safety on somebody's desk or coffee table.
Words and imagery used to describe the setting could suggest a plane crash. This is much more subtle and therefore much more effective than the other ways. Something leaning at a steep angle could be described as "taking a nose dive," for example. The colors on a sign could be "fiery reds and yellows," and so on.

Guided Practice

1. The teacher reads aloud to the class the climactic scene from a short story.

2. Together, the teacher and class brainstorm ways in which the setting of the opening scene could foreshadow this event, and the teacher records the list on the board.

3. Students are organized into working groups of three or four. Each group is to write an opening scene that will foreshadow the scene just read, using elements in the setting as well as words and images to hint at the climactic event.

4. Each group shares its opening scene with the rest of the class. Students should be encouraged to offer suggestions for improving the use of setting to foreshadow the ending of the story.

Practice and Product

1. Each student is instructed to review her/his Ideas File and find a completely plotted story (first draft, outline, or synopsis) with a climax that suggests foreshadowing possibilities.

2. The student then follows the process practiced above to plan and first-draft an opening scene for this story, using setting elements and descriptive language to hint at the climactic event.

3. When finished, students form groups of four. Each student reads her/his opening scene aloud to her/his group mates, who will then discuss whether the climax is well foreshadowed without giving away too much information.

4. Students should be instructed to place their stories with opening scenes attached in their Ideas Files for possible further development.

SKILL 5: WRITING ASSIGNMENT (1–2 WEEKS)

Introduction

Each student refers back to all the stories already first-drafted, outlined, or synopsized and selects one to develop, augment, and/or improve, using the skills practiced in this Skill Set.

If students are going to develop stories from ideas or outlines, the teacher may wish to remind them that they must follow the steps as outlined in Getting Started—developing the dramatic conflict, establishing the theme, and so on— before they begin writing.

Week 1: Complete the First Draft

1. The teacher explains to the students that over the next one or two weeks they are going to be producing a final-draft story and handing it in for evaluation.

2. Referring to AUTHORS NEED A WRITING PLAN, the teacher goes over with the class the steps in the writing process.

   Students should be reminded that although the emphasis in this assignment will be on maximizing the roles played by setting in their stories, the students will still be expected to follow the steps as outlined.

3. Referring to the AUTHORS NEED A WRITING PLAN handout, the teacher and class work backward from the final deadline to establish due dates for the various steps in the process: second-draft revision, proofreading with a partner, third-draft text editing, and submission of the final draft for evaluation. Students should write these due dates on their handouts to serve as a reminder.

4. Each student works independently to complete a revised first draft of her/his story by the due date, ensuring that the opening scene both sets the mood for the story and foreshadows the climax, that throughout the story setting details reveal character, and that person versus environment is a large part of the dramatic conflict.

   This work may be done in class, as homework, or both. The teacher should make available to those students who require them copies of any story-planning charts used in previous Skill Sets (e.g., CHARACTER BIO SHEETS, DRAMATIC CONFLICT CHART B, STORY OUTLINE SHEET, SCENE DEVELOPMENT CHART, and so on).

Week 2: Revise, Edit, and Polish

1. The teacher hands out PROOFREAD WITH A PARTNER CHECKLISTS for students' reference during the revising and editing process. The criteria on the sheet should be reviewed in class.

2. Using these criteria as a guide, students are to revise their first-draft work and produce a clean second draft of their stories by the due date established earlier.

3. On the due date, the teacher refers students to the PROOFREAD WITH A PARTNER CHECKLIST and puts up on the board (or on an overhead screen) the following guidelines for peer-assisted editing, going over them one at a time with the class:

1. *Editing partners are to work together, first on one author's story and then on the other author's story, discussing areas where improvements can be made. Editing partners are not to trade stories and work independently.*

2. *Editing partners are to check off each criterion on the author's sheet as soon as it has been discussed, using the left-hand column of the checklist. Authors will use the right-hand column while revising and editing their second drafts, to check off that each criterion has been considered and necessary improvements have been made. A checklist without check marks down both sides will be considered incomplete.*

3. *Editing partners may suggest improvements but are not allowed to make changes to an author's work. Authors are the owners of their work. Therefore, if changes are necessary, the author must be the one to make them.*

4. *Remember that the job of an editing partner is to help the author improve. All criticism of another writer's work must therefore be constructive (i.e., suggesting ways to make it better).*

4. Students then pair up with editing partners and work together to improve both their stories, following the instructions on the board or screen. Once the editing partner has signed off on her/his side of the sheet, each student author is responsible for making the necessary improvements to her/his second-draft work, checking off the other side of the sheet. The student then rewrites the story as a third draft.

5. The teacher hands out copies of the WORKING WITH SETTINGS ASSESSMENT SHEET for students to use as a reference while polishing their completed third drafts.

6. Polished work is then recopied in final-draft form, formatted in accordance with the teacher's instructions, and packaged together with the student author's planning materials, edited previous drafts, peer-editing checklist, and WORKING WITH SETTINGS ASSESSMENT SHEET. The entire package is submitted to the teacher for summative assessment.

TEACHING TIPS

As students practice revising their work, they must learn to identify any scenes or story elements that are not "pulling their weight" and ruthlessly eliminate them. Here are some questions that students can ask themselves as they cull the "dead wood" from their stories:

Are there any minor characters appearing only once in this story whose job could be done by others without sacrificing believability?

Are there any scenes that do not advance the plot (by impelling the protagonist to take some action that will move her/him closer to her/his goal) or reveal important information to the reader? Scenes in which "nothing much happens" should be cut from the story.

Are there any settings that do not perform at least two of the following functions: foreshadowing the climax, revealing character, creating a mood to enhance the effectiveness of the scene, and/or acting as an antagonist in the dramatic conflict?

Are there any scenes that duplicate each other in function and/or effect? If so, can one of them be eliminated? (For example, if the hero is challenged twice by the same opponent and defeats him the same way both times, one of these fights needs to be revised out of the story.)

REVISE, EDIT AND PROOFREAD WITH A PARTNER
CHECKLIST: WORKING WITH SETTINGS

AUTHOR'S NAME: _____

EDITING PARTNER: _____

Checked by editor	Editing Criteria	Improved by author
	1. Each major and minor character is introduced in a manner appropriate to his/her role in the story.	
	2. Minor characters have been effectively used in the story: as facilitators or complicators, foil, comic relief, logistics and/or reactive characters.	
	3. The main plot is compelling and has been developed around a strong and textured dramatic conflict.	
	4. Descriptive detail and figurative language have been effectively used to create the Illusion of Reality	
	5. The story has been enhanced by means of a well-developed subplot.	
	6. Setting detail has been effectively used to create a mood.	
	7. Setting details have been effectively used to reveal character information.	
	8. Setting adds texture and interest to the dramatic conflict by acting as an antagonist.	
	9. Details in the setting effectively foreshadow future events in the story.	
	10. The author has been considerate to the reader by making the story as well-written as possible: (a) spelling and grammar have been checked (not just on the computer); (b) there are no run-on sentences; (c) there is correct use of capital letters, commas and apostrophes; (d) there is agreement of subject and verb (both either singular or plural).	

WORKING WITH SETTINGS
ASSESSMENT SHEET

STUDENT AUTHOR: _____

STORY TITLE: _____

SCORING: **5 = OUTSTANDING**   **4 = VERY GOOD**   **3 = GOOD**
             2 = YOU CAN DO BETTER   **1 = POOR**

THIS AUTHOR HAS:	5	4	3	2	1
1. introduced each major and minor character in a manner appropriate to his/her role in the story					
2. made varied and effective use of minor characters in the story					
3. developed a compelling main plot around a strong and textured dramatic conflict					
4. made effective use of descriptive detail and figurative language to create the Illusion of Reality					
5. created a subplot which enhances but remains subordinate to the main plot					
6. used selected setting details to create a mood					
7. made effective use of setting details to reveal character information					
8. intensified the dramatic conflict by using the setting as an antagonist					
9. made effective use of setting to foreshadow future events in the story					
10. hooked the reader immediately with the opening scene of the story					
COLUMN TOTALS =					

TOTAL SCORE =   **/50**

COMMENTS:

Writing Longer Fiction: Skill Set 5

Step-Building Dramatic Tension

✍️ **YOU WILL NEED:**

- LSR 12—LONGER STORY OUTLINE SHEET—1 per student (Skill 1)
- Longer Story Outline diagram on the board (Skill 1)
- 3 story ideas (see Skill 1, Step 3)
- Students' Ideas Files (Skill 4)

PURPOSE

Authors of longer fiction depend on heightened dramatic tension to keep readers turning the pages of their stories. As students practice building tension using a tested story structure, they will gain a better understanding of both the structures underpinning various forms of literature and the elements that create and heighten tension in real life.

SKILL 1: BUILDING TENSION WITH STORY CRISES

Introduction and Modeling

1. The teacher reviews with the class the structure of a scene and the three possible ways for a scene to peak: *Confrontation, Revelation,* and *Achievement.*

   The following diagram and definitions can be written on the board:

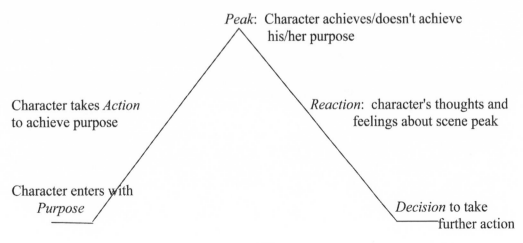

ACHIEVEMENT—the character achieves her/his goal in the scene.
CONFRONTATION—the character is prevented from achieving her/his goal in the scene.
REVELATION—the character learns something that renders her/his goal invalid or unimportant, forcing her/him to
choose a different goal.

It should be pointed out to the students that the purpose of each scene in a story should be the result of a decision made at the end of an earlier scene. This Decision = Purpose connection is what holds the plot of a story together.

2. The teacher then asks the class: Which of these three kinds of scene peaks do you think would build the most drama in a story and why? *(Either Confrontation or Revelation—Achievement does not create tension or suspense.)*

3. The teacher explains that in longer stories, there may be several points where a Confrontation or Revelation causes a major setback for the protagonist, forcing her/him to stop, rethink, and regroup.
   A Confrontation or Revelation that sets the protagonist back on her/his heels and turns the story in a different direction is called a CRISIS. A CRISIS ends a RISING ACTION and forces a FALLING ACTION, just as an ordinary scene peak ends the action of a scene, causing the main character to react and forcing her/him to decide what to do next.

4. The teacher reveals the Longer Story Outline diagram on the board and begins modeling how to use it by introducing the following story:

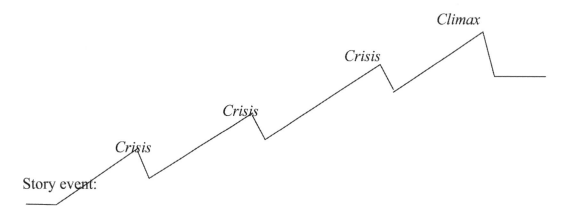

   Marilyn, a former drug addict, is home after spending six months in rehab. She wants to put the past behind her, finish her senior year of high school, and go on to college. To avoid looks and hassles from the people who knew her as an addict, she enrolls at a different high school than she attended before rehab. She's a very bright young lady and an excellent student, and soon her teachers are urging her to run for president of the student council. Marilyn decides to go for it. *(This is a Challenge story—her decision to run is the story event, and winning the election becomes her story goal.)*

5. The teacher and class brainstorm and list on the board the steps in running for school council: *assemble a campaign team, create materials and post or distribute them, deliver speeches, stage rallies, and so on. The final step before the election itself should be a speech to the entire student body at an assembly, and this should be the story climax.* These will be Marilyn's various Purposes at the beginning of each Rising Action, and the teacher puts them on the diagram in chronological order.

6. The teacher and class then brainstorm some obstacles that could get in the way of her achieving these Purposes and might even prevent her from remaining in or winning the election. Some of these could be revelations that cause her to reconsider her decision to run *(e.g., she learns that her main opponent is a boy she is romantically involved with, someone keeps tearing down or defacing her posters, she starts receiving nasty text messages, her parents are pressuring her to withdraw because they're afraid the stress might put her back on drugs, someone she knows from her previous school hears about her campaign and "outs" her as a former junkie, etc.)*

7. Referring to the chart on the board, the teacher points out that with each successive CRISIS, the stakes must go up, and the chances of success must seem worse than before, causing a build-up of DRAMATIC TENSION. The teacher can draw a dotted line on the board to show how each crisis builds higher tension than the previous one until the CLIMAX is reached with the highest tension level of all *(i.e., highest stakes, worst apparent chances of success)*.

8. The teacher and class now review the list of steps with their corresponding obstacles or revelations and select the four most interesting to develop. These are ranked in order from lowest stakes/best chance of success to highest stakes/worst chance of success and then charted on the diagram in ascending order, with the most dramatic obstacles or revelations leading up to the climax of the story.

9. Considering each crisis in turn and then the story climax, the teacher asks the students to identify all the types of antagonists Marilyn is facing at this point in the story. *(For example: parents who fear for her recovery or someone who tries to sabotage her campaign would be person vs. person; Marilyn's fear of hurting someone or doubts regarding her own ability to win the election would be person vs. self; and a school rule that forbids drug addicts from running for student council or negative public opinion once Marilyn is "outed" would be person vs. society/environment.)*

10. The teacher records and labels each set of antagonists (trying for all three kinds per step in the plot) beside the corresponding crisis or the climax on the chart.

Practice

1. The teacher hands out the LONGER STORY OUTLINE SHEET to each student, then organizes the class into groups of three or four. Each group receives one of the following stories to develop, following the process modeled by the teacher on the board:

   A teen who was always told her/his mother or father had died learns that s/he is actually alive and living in another city. The teen decides to find her/him.
   A (wo)man wakes up one morning with bruises all over, a terrible headache, and amnesia—s/he does not remember who s/he is and how s/he got the bruises. S/He needs to find out.
   A student is in love with an exchange student and gives herself/himself six months (the remaining length of the exchange student's stay) to make this person fall in love with her/him.

2. Each student group plots three crises for their assigned story idea, progressively increasing the DRAMATIC TENSION each time. The students should be instructed to state what the STEP-GOAL is and identify all the antagonists opposing the main character for each RISING ACTION on their chart.
   Each student should ensure that s/he has made a personal copy of the group's product.

3. The students are now organized in groups of three, ensuring that each group member has plotted a different story idea. Each student tells her/his three story steps to the rest of her/his group, who may offer positive suggestions for improvement.

4. Each student should hang on to her/his story outline for further development in Skill 2.

SKILL 2: PLOTTING THE CLIMAX OF THE STORY

Introduction and Modeling

1. Returning to the diagram on the board from Skill 1, the teacher describes the climactic scene of this story:

   The climactic scene takes place at a school assembly where each candidate is scheduled to give a final speech before ballots are cast. Being "outed" as a former drug addict has severely damaged Marilyn's campaign, even though she has been clean for nearly a year.

Her parents are terrified that the stress is going to cause a relapse, and they've been urging her to withdraw from the election. Her campaign manager has begun to believe the rumors about her and has quit. But Marilyn has a small core of loyal supporters, all marginalized for various reasons, and they refuse to give up on her. However it turns out, she has to finish this fight, for their sakes.

In a meeting with her campaign team, Marilyn solemnly promises to remain in the race and do her best to be elected. The odds against her are daunting, but Marilyn is not the same person she was at the beginning of her campaign. She has learned and grown, and so has her passion to win this contest. Perhaps she has a chance after all.

Marilyn goes onstage with the other candidates and hears some booing from the audience. She scans the auditorium and sees the former schoolmate who "outed" her, grinning smugly as he talks to everyone around him. His confidence shakes her resolve for a moment. When it's Marilyn's turn to speak, the booing resumes, louder than before. Determined to deliver her speech, however, Marilyn starts talking. She doesn't shout, and eventually the booers are shushed by the people around them who want to hear what she has to say.

Marilyn's speech is about change and how difficult it can be for some people to accept. She speaks with sincerity from the viewpoint of someone who has personally gone through great change. At some point in her speech, a voice in the audience says, "She's right." Marilyn speaks directly to that voice, getting the person to agree with her a couple more times. Then other voices join in, agreeing with her. By the time she has finished, Marilyn may not have delivered an election-winning speech, but she has certainly won the right to a fair chance at the polls.

2. The teacher points out that there are three important things to know about story climaxes and records them on the board as they are discussed:

    a. In fiction based on dramatic conflict, CLIMAXES must be seen by the reader to be inevitable. (Marilyn's past was going to follow her to her new school. It was just a matter of time before someone found out about it and she was going to have to deal with it once and for all.)

    b. The protagonist must not be allowed the choice of backing out of the confrontation; therefore, the CLIMAX is preceded by an IRREVOCABLE ACT that makes it impossible for her/him to default. (To ensure that the CLIMAX in Marilyn's story would take place, the author has her make a solemn promise to a group of people who are counting on her to stand up for them. There is no way for her to quietly drop out of the race after that.)

    c. The protagonist is brought to the CLIMAX with something important to fight for and is then made to look as though s/he is losing . . . until a critical moment when something unexpected happens. (A solitary voice agrees with Marilyn.) This FINAL REVERSAL turns the battle around by giving the protagonist a momentary opportunity, which s/he must be quick enough and brave enough and intelligent enough to take advantage of in order to reverse her/his situation and defeat the antagonist.

It should be pointed out to the students that when these three factors are present, the CLIMAX will be satisfying and complete for the reader.

Practice

1. Working independently, each student returns to the story s/he began plotting in the previous skill. Students are instructed to ensure that the three essential factors recorded on the board are present in the final rising action and climax of their stories.

2. Each student then plans and synopsizes the climactic scene of her/his story, recording it in point form on the back of the STORY OUTLINE CHART.

3. The students reassemble in their groups of three from the previous skill to share and discuss one another's climactic scenes.

SKILL 3: PLOTTING THE STORY DENOUEMENT

Introduction and Guided Practice

1. Referring to the Marilyn story plotted in the previous two skills, the teacher asks: How will Marilyn know that she's really won her fight? *(When her campaign manager stops her in the hall to apologize, when another candidate*

high-fives her, when the troublemaking former schoolmate is told by another student to stop being a jerk, when she receives a congratulatory note from the school principal, etc.) The teacher points out that there has to be a final scene after the climax in which the dust has settled and the protagonist—and reader—is assured that the antagonist has been soundly defeated and won't be making any more trouble.

2. Students can be reminded of the epilogue of any episodic show on television. At the end of the climax, there's a commercial break. Then we come back to the story for a minute or two so the audience can see how happy everyone is about how it turned out. The epilogue of a television show serves the same function as the DENOUEMENT of a written story.

3. Together, the teacher and class devise a suitable denouement for the Marilyn story and add it to the Longer Story Outline diagram on the board.

   The teacher should ask: Does Marilyn actually have to win the election in order to achieve her true goal and provide a satisfactory conclusion for the reader? *(No, it's enough that she has won her freedom from the demons of her past. Whether she wins or loses the election, Marilyn has achieved a major victory.)*

Practice

1. Working independently, each student returns to the story s/he began plotting two skill activities ago and adds a suitable denouement to follow the climactic scene of the story.

2. When done, the students assemble in groups of four to share and discuss their entire stories, with particular attention to the following questions (which may be written on the board):

   Do the crises build progressively higher as the plot unfolds?
   Is the climax the point of highest dramatic tension?
   Is the climax an inevitable confrontation if the story is to be satisfactorily resolved?
   Is the climax preceded by an irrevocable act?
   Is the climax won by the protagonist after a final reversal?
   Does the denouement scene let the reader know for certain that the protagonist has defeated the antagonist and achieved her/his story goal?
   Is the conclusion of the story a satisfying one for the reader?

SKILL 4: FIRST DRAFTING THE LONGER STORY

Product

1. The teacher explains to the students that they have now plotted an entire story and that it is time to write the story in first-draft form. This will not be handed in for evaluation but will be shared, if there is time, at the end of the week.

   Students may need to be reminded of the other longer fiction skills they have practiced, which they should try to incorporate into this story as well.

2. Each student proceeds to write the first draft of the longer story s/he has just finished plotting.

3. If there is time, students can get into groups of three or four and exchange stories for silent reading. Group mates can offer positive suggestions for improvement at this time.

   Each student's completed first draft should be placed in her/his Ideas File for possible revising, editing, and polishing later on.

LONGER STORY OUTLINE

Clarify your story idea by filling in
this diagram:

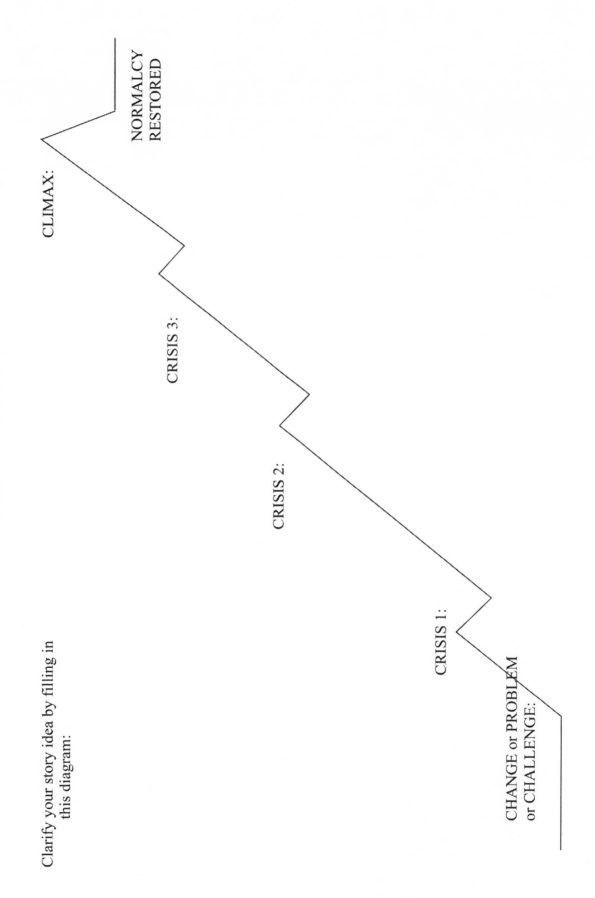

CLIMAX:

NORMALCY
RESTORED

CRISIS 3:

CRISIS 2:

CRISIS 1:

CHANGE or PROBLEM
or CHALLENGE:

Writing Longer Fiction: Skill Set 6
Major Writing Assignment

✍ **YOU WILL NEED:**

- WSR 14—AUTHORS NEED A WRITING PLAN—class set
- LSR 13—LONGER STORY COMPLETION—class set
- LSR 14—PROOFREAD WITH A PARTNER CHECKLIST—class set
- All the rough materials for the students' longer stories developed so far
- Students' Ideas Files
- Story-planning charts from previous Skill Sets
- LSR 15—WRITING LONGER FICTION: ASSESSMENT SHEET—1 per student

---

PURPOSE

Students are now ready to put together all the longer fiction writing skills they have learned in a story-writing assignment that will be revised, edited, and polished and handed in for evaluation.

Week 1: Complete the First Draft

1. The teacher explains to the students that over the next two weeks they are going to be producing a final-draft longer short story and handing it in for summative evaluation. Students may choose to work with a first draft or story outline from their Ideas Files, or they may decide to start from scratch with a fresh story idea. Regardless, there will be deadlines set, which students will be expected to meet.

   Students should be advised that a start from scratch will require them to plan their time carefully, as it will probably mean doing much of their first-drafting outside of class time.

2. The teacher hands out copies of AUTHORS NEED A WRITING PLAN and goes over with the class the steps in the writing process. Students are to keep this sheet handy to use as reference later on.

3. Referring to the AUTHORS NEED A WRITING PLAN handout, the teacher and class work backward from the final deadline to establish due dates for the various steps in the process: second-draft revision, proofreading with a partner, third-draft text editing, and submission of the final draft for evaluation. Students should write these due dates on their handouts to serve as a reminder.

4. Next, the teacher hands out copies of LONGER STORY COMPLETION and goes over the first part (Prepare Your First Draft) with the class.

5. Each student works independently to complete the first draft of her/his story by the due date. This may be done in class, as homework, or both. The teacher should make available to those students who require them copies of any story-planning charts used in previous Skill Sets (e.g., DRAMATIC CONFLICT CHART, STORY OUTLINE SHEET, SCENE DEVELOPMENT CHART, and so on).

Week 2: Revise, Edit, and Polish

1. The teacher refers each student who has completed her/his first-draft story to the self-editing criteria on the LONGER STORY COMPLETION sheet. Using these criteria as a guide, students are to revise their first-draft work and produce a clean second draft of their stories by the due date established earlier.

2. On the due date, the teacher hands out copies of the PROOFREAD WITH A PARTNER CHECKLIST and puts up on the board (or on an overhead screen) the following guidelines for peer-assisted editing, going over them one at a time with the class:

   1. Editing partners are to work together, first on one author's story and then on the other author's story, discussing areas where improvements can be made. Editing partners are not to trade stories and work independently.

   2. Editing partners are to check off each criterion on the author's sheet as soon as it has been discussed, using the left-hand column of the checklist. Authors will use the right-hand column while revising and editing their second drafts, to check off that each criterion has been considered and necessary improvements have been made. A checklist without check marks down both sides will be considered incomplete.

   3. Editing partners may suggest improvements but are not allowed to make changes to an author's work. Authors are the owners of their work. Therefore, if changes are necessary, the author must be the one to make them.

   4. Remember that the job of an editing partner is to help the author improve. All criticism of another writer's work must therefore be constructive (i.e., suggesting ways to make it better).

3. Students then pair up with editing partners and work together to improve both their stories, following the instructions on the board or screen. Once the editing partner has signed off on her/his side of the sheet, each student author is responsible for making the necessary improvements to her/his second-draft work, checking off the other side of the sheet. The student then rewrites the story as a third draft.

4. The teacher hands out copies of the WRITING LONGER FICTION: ASSESSMENT SHEET for students to use as reference while polishing their completed third drafts.

5. Polished work is then recopied in final-draft form, formatted in accordance with the teacher's instructions, and packaged together with the student author's planning materials, edited previous drafts, peer-editing checklist, and WRITING LONGER FICTION: ASSESSMENT SHEET. The entire package is submitted to the teacher for summative assessment.

LONGER STORY COMPLETION

Prepare Your First Draft: If you haven't already done so, establish the themes and dramatic conflict(s) of your story. Plot your story by brainstorming all the possible events that could take place and then selecting the most interesting ones and placing them in the most effective order. Repeat this step to develop an appropriate subplot. Diagram your story on SCENE DEVELOPMENT CHARTS, noting which scenes will provide the story crises. Then write each charted scene up in paragraph form, paying special attention to your opening scene. Write, type, or print the story out, double-spaced on one side of the page only. This is your first draft.

Self-Editing: Reread your story as often as necessary, watching for and correcting the following:

a. Theme: Is your story theme carried through from beginning to end? (If not, this usually means that a scene has become too involved with character, setting, or plot and has lost track of the main idea of the story. Once you have located the scene where the story began going off track, identify which element dominates the scene and remove the colorful but irrelevant details that have overshadowed the theme.)

b. Transitions: Is there a smooth transition from one scene to the next? (Check to be sure that the character's intent in each scene is the result of a decision s/he made in a previous scene.)

c. Main Characters: Are they realistic and three-dimensional, with both basic and secondary motivations? Do they interact with the setting and react "in character" to everything that they experience?

d. Minor Characters: Have they been put to effective use in the story? (Remember that minor characters must always be less important to the reader than the main characters. If a minor character is "stealing the show," her/his role may need to be reassigned to a less colorful personality.)

e. Setting: Do the settings of your story help to make it more effective by establishing mood, revealing character, foreshadowing future story events, and developing the conflict?

f. Plot and Subplot: Does the subplot fulfill its purpose effectively? Is the subplot brought to its conclusion before the climax of the main plot?

g. Dramatic Tension: Does tension build progressively from crisis to crisis? (Remember that the stakes must go up more each time, while the protagonist's chances of winning must seem to diminish.)

h. Opening Scene: Does the opening of your story "hook" the reader, introduce a main character, establish the setting, provide Important Background Information (IBI), and launch into the action?

i. Closing Scene/Denouement: Have you tied up all loose ends and shown that the story goal has been achieved and normalcy has been restored?

REVISE, EDIT, AND PROOFREAD WITH A PARTNER
CHECKLIST: THE LONGER STORY

AUTHOR'S NAME: _____

EDITING PARTNER: _____

Checked by editor	Editing Criteria	Improved by author
	1. Minor characters have been appropriately introduced and effectively put to work as: foil for the main character, plot facilitator or complicator, comic relief, logistics, reaction cue	
	2. The main character has been consistently developed and deepened: (a) with basic and secondary motivations; (b) with both ordinary and extraordinary characteristics; (c) with at least one minor problem not related to the plot; (d) in a subplot if necessary to reveal a hidden dimension.	
	3. Setting has been effectively used: (a) to create a mood by selection and description of details; (b) to reveal specific character traits; (c) to intensify dramatic conflict by acting as an antagonist; (d) to foreshadow future story events.	
	4. The story has been developed around a strong and textured Dramatic Conflict, enhanced by means of a well-developed subplot acting as: (a) a foil for the main plot; (b) a facilitator or complicator for the main plot.	
	5. Dramatic tension has been built throughout the story: (a) by plotting a progressively intensifying series of crises; (b) culminating in a climax that develops inevitably from the dramatic conflict; (c) and a denouement which satisfactorily resolves the story.	
	6. The story flows smoothly in scenes from start to finish: (a) effectively hooking the reader with the opening scene; (b) advancing the dramatic conflict one scene at a time; (c) linked in the best sequence by the Decision=Purpose bond; (d) using plot logic to create the Illusion of Reality.	
	7. The author has been considerate to the reader by making the story as well-written as possible: (a) spelling and grammar have been checked (not just on the computer); (b) there are no run-on sentences; (c) there is correct use of capital letters, commas and apostrophes; (d) there is agreement of subject and verb (both either singular or plural).	

WRITING LONGER FICTION: ASSESSMENT SHEET

STUDENT AUTHOR: _____

STORY TITLE: _____

SCORING: 5 = OUTSTANDING   4 = VERY GOOD   3 = GOOD
2 = YOU CAN DO BETTER   1 = POOR

THIS AUTHOR HAS:	5	4	3	2	1
1. introduced each major and minor character in a manner appropriate to his/her role in the story					
2. made varied and effective use of minor characters in the story					
3. developed a compelling main plot around a strong and textured dramatic conflict					
4. enhanced the story by means of a well-developed subplot that was resolved before the climax of the main plot					
5. if necessary, used a subplot to add dimension to the main protagonist					
6. used well-selected setting details to create a mood					
7. made effective use of setting details to reveal specific character information					
8. intensified the dramatic conflict by including the setting as an antagonist					
9. made effective use of setting to foreshadow future events in the story					
10. consistently portrayed the protagonists' basic and secondary motivations					
11. made characters interesting by giving them both ordinary and extraordinary characteristics					
12. deepened characterization by giving each main character a minor problem unrelated to his/her dramatic conflict					
13. added levels of meaning to the story by the use of archetypes					
14. plotted crises that built dramatic tension progressively higher, to a decisive and emotionally satisfying climax					
15. ensured that the climax developed inevitably from the dramatic conflict					
16. concluded with a well-chosen denouement scene					
17. made effective use of descriptive detail and figurative language to create and maintain the Illusion of Reality					
18. hooked the reader with an effective opening scene					
19. structured the story as a sequence of scenes strongly linked together by the Decision=Purpose connection					
20. demonstrated respect for the reader by ensuring that the writing is as clear and grammatically correct as possible.					
COLUMN TOTALS =					

TOTAL SCORE =   **/100**

Part IV

THE WRITING PROCESS:
A SUPPLEMENTARY
LIBRARY OF FICTION WRITING TOOLS

This module is designed as a multipurpose supplementary resource, suitable for use by and with young story crafters at any grade level. As the title implies, this series of checklists and worksheets guides students through the writing process, from the first draft of a story through revising, editing, and polishing to sharing/publication.

By phasing segments of The Writing Process into the Story Crafting Skills activities you have selected for your class, you can help your students to become competent and confident editors of their own work.

Depending on the needs and ability level(s) of your students, you may choose to accomplish this in a variety of ways:

1. Select individual segments to serve as the basis for discussion or for one or more formal whole-class writing lessons.
2. Select individual segments to enlarge and post around the classroom, to serve as reminders to students involved in revision and editing.
3. Assemble a package of applicable segments to hand out to students who are ready to revise and/or edit their work autonomously, or to students whose final drafts indicate the need for additional work in one or more editing areas.
4. Keep the entire module in the classroom, either in hard copy in a binder or electronically, and direct students to individual segments on an as-needed basis.
5. Implement the entire module in tandem with an entire Story Crafting module:

    The introductory pages (HOW TO GRAB THE READER WITH WORDS, BEFORE REVISING OR EDITING, and WRITING A SHORT STORY: A BASIC CHECKLIST) can be handed out to students for their personal reference or can be enlarged and displayed around the room as reminders to the entire class.

    The revision checklists (TESTING CHARACTERIZATION, TESTING CONFLICT, TESTING PLOT, TESTING SETTING, TESTING STYLE) can be introduced one at a time in the second-draft stage of writing a story. You may decide to focus on only one or two of them. Alternatively, you could have your students compile their own revision checklist(s), following a whole-class discussion on what makes for effective and realistic storytelling. These checklists work best if student authors use them to try to identify and correct major storytelling weaknesses *before* sharing work with a peer-editing partner.

    Continuity, unity, and pacing are revision areas that apply especially to longer fiction (5,000 words or more). These checklists will help an author improve the structure of her/his story and should be treated as a sixth area of focus for older or advanced students in the second-draft stage of writing novellas or novelettes.

    The editing checklists should be introduced at the third-draft editing stage. It is recommended that each item on a checklist be introduced separately as a mini-lesson before the entire list is given out.

    The exercises that accompany the editing checklists are designed for students who are having difficulty identifying and correcting particular writing flaws in their own work and the work of their peers. These exercises come with keys to permit the student to self-evaluate and thus work independently.

A TOUR OF THE WRITING PROCESS

WPR 1—HOW TO GRAB THE READER WITH WORDS
(the basic ingredients of interesting fiction)

WPR 2—BEFORE REVISING OR EDITING
(the prerequisites for effective editing—objectivity, alertness, and solitude)

WPR 3—WRITING A SHORT STORY: A BASIC CHECKLIST
(nine important points for every young author to remember)

WPR 4—REVISION: TESTING CHARACTERIZATION
(a checklist to help the writer pinpoint weaknesses in characterization)

WPR 5—REVISION: TESTING CONFLICT
(a checklist to help the writer gauge the strength of the conflict in the story)

WPR 6—REVISION: TESTING PLOT
(a checklist to help the writer determine whether the plot holds together)

WPR 7—REVISION: TESTING SETTING
(a checklist to help the writer determine the effectiveness of setting in the story)

WPR 8—REVISION: TESTING STYLE
(a checklist to help the writer gauge the overall success of her/his writing)

WPR 9—EDITING CHECKLIST 1: TRIM AWAY THE FAT (plus Worksheet for practice)
(First drafts are always in need of tightening. Eliminate extra words from your manuscript to help the reader focus on what is important in your writing.)

WPR 10—EDITING CHECKLIST 2: SHARPEN THE FOCUS (plus Worksheet for practice)
(How clearly are you communicating your message? Bring your writing into sharper focus by correcting: Unclear Pronoun References; Misplaced and Dangling Modifiers; Missing Commas; and Unexplained "Then," "There," or "That.")

WPR 11—EDITING CHECKLIST 3A: SMOOTH THE READ (plus Worksheet for practice)
(Well-written prose seems to flow from one sentence to the next. Edit to remove the bumps or jars caused by: Faulty Parallelism, Separated Sentence, Incorrectly Omitted Words, Incorrect Placement of Correlatives, and Weak Passive Voice.)

WPR 12—EDITING CHECKLIST 3B: SMOOTH THE READ (plus Worksheet for practice)
(continues Checklist 3A by dealing with: Rambling, Overlong Sentences; Sentence Fragments; Comma Splice; Circumlocutions)

WPR 13—EDITING CHECKLIST 4: CHOOSE POSITIONS OF STRENGTH (plus Worksheet for practice)
(If you want your writing to have an impact on the reader, then the message must have muscle. Make strategic use of: the Passive Voice; Periodic Sentences; and A Short, Powerful Statement at the End of a Paragraph of Longer Sentences.)

WPR 14—EDITING CHECKLIST 5: USE CALCULATED REPETITION (plus Worksheet for practice)

WPR 15—EDITING CHECKLIST 6: PAINT VIVID WORD PICTURES (plus Worksheet for practice)
(Use Flavorful Words; Use Specific, Concrete Words; Make Comparisons with Simile and Metaphor)

WPR 16—DO YOU HAVE CONTINUITY?—PART 1
(techniques for coupling sentences and paragraphs together like the cars of a train)

WPR 17—DO YOU HAVE CONTINUITY?—PART 2
(techniques for coupling scenes of a story together like the cars of a train)

WPR 18—DO YOU HAVE UNITY?—PART 1
(techniques for knitting paragraphs together using time, place, point of view, theme, and causality)

WPR 19—DO YOU HAVE UNITY?—PART 2
(techniques for knitting scenes and chapters together into a unified whole using parallels, contrasts, repetitions, time, causality, and point of view)

WPR 20—HOW'S YOUR PACING?
(how and when to use dialogue, description, action, flashback, and introspection to regulate the pacing of a story)

WPR 21—POLISHING CHECKLIST
(Be on the lookout for: Typographical Errors, Agreement of Subject to Verb and Pronoun to Antecedent, Brackets and Quotation Marks, Spacing and Paragraphing, Empty Spaces, Changes of Vocabulary, and Inconsistencies.)

WPR 22—MARKETING SHORT FICTION
(some do's and don'ts for young authors ready to submit their work to professional editors)

WPR 23—HOW TO WRITE A COVER LETTER
(to accompany the submitted manuscript)

HOW TO GRAB THE READER WITH WORDS

1. WRITE WHAT YOU YOURSELF WOULD ENJOY READING.

- The writing will be more fun.
- You'll bring more enthusiasm to the story.
- Your enthusiasm will come through in your writing and infect the reader.

2. Write a GREAT BEGINNING for your story.

- Get the reader involved in the action and identifying with the main character right away.

3. Put in plenty of ACTION.

- Make sure things keep happening and changing.
- Don't give the reader a chance to put the story down.

4. Season your writing—especially dialogues—with HUMOR caused by

- characters who react in unexpected ways or have odd quirks and/or
- misunderstandings that set up amusing situations.

5. Let SUSPENSE build steadily.

- Make the reader care about the main character.
- Then make the reader wonder what will happen to him/her.

6. Populate your story with INTERESTING, WELL-DEVELOPED CHAR-ACTERS.

BEFORE REVISING OR EDITING

1. HAVE YOU REGAINED YOUR OBJECTIVITY ABOUT YOUR WORK?
Take a break (at least 24 hours) from your writing before trying to revise or edit it. You need to put some emotional distance between yourself and the product of your imagination in order to see what needs improvement or correction.

2. ARE YOU FEELING WELL-RESTED AND IN A GOOD MOOD?
Ideally, you should be calm and alert while revising your work. If you are tired, you could easily miss or dismiss things that need to be improved. If you are upset, you could be too critical. You could even throw out something that was worth saving.

3. ARE YOU ALONE?
When you are self-editing, it really helps to read your manuscript aloud. Out of courtesy to others who might need to concentrate on something, you should find a private space where neither you nor others will be disturbed. In class, doing a group revision or a group edit, you and your group should be in a corner of the room far enough away from the others that you won't disturb them as you read, or be disturbed by them as *they* read.

4. HAVE YOU BEEN KEEPING UP YOUR READING?
This isn't as irrelevant as it may sound at first. To be a good writer, you must also be a voracious reader. Constantly exposing yourself to the written words of others will help you develop the degree of language sensitivity you need in order to write well, and also to edit well.

WRITING A SHORT STORY:
A BASIC CHECKLIST

1. Is there a strong DRAMATIC CONFLICT in your story? Remember, the back-bone of your story must be clearly defined, and the more serious the problem, the more exciting your story will be.

2. Does each scene tie in with the STORY GOAL?

3. Is your main character involved with three different antagonists? (VS PERSON, VS ENVIRONMENT, VS SELF)

4. Have you put sensory detail into your descriptions? (SIGHTS, SOUNDS, SMELLS, TEXTURES, TASTES)

5. Have you included a full bio for your main character, including physical description?

6. Does your main character have the three dimensions of life? (PHYSICAL, EMOTIONAL, PSYCHOLOGICAL)

7. Have you used dialogue to reveal character?

8. Did you establish the setting as quickly as possible, coincidentally with the action of the story?

9. Is your story a series of scenes that SHOW the story to the reader?

REVISION: TESTING CHARACTERIZATION

1. DO YOUR CHARACTERS ALWAYS REMAIN 'IN CHARACTER'? Or do they sometimes do or say things that don't match with their personalities?

   Refer back to the character bios you prepared before writing the story. Go through your story, double-checking the characters' words and actions against the bios, asking yourself, 'Would this character do or say this?' If the answer is NO, revise the scene to keep the character(s) in character.

2. IS YOUR HERO/INE A SYMPATHETIC (LIKABLE) CHARACTER? Or are this character's negative qualities a little too strong?

3. IS YOUR VILLAIN/ESS AN UNLIKABLE CHARACTER BY THE END OF THE STORY? Or do you find yourself warming to him/her as the story progresses?

   Remember that a character who is shown **liking** or **loving** becomes **likable** or **lovable** in turn. If your hero/ine is really unlikable, the villain/ess may *seem* sympathetic by comparison. So make sure there is at least one scene in which your hero/ine gets to express positive, caring feelings, and one scene (maybe even the same scene) where your villain/ess gets to show how *un*caring s/he is.

4. ARE THERE ANY MINOR CHARACTERS TRYING TO TAKE OVER THE STORY? This could mean that your hero/ine is too weak to be the main character, or that your minor characters have received too much attention.

   Look at how you introduced these minor characters. Minor or walk-on characters should be introduced by one name, a nickname, or no name ("the man in the doorway"). They should not be described in detail, and their thoughts and feelings should not be shown to the reader. That kind of attention should be paid to major characters only.

5. HAVE YOU GIVEN YOUR MAIN CHARACTERS A PAST, A PRESENT AND A FUTURE? They should give the impression that they were born somewhere and were shaped by life, not just by your imagination.

   Make sure you've done a bio on each major character - and then *use* it as a guide to how the character would act and speak in certain situations while you write.

(continued on other side)

6. DO YOUR MAIN CHARACTERS HAVE ALL THREE DIMENSIONS OF LIFE—PHYSICAL, EMOTIONAL, PSYCHOLOGICAL? If they exist but don't show any feelings or thoughts, they'll be flat and lifeless.

> You show a character's physical dimension in the way you describe his/her **setting**. You show a character's emotional dimension by describing his/her facial expressions, gestures, and so on in **reaction to change**, and as paralanguage in dialogue. You show a character's psychological dimension by letting him/her **think out loud in dialogue**, and by letting the reader into his/her thoughts by means of **internal monologue**. Be certain you're doing all this for the main character in your story.

7. DOES EVERY MINOR CHARACTER HAVE AT LEAST ONE JOB TO DO?

> Remember that every character, major or minor, is in your story for a reason. If you've created a character who isn't doing one or more of the following tasks, s/he needs to be eliminated: foil for the main character, plot facilitator or complicator, comic relief, logistics, reactive character in a scene.

8. IS YOUR MAIN CHARACTER DIFFERENT AT THE END OF THE STORY FROM WHAT S/HE WAS AT THE BEGINNING? Like a real person, s/he must learn and grow as a result of his/her experiences and must be emotionally affected by them.

> Remember that your story began with a **change, problem or challenge,** and that the main character's definition of normalcy must adjust to include the results of that change, problem or challenge by the end of the story.

9. HAVE YOU KEPT THE MAIN CHARACTERS' BASIC AND SECONDARY MOTIVATIONS IN MIND THROUGHOUT THE STORY? Remember that a basic motivation cannot be satisfied and will influence a person's every action, speech, thought, and decision.

> Be sure you know what your protagonist's motivations are. Write them down and refer to them as you revise the story, to keep the character constantly moving toward his/her personal goals.

REVISION: TESTING CONFLICT

1. IS THERE A CLEARLY-DEFINED PROTAGONIST? Or is it not quite clear whose story is being told to the reader?

   The protagonist is the character whose goals and needs motivate the plot of your story, the one who finally confronts the antagonist in the end. As the author, you must know who the hero/ine is and make it clear to the reader as well. It helps keep things straight if your hero/ine is much more sympathetic than your villain/ess. If you find your plot becoming muddled because another character's goals keep taking over the story, try charting the dramatic conflict as a 'Who wants to do What and Why and Why can't s/he' and keep that chart where you can see it as you write.

2. IS THERE A CLEARLY-DEFINED GOAL? Or is your protagonist not quite sure what s/he wants and where s/he is going?

   Don't let your story wander around because your hero/ine has no sense of direction. Refer back to the main character's bio charts and make sure that a goal has actually been established for this story. Then double-check that goal against your character's personality and past and make sure the goal arises naturally out of who s/he is and where s/he is coming from, so that s/he will really want to achieve it.

3. DOES THE PROTAGONIST HAVE A STRONG ENOUGH MOTIVATION TO CONTINUE TO PURSUE THIS GOAL AGAINST ALL ODDS? Or could he turn his back on it and walk away if the going got too rough?

4. IS THE MAIN CONFLICT STRONG ENOUGH TO CARRY THE WHOLE STORY? Is it important enough and are the stakes high enough to make the reader truly care about the outcome?

   If the main character's motivation is going to be strong, it must be based on the one thing that matters most to him/her in the whole world. Go back to the bio charts and figure out what this character would value more than his/her life. And then *put that thing, or person, or dream in danger, and give the character only one way to save it—by achieving the goal of the main conflict.*

5. ARE ALL THREE TYPES OF CONFLICTS PRESENT TO GIVE DEPTH AND TEXTURE TO THE STORY? You'll need Person vs. Person, Person vs. Environment, and Person vs. Self.

6. IF THE ANTAGONIST WERE TO DISAPPEAR, WOULD THE PROTAGONIST STILL FIGHT ON TOWARD THE GOAL? Or have you tried to build your story around two people who just don't like each other?

   Remember that the antagonist's job in the story is to throw obstacles in the protagonist's way **as the protagonist tries to reach his/her goal.** Eventually, the protagonist must defeat the antagonist in order to reach the goal, but the defeat itself must not be the goal.

REVISION: TESTING PLOT

1. **DOES THE PLOT MAKE SENSE?** Is there an effect to go with every cause and a cause to explain every effect in your story?

   In real life there can be unexplained coincidences, but not in fiction. The reader of fiction expects a story to proceed along a logical chain of cause and effect, which can be traced backwards, to the opening paragraphs of the story, or forwards, to the conclusion where everything is tied up neatly. Make sure that every event in your story has a believable reason for happening, either shown to the reader beforehand or revealed afterward by the characters.

2. **DOES YOUR FIRST SCENE CONTAIN ALL THE INFORMATION THE READER NEEDS TO BECOME INTERESTED IN THE STORY?** You have to introduce the main character, introduce the main conflict, establish the setting, *and* snag the reader's attention to keep him/her reading.

   Remember that the best way to introduce information to the reader is *coincidentally*, and the best way to snag a reader's interest is with *action*. Therefore, begin your story with a scene in which a main character is busy doing something. Establish the setting coincidentally with that action; and by the way you describe your character, also reveal what her/his goals and motivations are.

3. **IS YOUR PLOT PRESENTED TO THE READER AS A SERIES OF SCENES WHICH SHOW, RATHER THAN TELL, THE STORY?** Or do you, the narrator, keep intruding to sum up or interpret for the reader?

   First of all, decide from whose point of view the story is going to be shown to the reader. Then, while showing the story, be as **sensory** as possible in your descriptions. Show the reader at any given moment in the story what that point-of-view character is seeing, hearing, smelling, feeling. As you reread your work, look for words that name emotions (happy, sad, nervous, furious, and so on). These tend to come from the narrator instead of the character, and can signal when a story is being *told* rather than *shown*.

4. **DOES EVERY SCENE BEGIN WITH A PURPOSE, PEAK WITH A REVELATION, A CONFRONTATION OR AN ACHIEVEMENT, AND END WITH A DECISION?** If not, it probably isn't a scene, but rather a *summing up* by the narrator.

   It isn't always effective to include every part of every scene in a story, but the reader ought to be able to figure out that the missing part did happen. Sometimes the action of a scene can slow a story down, and so the author decides to jump from the **decision** of one scene directly to the **peak** of the next one.

For example, if the hero decides he must go to the battle zone to warn his commanding officer, the action of the next scene will involve travelling. A full description of the soldier's travels would probably slow the story down and bore the reader, so the author leaps from decision to peak with a single sentence: *"He was almost there when he heard the tramping of boots close behind him, and a sharply-issued command . . . in German."*

5. DOES YOUR STORY BEGIN SHORTLY BEFORE A MAJOR CHANGE IN THE MAIN CHARACTER'S LIFE? Be sure that it's a change s/he cannot possibly ignore.

Remember that the conflict of your story depends on the main character having a strong motivation for pursuing her/his goal. If the change that begins the story is one that the character can ignore, then there is no disruption of the normalcy of her/his life, and therefore no reason for the protagonist to set out in pursuit of a goal, and therefore no conflict.

6. DOES EACH SCENE DEAL WITH A PROBLEM ARISING FROM THAT CHANGE? Everything in your story must lead inevitably to the climax.

7. HAVE YOU KEPT THE WORST PROBLEM FOR THE CLIMAX? DOES THE SOLUTION TO THIS PROBLEM ALSO RESOLVE THE MAJOR CHANGE AND RETURN THE MAIN CHARACTER'S LIFE TO AN ACCEPTABLE NORM **FOR THAT CHARACTER?** Or is there a nagging feeling that there must be more to the story?

Remember that in order to adjust to the change in her/his life, the character has to learn something from it and change him/herself. If your story feels incomplete at the end, it may be because your main character has still not adjusted her/his idea of **normalcy**, and therefore cannot reach normalcy again to bring the story to a satisfying conclusion.

8. IS THE MAIN PLOT ENHANCED BY MEANS OF A WELL-CONSTRUCTED SUBPLOT? Remember that subplots, like minor characters, can act as foils, as facilitators or as complicators to the main plot. As well, you need to ensure that the subplot is resolved before the main plot reaches its climax.

9. IN A LONGER STORY, IS EACH CRISIS TRULY A TURNING POINT IN THE STORY? A crisis is a confrontation or revelation that skews the story around, forcing the protagonist to take a step back and seriously rethink his/her plan.

REVISION: TESTING THE SETTING

1. DID YOU ESTABLISH THE SETTING OF THE STORY RIGHT AWAY? Or did you make the reader guess where and when it was supposed to be taking place?

2. DID YOU MAKE THE SETTING AN ANTAGONIST TO ADD TEXTURE TO THE DRAMATIC CONFLICT?

3. DID YOU MAKE THE SETTING FEEL REALISTIC BY USING SENSORY DETAIL AND FIGURATIVE LANGUAGE TO DESCRIBE IT?

4. DID YOU MAKE USE OF PARTS OF THE SETTING TO REVEAL THE MOOD AND NATURE OF YOUR MAIN CHARACTERS? Remember that every character in a setting must react to that setting, in character, and every character will imprint those places in which s/he "lives."

   Often, what a character *doesn't* notice or react to about the setting can be just as important as what s/he does notice. For example, if you have two people walking along a country road, and one of them is totally absorbed by the animals grazing in the fields and the other worries constantly about the traffic and hardly notices that there *is* anything happening on either side of the road, what does that tell you about these two people?

5. HAVE YOU MADE EFFECTIVE USE OF THE SETTING TO FORE-SHADOW LATER EVENTS? Or are there no hints in the opening scenes of the climax to come?

   Remember that the most effective kind of foreshadowing is the kind that brings a story around full-circle by hinting in the opening scene at what is going to happen in the climax. It ties the story together and gives the reader a feeling of completion at the end.

REVISION: TESTING THE STYLE

1. DOES YOUR STORY HAVE A GREAT BEGINNING? Or does it take a while to really get started?

2. IS THERE PLENTY OF ACTION? Remember, action will keep the story moving along quickly, but too much *re*action will slow it down.

3. ARE YOUR CHARACTERS INTERESTING AND RELATABLE? This makes it easy for a reader to *care about* your characters and become emotionally involved in their story.

    If you've constructed your characters with all three dimensions (physical, emotional, psychological) and given them feelings and reactions that the reader can identify with, then they will be **relatable**. If you've also given them a sense of humor, an unusual job or hobby, or a problem or characteristic that few people (including the reader) are allowed to see, then the characters will be interesting.

4. DOES THEIR DIALOGUE SOUND NATURAL WHEN SPOKEN ALOUD AND YET NOT TOO WORDY? Or do they sound as though they're reading the words for the first time?

    Try reading your dialogue aloud to hear how it sounds when spoken. Often the ear catches what the eye misses.

5. DOES THE STORY SEEM TO FLOW? Or is the writing choppy and disconnected?

    Make sure that the purpose of each scene has come from the decision of a scene before it. This linking together of scenes will give your story continuity and make it move more smoothly.

6. DO YOU, THE AUTHOR, ENJOY REREADING THIS STORY? Or do you feel it needs to be improved?

EDITING CHECKLIST 1: TRIM AWAY THE FAT

First drafts are always in need of tightening. By removing the extra words from your manuscript, you will direct the reader's attention to the important words and ideas in your writing.

1. TAKE OUT UNNECESSARY DUPLICATION OF MEANING. For example:

    "In my opinion, I think" should just be "I think";

    "quite a far distance" should be *either* "far" *or* "quite a distance."

   BUT don't take out duplications which have been put in deliberately, for emphasis:

    You'll get nothing from me, Harry—nothing, zero, zip, nada, forget it!

2. TAKE OUT WORDS WHICH OCCUPY SPACE BUT ARE NOT NECESSARY TO THE MEANING OF THE SENTENCE. For example:

    Come and have a look at this" should be "Come look at this."

3. GET RID OF WORDS OR PHRASES WHICH CROWD OTHERS OUT OF THEIR RIGHTFUL PLACE OF EMPHASIS OR IMPORTANCE. For example:

    "the field of anthropology" should just be "anthropology";

    "It was Gina who created . . ." should just be "Gina created. . . ."

4. CHANGE AS MANY PASSIVE VERBS TO ACTIVE AS POSSIBLE. For example:

    "The book was read by him" should be "He read the book."

5. SHRINK CLAUSES AND PHRASES IF YOU CAN.

   A clause is a group of words which contains a subject and verb. A *sentence*, therefore, is a kind of clause. But there are other clauses, known as *subordinate clauses*, which cannot stand by themselves as sentences. Instead, depending on what kind of questions they answer, these clauses function inside a sentence *as if they were single words.*

Clauses that answer the questions WHERE, WHEN, HOW, WHY are ADVERB CLAUSES:

You may leave <u>when you have finished your work</u>. (Compare: You may leave <u>soon</u>.)

He is grouchy <u>because he is so hungry</u>.

<u>If you hurry</u>, you can still catch the bus.

Why are you sitting <u>where it is so cold</u>?

Clauses that answer the questions WHICH, WHAT KIND are ADJECTIVE CLAUSES:

There is a man <u>who knows what he wants</u>. (Compare: There is a <u>decisive</u> man.)

We ate lunch, <u>which by now was quite cold</u>.

Clauses that answer the question WHAT are NOUN CLAUSES:

I never noticed <u>that you limped</u>. (Compare: I never noticed <u>your limp</u>.)

<u>What you see</u> is <u>what you get</u>.

Very often, a SUBORDINATE CLAUSE can be reduced to a PHRASE or even a single word. For example:

"if you're lucky" becomes "with luck";

"a day <u>when it rained</u>" becomes "a <u>rainy</u> day";

"She came indoors <u>so that she could</u> get warm" becomes
"She came indoors <u>to</u> get warm."

Also frequently, a PHRASE, which is a group of words without a subject or verb, can be reduced to a single word. For example:

"He spoke to her <u>in a brusque voice</u>" becomes
"He spoke <u>brusquely</u> to her."

EDITING WORKSHEET 1: TRIM AWAY THE FAT

On a separate sheet of paper, tighten up each of the following sentences:

1. The decision was unanimous, without a single opposing voice.

2. Fear made him blind and he couldn't see.

3. The people who are located in Thornhill seem to buy more paper products, for some reason.

4. I've decided to do a study of bees.

5. Paulo was told by his English professor about a new novel just coming out which is supposed to be very exciting.

6. Lucie was a child one could easily love.

7. All the cars which are sold in the month of February will carry a special guarantee.

8. Nellie ran outside so that she could see where Jason was.

9. The level of the river is rising.

10. This product is recommended by my dentist.

11. Let's hurry up and get a move on!

12. All they found was his lifeless corpse.

13. There is nothing which is more refreshing on a hot day than the cool breeze off the lake.

14. He went to Brussels in order to do business.

15. I've always been fascinated by the field of astronomy.

16. We'll set out when the sun rises.

17. Go and see what your brother is up to.

18. It was Eve who chose to move to a farm in the country.

19. She told him in a loud voice what her reason was for leaving.

20. That teddy bear is my sister's single most favorite toy.

EDITING WORKSHEET 1: KEY

The following are tightened versions of the sentences on the other side of the sheet:

1. The decision was unanimous.

2. Fear made him blind.

3. The people in Thornhill buy more paper products, for some reason.

4. I've decided to study bees.

5. Paulo's English professor told him about an exciting new novel.

6. Lucie was a lovable child.

7. All cars sold in February will carry a special guarantee.

8. Nellie ran outside to see where Jason was.

9. The river is rising.

10. My dentist recommends this product.

11. Let's hurry up! *or* Let's get a move on!

12. All they found was his corpse.

13. Nothing is more refreshing on a hot day than the cool breeze off the lake.

14. He went to Brussels on business.

15. Astronomy has always fascinated me.

16. We'll set out at dawn.

17. Go see what your brother is up to.

18. Eve chose to move to a farm.

19. She told him loudly why she was leaving.

20. That teddy bear is my sister's favorite toy.

EDITING CHECKLIST 2: SHARPEN THE FOCUS

Now turn your attention to how clearly you are communicating your message. Bring your writing into sharper focus by correcting the following:

1. UNCLEAR PRONOUN REFERENCES.

Be sure that each pronoun is securely connected to a **preceding** noun. For example:

When <u>Jane</u> arrived, <u>she</u> hung <u>her</u> coat in the closet.

This is clearly Jane hanging her own coat in the closet. But compare it with the following:

When <u>she</u> arrived, <u>Jane</u> hung <u>her</u> coat in the closet.

NOW whose coat is it? And who just arrived, Jane or somebody else?

2. BADLY PLACED MODIFIERS.

These can result in a great deal of unintentional humor. For example:

"a handkerchief from a lady soaked in perfume."

To make it clear that the handkerchief, not the lady, has been made aromatic, this should be:

"a perfume-soaked handkerchief from a lady."

WATCH OUT for the position in your sentence of the words ONLY, NEARLY, ALMOST. Compare:

<u>Only</u> he came to my house. (nobody else did)
He <u>only</u> came to my house. (that's all he did)
He came <u>only</u> to my house. (not a step farther)
He came to <u>only</u> my house. (nobody else's)
He came to my <u>only</u> house. (I just have one)
He came to my house <u>only</u>. (not to my office)

3. DANGLING CONSTRUCTIONS.

When a word, phrase or clause comes before the rest of a sentence and is separated from it by a comma, then the word(s) involved always try to attach themselves to the **subject** of the sentence. If they can't, then they dangle, creating confusion and frequently humor:

At the age of three, his parents died.

Obviously, his parents died when *he* was three years old. But "he" isn't mentioned in the sentence, giving this opening phrase nothing to hang onto. Correct by putting "he" back in:

At the age of three, he lost his parents.

OR

When he was three years old, his parents died.

4. MISSING COMMAS.

Commas tell the reader when to pause. Changing the placement of a comma can radically change the meaning of a sentence, and leaving one out can greatly confuse the reader. For example:

> We keep our radio going often without paying any attention to it.

Do we keep the radio going often, or do we ignore it often? Where should the comma be placed in this sentence? Here is another example:

> Flying debris struck the building heavily damaging the roof.

Was the building struck heavily, or was the roof heavily damaged? Where should the comma be placed in this sentence?

5. UNEXPLAINED "THEN," "THERE," OR "THAT."

For example:

> The subject isn't mentioned in the book since there were no heavier-than-air craft at <u>that</u> time.

When? When the book was published? Or during the historical era being described in the book? The reader is confused—be specific!

EDITING WORKSHEET 2: SHARPEN THE FOCUS

On a separate sheet of paper, get rid of any confusion or ambiguities in each of the following:

1. Rain spoiled our picnic. It lasted three days.

2. Everyone should know their phone number.

3. Having eaten our lunch, the bus left.

4. As this town's first woman fire chief, I wish to congratulate you.

5. He left that scene out because he couldn't remember where it went.

6. Nana is sad because we don't go there very often anymore.

7. Geordie took his hankie out, blew his nose and put it back in his pocket.

8. If she wins the spelling contest, Glynis will be very happy.

9. Germany's exports of building tools have more than doubled this year. The reason is their insistence on quality workmanship.

10. My father tripped on his way back from the hardware store yesterday and we were nearly picking up nails from the driveway for two hours.

11. Enraged, nothing could stop him.

12. Wang Lo would come home from school, eat dinner, do his homework, and be in bed by 9:00 p.m. Things were much simpler then.

13. In all the robbers took more than $500.

14. I am looking for bunk beds for two active youngsters with safety rails on them.

EDITING WORKSHEET 2: KEY

The following are improved versions of the sentences on the other side of this sheet:

1. The picnic was spoiled by rain, which lasted three days.

2. Everyone should know his/her own phone number.

3. After we had eaten lunch, the bus left.

4. I wish to congratulate you on becoming this town's first woman fire chief.

5. (Depending on meaning:) He left that scene out because he had misplaced it. OR He left that scene out because he couldn't remember where it fit in the story.

6. Nana is sad because we don't visit her very often anymore.

7. Georgie took his hankie out and blew his nose. Then he put the hankie back in his pocket.

8. If Glynis wins the spelling contest, she will be very happy.

9. Germany's exports of building tools have more than doubled this year, because of the Germans' insistence on quality workmanship.

10. My father tripped on his way back from the hardware store yesterday, and we were picking up nails from the driveway for nearly two hours.

11. Enraged, he was unstoppable. OR When he was enraged, nothing could stop him.

12. Wang Lo would come home from school, do his homework, and be in bed by 9:00 p.m. Things were much simpler when he was a child.

13. In all, the robbers took more than $500.

14. I am looking for bunk beds with safety rails, for two active youngsters.

EDITING CHECKLIST 3A: SMOOTH THE READ

Readers are looking for a "smooth read," meaning prose that flows from one sentence to the next. As you edit, remove any bumps or jars from *awkward sentence structures* such as:

1. FAULTY PARALLELISM. Logic says that things on a list must all fall into the same category, or else you don't have a list. For example, a list of things to do at the cottage might include: clean the boathouse, fix the front step, paint the eaves, defrost the refrigerator. These are all phrases consisting of a verb plus an object.

   In your writing, if you begin a list with nouns, then all the items in the list should be nouns:

   > Weight training gives a boy strength, confidence, and <u>builds up his muscles</u>.

   The edited version of this sentence is:

   > Weight training gives a boy strength, confidence, and <u>greater bulk</u>.

2. SEPARATED SENTENCE. The subject of a sentence mustn't be so far away from the verb that the reader loses track of what the sentence is saying:

   > *The basement*, looking like the aftermath of a tornado, and which was adorned with cobwebs strung across every corner, *was my job that week*.

   The edited version of this sentence is:

   > *The basement was my job that week*—it looked like the aftermath of a tornado and was adorned with cobwebs strung across every corner.

3. INCORRECTLY OMITTED WORDS. Sometimes you can leave words out of a sentence without losing any of the meaning:

   > When (I was) only two years old, I taught myself to read.

   > Walls do not a prison make, nor (do) iron bars (make) a cage.

   Notice that the words which have been left out appear elsewhere in the sentence and will be automatically filled in, correctly, by the reader. Now compare:

   > I never have (understand?) and I never will understand chemistry.

   The omitted word ought to be "understand"—but it isn't. The sentence becomes a little jarring to the reader as s/he realizes that something is not right with it. Here is the edited version:

   > I never did understand chemistry, and I never will (understand chemistry).

4. INCORRECT PLACEMENT OF CORRELATIVES. Correlatives are pairs of words or expressions that offer the reader first one hand and then the other: EITHER . . . OR, NEITHER . . . NOR, BOTH . . . AND, NOT ONLY . . . BUT ALSO. If you think of them as the two sides of an old balancing scale, then you realize that whatever follows the first correlative must be balanced or equaled by what follows the second:

> Being <u>neither</u> stubborn <u>nor</u> a troublemaker, he followed the others into the building.

You can say "being stubborn" and you can say "being a troublemaker" and they both balance. But compare this to the awkward sentence following:

> Being <u>neither</u> stubborn <u>nor</u> wanting to make trouble, he followed the others into the building.

You can say "being stubborn," but "being wanting to make trouble" does not make sense.

5. WEAK PASSIVE VOICE. In the ACTIVE VOICE, the subject performs the action of the verb:

> A mugger assaulted my friend.

In the PASSIVE VOICE, the subject receives the action of the verb:

> My friend was attacked recently by a guard dog.

There are times when the passive voice should be used. It is often the best way to put an important idea at the end of a sentence, for example (see above). And sometimes it is necessary to use the PASSIVE VOICE because the doer of the action is unknown or cannot be expressed:

> When all the votes were counted, the winner was . . .

However, in most other cases, using the PASSIVE VOICE tends to weaken the sentence. For example:

> When we arrived at the farm, a beautiful sunset was seen.

EDITING WORKSHEET 3A: SMOOTH THE READ

On a separate sheet of paper, get rid of the awkward sentence structures in each of the following:

1. There goes my dream man—he's got looks, brains, and he's rich.

2. Karl is as short or shorter than Yussuf.

3. As we walked to the corner, an explosion was heard.

4. Mrs. DeLeon—and I want you to know it took a great deal of persuasion to accomplish this, not to mention all the nights that I lay awake chewing my nails over it—has finally given her consent.

5. Either you can take the bus or go on the train.

6. Karate teaches strength, quickness, and how to keep your temper.

7. That infernal machine, which gobbles electricity like there's no tomorrow and has already broken down three times this month, has got to go!

8. Not only was the cabin a four-hour drive from the house, but also filthy inside.

9. Varino will make as much or more than Griffin playing for the Blue Jays next year.

10. When we woke up this morning, the growl of a bulldozer could be heard on the street.

EDITING WORKSHEET 3A: KEY

The following are improved versions of the sentences on the other side of this sheet:

1. There goes my dream man—he's got looks, brains, and money. OR There goes my dream man—he's handsome, intelligent, and rich.

2. Karl is as short as or shorter than Yussuf. OR Karl is at least as short as Yussuf, if not shorter.

3. As we walked to the corner, we heard an explosion.

4. Mrs. DeLeon has finally given her consent. I want you to know it took a great deal of persuasion to win her over, not to mention all the nights that I lay awake chewing my nails.

5. You can either take the bus or go on the train. OR Either you can take the bus, or you can go on the train.

6. Karate teaches strength, quickness, and self-control.

7. That infernal machine has got to go! It gobbles electricity like there's no tomorrow and has already broken down three times this month.

8. Not only was the cabin a four-hour drive from the house, but it was also filthy inside.

9. Varino will make as much as or more than Griffin playing for the Blue Jays this year. OR Varino will make at least as much as Griffin playing for the Blue Jays this year.

10. When we woke up this morning, we could hear the growl of a bulldozer on the street.

EDITING CHECKLIST 3B: SMOOTH THE READ

Readers are looking for a 'smooth read', meaning prose that flows from one sentence to the next. As you edit, remove any bumps or jars from *awkward sentence structures* such as:

1. RAMBLING, OVERLONG SENTENCES. Sentences can ramble in two ways—they can go off topic and forget the point they were supposed to be making, or they can just be too long and contain too many thoughts for the reader to digest. For example:

> Andre took the shopping list and went to the store, thinking that he would add a few items once he got there, but on the way he did some counting in his head and realized he hadn't brought enough money, so he had to go home and dig out his wallet again.

Correct this by breaking it up into smaller sentences:

> Andre took the shopping list and went to the store, thinking that he would add a few items once he got there. On the way, however, he did some counting in his head and realized he hadn't brought enough money. With a sigh, he returned home and dug out his wallet again.

2. SENTENCE FRAGMENTS. This does not refer to fragments used deliberately for effect, or found between quotation marks in dialogue:

> The tree had fallen over. Again. Janette moaned in disgust.

The fragments that weaken your writing are the ones you insert mistakenly, thinking they are complete sentences:

> My neighbor, an avid fossil collector, who once showed me a dinosaur footprint.

Correct this by EITHER removing the subordinating word "who," if the emphasis is on the past:

> My neighbor, an avid fossil collector, once showed me a dinosaur footprint.

OR by replacing the first comma with a verb, if the emphasis is on the present:

> My neighbor is an avid fossil collector who once showed me a dinosaur footprint.

An entire category of SENTENCE FRAGMENTS is created by a punctuation error called the PERIOD FAULT, in which a period slips in where there ought to be a comma:

> I shall always remember my cousin Harvey. Because he was such an eccentric character.

Correct this by changing the period to a comma:

> I shall always remember my cousin Harvey, because he was such an eccentric character.

3. COMMA SPLICE. This is the opposite of the PERIOD FAULT. Instead of a period replacing a comma, a comma incorrectly replaces a period (or colon, or dash, or semicolon). The result is sometimes known as a RUN-ON SENTENCE:

> I am not going back to that hairdresser, I don't like her attitude.

Correct this by replacing the comma with some sort of full-stop punctuation:

> I am not going back to that hairdresser. I don't like her attitude.
> I am not going back to that hairdresser—I don't like her attitude.
> I am not going back to that hairdresser; I don't like her attitude.

4. CIRCUMLOCUTIONS. These are tortured, roundabout ways of saying simple, everyday things. The Canadian Broadcasting Corporation used to have a broadcast style regulation that forbade newswriters from using a noun twice in a row in a story. The second time, the writer had to use a descriptive phrase instead.

> For example, in a story about Sophia Loren visiting the country, the reporter might say, "Sophia Loren" in the first sentence, and switch to "the famous Italian actress" in the second.

> The rule was changed immediately after a broadcast in which there was a story about the banana, and the announcer, following the regulations, referred to it the second time as "the elongated yellow fruit."

> That is CIRCUMLOCUTION.

EDITING WORKSHEET 3B: SMOOTH THE READ

On a separate sheet of paper, get rid of all the awkward sentence structures in the following:

1. Emily did all her homework at school that day. To free up her evening in case Dexter called.

2. Mrs. Esterhaus was entertaining her sister, an Arctic explorer who, on her last expedition, had discovered an Inuit house dating back to 1894 and had spent the entire three weeks taking it apart stone by stone and doing autopsies and then putting everything back together again.

3. He doesn't like catching fish, I don't like cleaning and cooking them, so we're even.

4. Now is the time to honor our comrades who have shucked off their mortal shells and set out on that great trek to eternity.

5. Roger Bannister, the greatest runner I had ever actually seen in action.

6. Don't you talk to that man, he doesn't know anything.

7. Sukie felt a chill as she read the story in the magazine. Because it was exactly what she had written in her diary the week before.

8. I knew I had to get my homework done fast and change my clothes in time for the party, so I rushed home from school only to find that my little brother had been home sick all day and if my mother didn't get the night out herself she was going to kill someone slowly, and there was no clean laundry, and guess whose turn it was to make dinner and wash up afterwards, so guess who couldn't make it to the party?

9. A little girl with brand new shoes, happily skipping down the street.

10. Duncan ingested a great amount of nourishment without properly masticating it.

EDITING WORKSHEET 3B: KEY

The following are improved versions of the sentences on the other side of this sheet:

1. Emily did all her homework at school that day, to free up her evening in case Dexter called.

2. Mrs. Esterhaus was entertaining her sister, an Arctic explorer. On her last expedition, she had discovered an Inuit house dating back to 1894, and had spent three weeks taking the house apart stone by stone, doing autopsies on the bodies found inside, and then putting everything back together again.

3. He doesn't like catching fish, and I don't like cleaning and cooking them. So, we're even.

4. Now is the time to honor our dead comrades.

5. Roger Bannister was the greatest runner I had ever actually seen in action.

6. Don't you talk to that man! He doesn't know anything.

7. Sukie felt a chill as she read the story in the magazine, because it was exactly what she had written in her diary the week before.

8. I knew I would have to get my homework done fast and change my clothes in time for the party, so I rushed home from school . . . only to find that my little brother had been home sick all day, and my mother was ready to kill someone slowly if she didn't get the night out herself. On top of that, there was no clean laundry, and guess whose turn it was to make dinner and wash up afterwards? So guess who couldn't make it to the party?

9. A little girl with brand new shoes skipped happily down the street.

10. Duncan wolfed down a huge meal.

EDITING CHECKLIST 4:
CHOOSE POSITIONS OF STRENGTH

If you want your writing to have an impact on the reader, then the message must have muscle. And if you've ever had to prepare arguments for a formal debate, then you already know that the end of your speech is the position of greatest strength, and the opening is the position of second greatest strength.

The same rule holds true for sentences, paragraphs, and chapters: *Put your most important word, thought, or idea at the end, and your second most important word, thought or idea at the beginning* to give them the proper emphasis in your writing. Compare the emphasis in the following sentences:

> *The book was what I really wanted.*

> *The book was what mattered to me.*

> *To me, what mattered most was the book.*

Therefore, when you are EDITING, be sure that the words/ideas you want to stress are in that strong final position. *Rearrange sentences or paragraphs if necessary to put them there.*

1. MAKE STRATEGIC USE OF THE PASSIVE VOICE.

   That order may have been given by a general, but it was countermanded by a much higher authority, namely, one of the civilians who paid his salary.

2. PERIODIC SENTENCES WITHHOLD THEIR MEANING UNTIL THE END.

   Gaunt with hunger, covered with burrs, filth and scratches, and smelling like three week old garbage, the stubborn hound finally reappeared at my back door.

3. PUT A SHORT, POWERFUL STATEMENT AT THE END OF A PARA-GRAPH OF LONGER SENTENCES.

   The lake glowed like molten gold as the fiery disk of the sun sank wearily behind a thick stand of spruce and red maple. In the air hung the warm tang of spring and the last nip of winter, and all around me was the healing silence of the mountains. I was home.

EDITING WORKSHEET 4: CHOOSE POSITIONS OF STRENGTH

On a separate sheet of paper, rearrange each of the following to put the most important idea at the end:

1. Astronomy has always fascinated me.

2. Married couples tend to buy more paper toweling, for some reason.

3. It was your idea to invest in those stocks.

4. No, silly, <u>ponds</u> are where ducks live.

5. That antique car is David's favorite toy.

6. Family pets have attacked more than fourteen children this year.

7. The horse came in last, in spite of all that the owner and trainer had done, and in spite of its natural talent and desire to win.

8. The cottage looked as though it had sat empty for ten winters, at least, with its dilapidated roof, its rotting plank floor, and its cracked, grime-encrusted windows.

On a separate sheet of paper, write a long sentence which might come just before each of the short statements below, to increase its power. Then show your sentences to a classmate:

1. He was gone.

2. It was empty.

3. I couldn't leave.

4. They didn't understand.

EDITING WORKSHEET 4: KEY

The following are improved versions of the sentences on the other side of this sheet:

1. I have always been fascinated by astronomy.

2. For some reason, married couples tend to buy more paper toweling. OR For some reason, more paper toweling is bought by married couples.

3. Investing in those stocks was your idea.

4. No, silly, ducks live around ponds.

5. David's favorite toy is that antique car.

6. This year, more than fourteen children have been attacked by family pets.

7. In spite of all that the owner and trainer had done, and in spite of its natural talent and desire to win, the horse came in last.

8. With its dilapidated roof, its rotting plank floor, and its cracked, grime-encrusted windows, the cottage looked as though it had sat empty for at least ten winters.

EDITING CHECKLIST 5: USE CALCULATED REPETITION

Deliberate repetition is an effective way to stress your main ideas. By repeating key words or phrases, you bring them into much clearer focus for the reader. As you read the following examples, remember the number 3:

> . . . government of the people, by the people, for the people, shall not perish from the earth.
>
> *(Abraham Lincoln)*

> Victory at all costs, victory in spite of all terror, victory however long and hard the road may be; for without victory there is no survival.
>
> *(Winston Churchill, in a speech to the House of Commons, 13 May 1940)*

> . . . wet roads, wet fields, wet housetops; not a beautiful, scarcely a picturesque object met my eyes along the whole route; yet to me, all was beautiful, all was more than picturesque.
>
> *(Charlotte Bronte)*

Did you notice that in each case, the repetitions occurred three times? There is something especially effective about three things together—the same adjective to describe three different nouns in a row, three rhythmic phrases with the same last word, coming one after the other. . . . Nobody knows exactly why or how it works, but it's something that every writer can and should take advantage of in order to add power to his/her writing.

EDITING WORKSHEET 5: USE CALCULATED REPETITION

On a separate sheet of paper, rewrite each of the following to make it more effective by using repetition:

1. The rain was dripping off the eaves outside my bedroom window, falling on the edge of the porch and the porch railing. The plopping sound was keeping me awake.

2. Giggling, the children raced all over the house, looking for Easter eggs to fill their little straw baskets. And they found them, in every room.

3. Dinah sat on her father's shoulder, staring wide-eyed at the parade passing by. Every float was based on the theme of Santa's workshop.

4. My grandmother's attic was a treasure cave when I was small—a place where I could curl up with the many things she had saved over the years, and let them transport me, on the magic carpet of my imagination, to other times and places.

5. The tailor took down a large cardboard box and opened it carefully. Sarina gasped softly in disbelief. She had never seen so many buttons in one place.

EDITING WORKSHEET 5: KEY

No, I'm not going to do them all for you, but I will show you how the first one might be done, just to get you started:

1. Rain dripped off the eaves outside my bedroom window. Plop-plop, onto the carved porch railing . . . plop-plop, onto the protruding edge of the verandah . . . plop-plop, right into my head, it seemed . . . plop-plop, plop-plop, keeping me awake all night.

Now you try the rest. When you're satisfied with what you've done, why not share it with one of your classmates, or with your teacher?

EDITING CHECKLIST 6: PAINT VIVID WORD PICTURES

Your purpose in writing is to communicate thought-images from your head to the reader's, and that means painting pictures with words. Strong images are painted with bold verbal brushstrokes. Therefore, as you edit your work, look for weak, colorless words and phrases that you can exchange for more vivid and energetic ones.

1. USE "FLAVORFUL" WORDS. Don't settle for vanilla when you can have your pick of 31 different flavors out of a Thesaurus. Don't settle for WALKED when you can use STROLLED, AMBLED, STRUTTED, STALKED. Don't settle for RED when there's CRIMSON, SCARLET, RUBY, VERMILION.

    Jacques <u>ran</u> across the street and through the park.

    How flavorless of him! Use a different word that will also tell us something more about his reason for running and help the reader visualize how he is moving:

    Jacques <u>jogged</u> across the street and through the park.
    (He was getting his morning exercise.)

    Jacques <u>raced</u> across the street and through the park.
    (He was trying to catch up with someone.)

    Jacques <u>scurried</u> across the street and through the park.
    (He had to return a backpack full of heavy books before the library closed.)

2. USE SPECIFIC, CONCRETE WORDS. Writing is more powerful—and much easier for the reader to visualize—when it avoids the general, vague, and abstract.

    So don't say "hat" if the character is wearing a red hand-knitted tuque.

    Don't say "car" if she is behind the wheel of a twelve-year-old Volkswagen beetle.

    Don't say "drink" if she's sipping a tall glass of iced tea.

3. MAKE COMPARISONS. Similes and metaphors paint the most vivid pictures of all.

    A simile is a single-point comparison which includes the word *like* or *as*:

    The ship's prow sliced through the water *like* a scalpel.
    As fierce *as* a mother bear protecting a cub . . .

(continued on other side)

In each case above, only one characteristic is being compared. The SIMILE is a more restricted form of comparison than the METAPHOR, which can compare several points at once, without using *like* or *as*, and which can also plant suggestions for further points of comparison later on in the text:

> After less than a year, the company was a hive of activity. Sales staff were on the phone or on the road, selling. Managers were managing. Warehouses were shipping. Accountants were tallying. And Regina, at the center of it all, was basking in her success.

Clearly, the company is being compared to a beehive, with each worker focusing on his or her specific job and Regina, which means "queen" in Latin, benefiting from her employees' diligent labor. Later on, you might describe a lazy male worker as a drone, or a competitor as being 'stung' by Regina's sarcastic tongue, and this will add more and finer detail to the image in the reader's mind of Regina as the queen bee of a hive.

Enjoy putting simile and metaphor into your writing, but beware of mixing metaphors:

> He mowed down the enemy like a field of sitting ducks.

EDITING WORKSHEET 6: PAINT VIVID WORD PICTURES

On a separate sheet of paper, rewrite each of the following so that it paints a picture inside the reader's head:

1. Watching for signs of a trap, Luis walked into the alley.

2. Monique fell overboard.

3. Jill always moves very carefully and quietly through a room.

4. She wore a very attractive dress that showed off all her charms.

5. They drew everyone's attention when they arrived at the party, arguing.

6. Even though she detested Nadia, Zofia acted very friendly toward her.

7. Marcel could tell by looking at him that the old man was drunk.

No, there is no key to this worksheet—this is a writing exercise that depends on your own imagination, so there are no "right answers," just thousands of possibilities.

Pick a sentence that calls up an image in your mind's eye. Then, use the three techniques on the checklist to paint that image, as clearly and colorfully as possible, onto the page for the reader.

When you're satisfied with what you've done, you may decide to share it, with your teacher and/or your classmates.

DO YOU HAVE CONTINUITY?—PART 1

Picture your story as a train, with the opening scene, like the train's engine, pulling all the other scenes behind it. Now picture each scene as a train, with the first paragraph as the engine and the following paragraphs as the line of cars it is pulling. And now imagine that each paragraph is a train, with the opening (topic) sentence determining the train's direction and pulling the remaining sentences, like the cars of the train, along behind it.

The engine is able to pull the train only if all the cars are coupled together. When everything is properly hooked up and the engine is pulling the entire train behind it, with each car attached to the next, you have continuity.

Make sure that there is continuity between the sentences and paragraphs of your story, using the following writing techniques.

1. REPETITION OF WORDS OR IDEAS. Words or phrases which are repeated from one sentence/paragraph to the next act like grappling hooks, coupling those sentences/paragraphs together:

    Jimmy wanted a dog, all right, but not that wimpy mutt his mother had brought home from the pound. He wanted a real dog. A hunting dog would be perfect, he figured.

Ideas can also be repeated to create continuity between sentences and paragraphs. So, "dog" in the first sentence, "hunting companion" in the second sentence and "bloodhound" in the third sentence would have coupled them together equally well.

2. REFERENCE. This means that a noun in the first sentence is referred to by a pronoun or an adjective in the second:

    Another sport which is growing in popularity is wind-surfing. Enthusiasts describe its many benefits to the cardiovascular system.

3. EXPANSION/SUMMATION. This means that the second sentence either expands or sums up an idea contained in the first sentence:

    We are blessed with generous neighbors. Mr. Green minds our apartment whenever we're away, and Mrs. Oh is constantly sending over samples of her delicious baking.

    Yesterday, Mr. Jones made me work right through my coffee and lunch breaks. The man is a tyrant!

4. COMPARISON/CONTRAST. You can't have comparison or contrast without putting two things side by side. This relationship will effectively link two sentences/paragraphs together:

    Mrs. Doherty puts eggshells and coffee grounds in her flowerbeds. My mother grows roses too, but she never feeds them kitchen scraps.

DO YOU HAVE CONTINUITY?—PART 2

Picture your story as a train, with the opening scene, like the train's engine, pulling all the other scenes behind it. The engine is able to pull the train only if all the cars are coupled together. When everything is properly hooked up and the engine is pulling the entire train behind it, with each car attached to the next, you have continuity.

Make sure that there is continuity between the scenes of your story, using the following storytelling techniques.

1. SAMENESS OF CHARACTERS

   One or more characters appearing in consecutive scenes may act as a coupling device to hold them together. If your hero questions a secondary character in the first scene, for example, the next scene can feature either the hero or the secondary character.

2. SAMENESS OF TIME

   Two consecutive scenes which have happened to different characters, in different locations, but at the same time, can be coupled together by an introductory clause such as, "While Kevin was getting dressed for his big date . . ."

3. SAMENESS OF PURPOSE

   Two consecutive scenes may be coupled by the fact that the main character's purpose in each one is the same. If your hero is a private detective tracking down a missing person, for example, s/he may visit several different people in different locations at different times, to question them all about the same missing person. Her/His unchanging purpose is what provides the continuity and couples all these scenes together.

4. SAMENESS OF EMOTION

   A character's unchanging emotion can be used to couple scenes or parts of scenes together, especially if the action and reaction of a scene take place at different times and/or in different locations.

5. CAUSALITY

   The strongest way to couple two consecutive scenes together is by having the first scene CAUSE or MAKE POSSIBLE the second one. The most common way this happens is through the Decision = Purpose connection, in which a character's decision to take action is followed by the scene in which the action occurs.

DO YOU HAVE UNITY?—PART 1

There are four unities of writing. We tend to connect in our minds things that happened at the same time, or in the same place, or because of one another, or things that develop or follow a particular theme or idea. Use the following writing techniques to ensure that there is unity within and between the paragraphs of your story:

1. UNITY OF TIME

    Are there key phrases in the text to indicate to the reader that events are happening simultaneously or are following a time sequence?

    Is there a countdown to a deadline?

    Do things happen in chronological order?

2. CAUSALITY

    Are events reported in logical order, going from cause to effect?

3. UNITY OF PLACE

    Does everything happening in a single paragraph take place in the same location?

    Is there a new paragraph started whenever the location changes?

    Is the new location indicated to the reader in the opening sentence of the paragraph?

4. UNITY OF POINT OF VIEW

    Is everything that is reported in a single paragraph seen from the same point of view (i.e., experienced through the senses of the same character)?

    Is there a new paragraph started whenever the point of view changes?

    Does the camera eye see only what the point of view character can see?

5. UNITY OF THEME

    Does each paragraph have a central idea that holds it together?

    Does each paragraph develop only the idea expressed by the topic sentence?

DO YOU HAVE UNITY?—PART 2

In longer fiction, unifying devices are threads that run all the way through a story, surfacing at intervals to remind the reader that they're there, and tying everything together neatly at the end.

Ensure that there is unity within and between the scenes and chapters of your story by making use of the following common storytelling techniques:

1. PARALLEL CHARACTERS/SITUATIONS

    Do characters and/or events develop in similar ways in your story, to provide an ongoing comparison?

2. CONTRASTING CHARACTERS/SITUATIONS

    Do similar things happen to dissimilar characters, pointing up their differences? OR Do similar characters become involved in dissimilar situations?

    Is there an ongoing contrast in your story?

3. UNITY OF TIME

    Is the story told in chronological order, maintaining logical cause and effect relationships?

    Are flashbacks clearly marked and solidly coupled to the present at beginning and end?

    In a suspenseful situation, is there a countdown to a deadline?

4. CHAIN OF CAUSALITY

    Is there an effect for every cause in the story?

    Is there a logical cause for every effect in the story?

    Are all the loose ends tied up by the end of the story?

5. POINT OF VIEW

    Is there a single dominating point of view in the story?

6. RECURRING IMAGE

    Is there an image which reappears at intervals throughout the story? If so, does it have the same meaning or value each time?

7. REFRAIN

    Is there a sound, a saying, or a snatch of a poem or song that recurs at intervals throughout the story? If so, have you assigned a meaning to it?

HOW'S YOUR PACING?

ON THE RISING ACTION:

1. **Dialogue**: Keep speeches short and have them express your characters' reactions and feelings, rather than introducing huge chunks of information. Bursts of rapid-fire dialogue make for a very fast read. Short words, short sentences, single sentences of dialogue per speaker will convey a mood of impatience and tension.

2. **Description**: Again, keep it short and connected to the emotional state of the point-of-view character. One or two details interspersed with the action description will indicate that the main character is too busy to take in more than one impression at a time.

3. **Action/Movement**: Have your characters doing things but not analyzing them in depth.

ON THE FALLING ACTION:

1. **Dialogue**: The slow pace of FALLING ACTION permits lengthy discussions between characters, involving analysis, philosophy, and remembrance of past events.

2. **Description**: Lengthy descriptions slow the story down. FALLING ACTION, while your hero/ine is mulling over the crisis just past, is a good place to have him/her also notice and appreciate his/her surroundings.

3. **Flashback**: Recalling the past tends to bring the present to a halt. FALLING ACTION is the only place in the story where it's all right to stop and reminisce about what happened earlier, as long as the flashback is securely coupled to the present action, at beginning and end.

4. **Introspection**: This is a time when the main character retreats into his/her thoughts to reason out what has happened and what can be expected to happen next. All action stops. Reserve this for the FALLING ACTION, with its much slower pace.

POLISHING CHECKLIST

Polishing is concerned with the *sound* and *surface* of your writing, rather than with its meaning. Therefore, as you go over your manuscript one last time, be on the lookout for:

1. TYPOGRAPHICAL ERRORS. Correct all the spelling or typing mistakes you can find. If in doubt, consult a good dictionary. Don't rely on your computer's spell-checker! All it does is compare each word against its own internal dictionary, so if a misspelled word is a real word in the dictionary (e.g., "strangler" instead of "stranger"), it won't catch the mistake.

2. AGREEMENT OF SUBJECT TO VERB AND PRONOUN TO ANTECEDENT. While you were making all those editorial changes earlier on, you may have changed a subject from singular to plural but forgotten to change the verb. Or, you may have changed a noun but forgotten to make the same change to the pronoun that followed it.

3. BRACKETS AND QUOTATION MARKS. Have you remembered to close them all?

4. SPACING AND PARAGRAPHING. Look at the way your writing *looks* on the page. Have you double-spaced where necessary? Are all your paragraphs properly indented? Have you started a new paragraph for each new speaker in a dialogue?

5. EMPTY SPACES. Did you remember to hand-draw that weird symbol that you had to leave a space for because it doesn't appear on your keyboard? Are there still any spaces or space-holding strings of letters in your text where you meant to insert information once you'd looked it up?

6. CHANGES OF VOCABULARY. As you read the text aloud, you may encounter words or groups of words that don't look or sound right, or suddenly strike you as being unintentionally comical. Change them.

7. INCONSISTENCIES. If you revised your heroine from blond to brunette, be sure that there aren't any forgotten references to blond hair buried in the text. Also look for people who suddenly switch from right-handed to left-handed, eyes that change color from one chapter to the next, rings that move from one finger to another all by themselves, and so on.

MARKETING SHORT FICTION

Here are some DOs and DON'Ts for young authors who wish to send their work out to be evaluated by professional editors:

DO:

1. Do submit your work appropriately. Read some back issues of a targeted magazine before you send anything in, to get a sense of who reads the publication and what sort of material it usually publishes. Then, if you feel that your story will fit in, either consult the formatting and submission instructions provided on the web site (if it's an emagazine), or check out the masthead inside the front cover (if it's a print magazine), to determine how and to whom you should be sending your work.

2. Do submit your story in standard professional format. Whether you are submitting via email attachment or via regular post, aka snail mail, the formatting will be the same: clean final copy, double-spaced on one side only of white, 8-1/2" x 11", 16- or 20-pound bond paper. Leave at least 1" of margin all around the page, left-justify the text, and use an easily readable serifed font (such as Courier 12 pt or Times New Roman 12 pt). Pages should be consecutively numbered in the upper right corner, and the author's last name and the story title should appear in a header in the upper left or upper right corner of each page after the first one—see below).

3. Do make sure you've put your full name and contact information on the first page of the story, in the upper lefthand corner, as shown:

Full name   **Appr. 650 words**
Street Address
City, State/Province
Country   Zip/Postal Code
Telephone number
E-mail address

TITLE OF YOUR STORY
by A. Writer

It was a dark and stormy night . . .

4. Do submit your story to the fiction editor, by name.

5. As a courtesy, do include a covering letter, even if all it says is: "I'm sending you my story for consideration. I would appreciate any comments you might care to offer."

6. Do send the full manuscript, making sure you keep a copy for your files, along with a copy of the covering letter that accompanied the submission.

7. If you are submitting your story by regular post (aka snail mail), do enclose a self-addressed stamped envelope (SASE) for the editor's reply. Address the envelope to yourself and make sure you've attached the right amount of postage. If you want the story returned along with

the editor's letter, make sure the envelope is the right size to hold them both and has the right amount of postage.

**If you are snail-mailing your story to a publication in another country, you will need to either put the postage of that country on your SASE or buy an International Reply Coupon at the post office and enclose the IRC with your submission.

8. Do keep writing, do keep submitting, do keep your fingers crossed.

DON'T:

1. Don't send anything less than your best work, edited and polished.

2. Don't expect an immediate reply, or even an acknowledgment that your story has arrived. When the editor gets around to your story, s/he will.

3. Don't be discouraged if the story is rejected. Short stories are much harder to write well than novels, but practice *will* make perfect, so keep trying. And don't take the rejection personally. There are many reasons for a submission to be turned down, and most of them have nothing to do with the quality of the writing.

HOW TO WRITE A COVER LETTER

Your covering letter is a way of introducing yourself to the editor who will be reading your story. It might be printed out to accompany a hard copy submission, or it might be the body of the email to which you've attached the .doc or .rtf file. Either way, it should be short, and should say things about you and about your story that the editor might find interesting.

Don't forget that a covering letter is a business letter, and must therefore be set up on the page like any other business letter. Here is an example of a hard copy covering letter:

A. Writer
123 Somewhere Lane
Anywhere, Province/State
Country Postal/Zip Code

Date (written out)

Powerhouse Publications
11 Printing Street, Suite 609
Big City, Province/State
Country Postal/Zip Code

ATTN: J. R. Wordman
Editor, *Magazine Name*

Dear J. R. Wordman,

I am sending for your consideration my short story, titled "Galloping in Circles," approximately 2,500 words long. It is about a teenage girl from the city who visits a horse ranch and learns that horses, like people, have different personalities. In the process, she makes a special connection with an orphaned colt and learns something about herself as well.

I am 15 years old, in Grade 10 at ——— High School, and I've lived around horses all my life. My English teacher, Ms. ———, suggested that I enter "Galloping in Circles" in your magazine's writing contest.

Thank you for taking the time to read my submission. I have enclosed an SASE and look forward to hearing back from you in the near future.

Sincerely,

(*sign your name*)

A. Writer

Encl.

Made in the USA
Middletown, DE
18 April 2021